Rick Steves'
SNAPSHOT

Norway

D1308041

CONTENTS

▸ **INTRODUCTION**........................V
▸ **NORWAY**.............................2
▸ **OSLO**..............................**10**
   Orientation to Oslo........................11
   Tours in Oslo...........................16
   Self-Guided Tram Tour..................17
   Self-Guided Walk......................19
   Sights in Oslo........................28
   Shopping in Oslo......................57
   Sleeping in Oslo......................58
   Eating in Oslo........................64
   Oslo Connections......................70
▸ **NORWAY IN A NUTSHELL**..........**72**
   Orientation to the Nutshell..............74
   Self-Guided Tour......................78
  ▸ **FLÅM**............................84
    Orientation to Flåm.....................84
    Sights near Flåm.......................85
    Sleeping and Eating in Flåm.............89
  ▸ **AURLAND**.........................90
    Orientation to Aurland.................91
    Sleeping in Aurland...................91
    Eating in Aurland.....................92
  ▸ **UNDREDAL**........................93
▸ **MORE ON THE SOGNEFJORD**......**94**
  ▸ **BALESTRAND**......................95
    Orientation to Balestrand..............98
    Sights in Balestrand..................100
    Sleeping in Balestrand................105
    Eating in Balestrand.................107
    Balestrand Connections..............108
  ▸ **THE LUSTRAFJORD**................110
    Sights on the Lustrafjord..............111
    Sleeping on the Lustrafjord............117
    Lustrafjord Connections.............119
  ▸ **SCENIC DRIVES FROM**
    THE SOGNEFJORD.................120

▸ **GUDBRANDSDAL VALLEY AND
JOTUNHEIMEN MOUNTAINS**..........**123**

  ▸ **LILLEHAMMER AND THE
GUDBRANDSDAL VALLEY**..............124

    Orientation to Lillehammer..............124

    Sights in Lillehammer 124

    Sleeping in the Gudbrandsdal Valley.....127

    Eating in the Gudbrandsdal Valley.......129

  ▸ **JOTUNHEIMEN MOUNTAINS** 130

    ▸ **LOM**.................................130

    Orientation to Lom......................130

    Sights in Lom 131

    Sleeping near Lom 132

    ▸ **DRIVES AND HIKES IN THE
JOTUNHEIMEN MOUNTAINS**...........134

    Gudbrandsdal and Jotunheimen
Connections 136

▸ **BERGEN**....................................**137**

    Orientation to Bergen...................139

    Tours in Bergen 144

    Sights in Bergen 145

    Shopping in Bergen....................157

    Sleeping in Bergen.....................157

    Eating in Bergen 163

    Bergen Connections 166

▸ **SOUTH NORWAY** **169**

  ▸ **STAVANGER**...........................170

    Orientation to Stavanger 170

    Sights in Stavanger.....................172

    Sleeping in Stavanger 175

    Eating in Stavanger 176

    Stavanger Connections 176

  ▸ **THE SETESDAL VALLEY**.............177

    ▸ **FROM ODDA TO HOVDEN**.............177

    Sights and Activities in Hovden.........179

    Sleeping and Eating in Hovden 180

    ▸ **FROM HOVDEN TO KRISTIANSAND** 180

▶ **KRISTIANSAND** 181
   Orientation to Kristiansand 181
   Sleeping in Kristiansand 182
   Eating in Kristiansand 184
   Kristiansand Connections 184
▶ **PRACTICALITIES** **187**
   Money 187
   Phoning 188
   Making Hotel Reservations 188
   Eating 189
   Transportation 190
   Helpful Hints 190
   Resources from Rick Steves 191
   Additional Resources 191
   How Was Your Trip? 191
   Norwegian Survival Phrases 192
▶ **INDEX** **193**

INTRODUCTION

This Snapshot guide, excerpted from my guidebook *Rick Steves' Scandinavia,* introduces you to a land with immigrant roots, modern European values, and the great outdoors like nowhere else—Norway. Start in Oslo, Norway's sharp capital city, with its historic and walkable core, mural-slathered City Hall, and inspiring Nobel Peace Center. Oslo's excellent museums are dedicated to Norwegian art, the paintings of Edvard Munch, Viking ships, traditional folk life, Norway's WWII resistance, and more. Ogle the celebration-of-humanity statues at Vigeland Park, and relive Olympic memories at Holmenkollen Ski Jump.

Then head for Norway's countryside for a dose of natural wonder. The famous "Norway in a Nutshell" ride—by train, ferry, and bus—showcases the scenic splendor of the country, from snowcapped mountains to the striking Sognefjord. Choose a cozy fjordside hamlet (such as Balestrand, Solvorn, or Aurland) as your home base for touring mighty glaciers and evocative stave churches. Explore the Gudbrandsdal Valley, Lillehammer's excellent open-air folk museum, and the impressive Jotunheimen Mountains.

Dip into Bergen, Norway's salty port town, with its lively fish market, colorful Hanseatic quarter, and a funicular to the top of Mount Fløyen. You can round out your Norwegian experience in the lively city of Stavanger, the time-passed Setesdal Valley, and resorty Kristiansand.

To help you have the best trip possible, I've included the following topics in this book:

• **Planning Your Time,** with advice on how to make the most of your limited time

• **Orientation,** including tourist information (abbreviated as TI), tips on public transportation, local tour options, and helpful hints

- **Sights** with ratings:
  - ▲▲▲—Don't miss
  - ▲▲—Try hard to see
  - ▲—Worthwhile if you can make it
  - No rating—Worth knowing about
- **Sleeping** and **Eating,** with good-value recommendations in every price range
- **Connections,** with tips on trains, buses, and driving

Practicalities, near the end of this book, has information on money, phoning, hotel reservations, transportation, and more, plus Norwegian survival phrases.

To travel smartly, read this little book in its entirety before you go. It's my hope that this guide will make your trip more meaningful and rewarding. Traveling like a temporary local, you'll get the absolute most out of every mile, minute, and dollar.

Ha en god tur!
Rick Steves

NORWAY

NORWAY

Norge

Norway is stacked with superlatives—it's the most mountainous, most scenic, and most prosperous of all the Scandinavian countries. Perhaps above all, Norway is a land of intense natural beauty, its famously steep mountains and deep fjords carved out and shaped by an ancient ice age.

Norway is also a land of rich harvests—timber, oil, and fish. In fact, its wealth of resources is a major reason why Norwegians have voted *"nei"* to membership in the European Union. They don't want to be forced to share fishing rights with EU countries.

The country's relatively recent independence (in 1905, from Sweden) makes Norwegians notably patriotic and proud of their traditions and history.

Norway's Viking past (c. A.D. 800-1050) can still be seen today in the country's 28 remaining stave churches—with their decorative nods to Viking ship prows—and the artifacts housed in Oslo's Viking Ship Museum.

The Vikings, who also lived in present-day Denmark and Sweden, were great traders, shipbuilders, and explorers. However, they are probably best known for their infamous invasions, which terrorized much of Europe. The sight of their dragon-prowed ships on the horizon struck fear into the hearts of people from Ireland to the Black Sea.

Named for the Norse word *vik*, which means fjord or inlet, the Vikings sailed their sleek, seaworthy ships on extensive voyages, laden with amber and furs for trading—and weapons for fighting. They traveled up the Seine and deep into Russia, through the Mediterranean east to Constantinople, and across the Atlantic to Greenland and even "Vinland" (Canada). In fact, they touched the soil of the Americas centuries before Columbus, causing proud "ya sure ya betcha" Scandinavian immigrants in the US to display bumper stickers that boast, "Columbus used a Viking map!"

Both history and Hollywood have painted a picture of the Vikings as fierce barbarians, an image reinforced by the colorful names of leaders like Sven Forkbeard, Erik Bloodaxe, and Harald Bluetooth. Unless you're handy with an axe, these don't sound like

South Norway

To Kirkenes

To Bodø
To Östersund
& Stockholm

COASTAL STEAMER

Trondheims-fjord

Hell

Trondheim

Kristiansund

Atlantic Ocean

500 KM

250 MI

Molde

SWE.

FIN.

NOR.

Ålesund

Åndalsnes

DEN.

Geiranger-fjord

Dombås

Gudbrandsdal Valley

Nordfjord

Lom

Florø

Jostedal Glacier

Sognefjell

Kvam

Lustra-fjord

Jotunheimen Mountains

Lillehammer

Balestrand

Lærdal

Sognefjord

Flåm

Aurland

Lake Mjøsa

Hamar

100 Kilometers

Voss

Myrdal

50 Miles

Bergen

Hardangervidda (Plateau)

Eidsvoll

Hardanger-fjord

Kongsvinger

NORWAY

Oslo

Charlotten-berg

To Stockholm

Bokna-fjord

Hovden

Drammen

Drøbak

Stavanger

Tønsberg

Frederikstad

Setesdal Valley

Larvik

Lake Vänern

Arendal

Flekke-fjord

Kristiansand

SWEDEN

Skagerrak Strait

Göteborg

North Sea

Hirtshals

To Malmö & Copenhagen

Frederikshavn

To Cope.

DENMARK

the kind of men you want to hoist a tankard of mead with. They kept slaves and were all-around cruel (though there is no evidence that they forced their subjects to eat lutefisk). But the Vikings also had a gentle side. Many were farmers, fishermen, and craftsmen who created delicate works with wood and metal. Faced with a growing population constrained by a lack of arable land, they traveled south not just to rape, pillage, and plunder, but in search of greener pastures. Sometimes they stayed and colonized, as in northeast England, which was called the "Danelaw," or in northwest France, which became known as Normandy ("Land of the North-men").

The Vikings worshipped many gods and had a rich tradition of mythology. Epic sagas were verbally passed down through generations or written in angular runic writing. The sagas told the heroic tales of the gods, who lived in Valhalla, the Viking heaven,

Norway Almanac

Official Name: Kongeriket Norge—"The Kingdom of Norway"—or simply Norge (Norway).

Population: Norway's 4.8 million people (about 31 per square mile) are mainly of Nordic and Germanic heritage, with a small population of indigenous Sami people in the north. The rapidly growing immigrant population is primarily from Pakistan, Sweden, Denmark, Iraq, Vietnam, and Somalia. Most Norwegians speak one of two official forms of Norwegian (Bokmål and Nynorsk), and the majority speak English as a second language. While church attendance is way down, the vast majority of Norwegian Christians consider themselves Lutheran.

Latitude and Longitude: 62°N and 10°E, similar latitude to Canada's Northwest Territories.

Area: 148,900 square miles, slightly larger than Montana.

Geography: Sharing the Scandinavian Peninsula with Sweden, Norway also has short northern borders with Finland and Russia. Its 51,575-mile coastline extends from the Barents Sea in the Arctic Ocean to the Norwegian Sea and North Sea in the North Atlantic. Shaped by glaciers, Norway has a rugged landscape of mountains, plateaus, and deep fjords. In the part of Norway that extends north of the Arctic Circle, the sun never sets at the height of summer, and never comes up in the deep of winter.

Biggest Cities: Norway's capital city, Oslo, has a population of 580,000; more than a million live in its metropolitan area.

Economy: The Norwegian economy grows around 4 percent each year, contributing to a healthy $255 billion Gross

presided over by Odin, the god of both wisdom and war. Like the Egyptians, the Vikings believed in life after death, and chieftains were often buried in their ships within burial mounds, along with prized possessions such as jewelry, cooking pots, food, and Hagar the Horrible cartoons.

Like the Greeks and Etruscans before them, the Vikings never organized on a large national scale and eventually faded away due to bigger, better-organized enemies and the powerful influence of Christianity. By 1150, the Vikings had become Christianized and assimilated into European society. But their memory lives on in Norway.

Beginning in the 14th century, Norway came under Danish rule for more than 400 years, until the Danes took the wrong side in the Napoleonic Wars. The Treaty of Kiel forced Denmark to cede Norway to Sweden in 1814. Sweden's rule of Norway lasted until 1905, when Norway voted to dissolve the union. Like many European countries, Norway was taken over by Germany during

Domestic Product and a per capita GDP of $54,600. Its primary export is oil—Norway ranks behind only Saudi Arabia and Russia in the amount of oil exported, making it one of the world's richest countries. Thanks to this oil wealth, and the country's generally prudent approach to debt, the recent economic crisis has been relatively easy on Norway.

Currency: 5 Norwegian kroner (kr, officially NOK) = about $1.

Government: As the leader of Norway's constitutional monarchy, King Harald V has largely ceremonial powers. Since October 2005 the government has been led by Prime Minister Jens Stoltenberg, who survived a narrow election in 2009. The legislative body is the Stortinget, with 169 members elected for four-year terms. The Labor Party currently holds 64 seats, followed by the Progress Party with 41, the Conservative Party with 30, and the Socialist Left Party with 11. The remaining seats are divided among smaller political parties.

Flag: The Norwegian flag is red with a blue Scandinavian cross outlined in white.

The Average Norwegian: He or she is 39 years old, has 1.78 children, and will live to be 81. One in three Norwegians is employed in the service sector, one in four in industry, and only 3 percent in agriculture.

World War II. April 1940 marked the start of five years of Nazi occupation, during which a strong resistance movement developed, hindering some of the Nazi war efforts.

Each year on May 17, Norwegians celebrate their ill-fated but idealistic 1814 constitution with fervor and plenty of flag-waving. Men and women wear folk costumes *(bunads),* each specific to a region of Norway. Parades are held throughout the country. The parade in Oslo marches past the Royal Palace, where the royal family waves to the populace from their balcony. While the king holds almost zero political power (Norway has a parliament chaired by a prime minister), the royal family is still highly revered and respected.

Several holidays in spring and early summer disrupt transportation schedules: the aforementioned Constitution Day (May 17), Ascension Day (May 9 in 2013), and Whitsunday and Whitmonday (a.k.a. Pentecost and the following day, May 19-20 in 2013).

High taxes contribute to Norway's high standard of living. Norwegians receive cradle-to-grave social care: university education, health care, nearly yearlong maternity leave, and an annual six weeks of vacation. Norwegians feel there is no better place than home. Norway regularly shows up in first place on the annual UN Human Development Index.

Visitors enjoy the agreeable demeanor of the Norwegian people—friendly but not overbearing, organized but not uptight, and with a lust for adventure befitting their gorgeous landscape. Known for their ability to suffer any misfortune with an accepting (if a bit pessimistic) attitude, Norwegians are easy to get along with.

Despite being looked down upon as less sophisticated by their Scandinavian neighbors, Norwegians are proud of their rich folk traditions—from handmade sweaters and folk costumes to the small farms that produce a sweet cheese called *geitost*. Less than 7 percent of the country's land is arable, resulting in numerous small farms. The government recognizes the value of farming, especially in the remote reaches of the country, and provides rich subsidies to keep this tradition alive. These subsidies would not be allowed if Norway joined the European Union—yet another reason the country remains an EU holdout.

Appropriate for a land with countless fjords and waterfalls, Norway is known for its pristine water. Norwegian-bottled artisan water has an international reputation for its crisp, clean taste. Although the designer Voss water—the H_2O of choice for Hollywood celebrities—comes with a high price tag, the blue-collar Olden is just as good. (The tap water is actually wonderful, too—and much cheaper.)

While the Norwegian people speak a collection of mutually understandable dialects, the Norwegian language has two official forms: *bokmål* (book language) and *nynorsk* (New Norse). During the centuries of Danish rule, people in Norway's cities and upper classes adopted a Danish-influenced style of speech and writing (called Dano-Norwegian), while rural language remained closer to the Old Norse. After independence, Dano-Norwegian was renamed *bokmål*, and the rural dialects were formalized as *nynorsk*, as part of a nationalistic drive for a more purely Norwegian language. Despite later efforts to combine the two forms, *bokmål* remains the most commonly used, especially in urban areas, books, newspapers, and government agencies. Students learn both.

The majority of the population under 70 years of age also speaks English, but a few words in Norwegian will serve you well. If you visit a Norwegian home, be sure to leave your shoes at the door; indoors is usually meant for stocking-feet only. At the end of a meal, it's polite to say "Thanks for the food"—*"Takk for maten"* (tahk for MAH-ten). Norwegians rarely feel their guests have eaten enough food, so be prepared to say *"Nei, takk"* (nigh tahk; "No, thanks"). You can always try *"Jeg er met"* (yigh ehr met; "I am full"), but be careful not to say *"Jeg er full"*—"I am drunk."

Stave Churches

Norway's most distinctive architecture is the stave church. These medieval houses of worship—tall, skinny, wooden pagodas with

dragon's-head gargoyles—are distinctly Norwegian and palpably historic, transporting you right back to the Viking days. On your visit, make it a point to visit at least one stave church.

Stave churches are the finest architecture to come out of medieval Norway. Wood was plentiful and cheap, and locals had an expertise with woodworking (from all that boat-building). In 1300, there were as many as 1,000 stave churches in Norway. After a 14th-century plague, Norway's population dropped, and many churches fell into disuse or burned down. By the 19th century, only a few dozen stave churches survived. Fortunately, they became recognized as part of the national heritage and were protected. Virtually all of Norway's surviving stave churches have been rebuilt or renovated, with painstaking attention to the original details.

A distinguishing feature of the "stave" design is its frame of tall, stout vertical staves (Norwegian *stav*, or "staff"). The churches typically sit on stone foundations, to keep the wooden structure away from the damp ground (otherwise it would rot). Most stave churches were made of specially grown pine, carefully prepared before being felled for construction. As the trees grew, the tips and most of the branches were cut off, leaving the trunks just barely alive to stand in the woods for about a decade. This allowed the sap to penetrate the wood and lock in the resin, strengthening the wood while keeping it elastic. Once built, a stave church was slathered with black tar to protect it from the elements.

Stave churches are notable for their resilience and flexibility. Just as old houses creak and settle over the years, wooden stave churches can flex to withstand fierce winds and the march of time. When the wind shifts with the seasons, stave churches groan and moan for a couple of weeks...until they've adjusted to the new influences, and settle in.

Even after the Vikings stopped raiding, they ornamented the exteriors of their churches with warlike, evil spirit-fighting dragons reminiscent of their ships. Inside, a stave church's structure makes you feel like you're huddled under an overturned ship. The churches are dark, with almost no windows (aside from a few small "portholes" high up). Typical decorations include carved, X-shaped crossbeams; these symbolize the cross of St. Andrew (who was crucified on such a cross). Round, Romanesque arches near the tops of the staves were made from the "knees" of a tree, where the roots bend to meet the trunk (typically the hardest wood in a tree). Overall, these churches are extremely vertical: the beams inside and the roofline outside both lead the eye up, up, up to the heavens.

Most surviving stave churches were renovated during the Reformation (16th and 17th centuries), when they acquired more horizontal elements such as pews, balconies, pulpits, altars, and other decorations to draw attention to the front of the church. In some (such as the churches in Lom and Urnes), the additions make the church feel almost cluttered. But the most authentic (including Hopperstad near Vik) feel truly medieval. These time-machine churches take visitors back to early Christian days: no pews (worshippers stood through the service), no pulpit, and a barrier between the congregation and the priest, to symbolically separate the physical world from the spiritual one. Incense filled the church, and the priest and congregation chanted the service back and forth to each other, creating an otherworldly atmosphere that likely made worshippers feel close to God. (If you've traveled in Greece, Russia, or the Balkans, Norway's stave churches might remind you of Orthodox churches, which reflect the way all Christians once worshipped.)

When traveling through Norway, you'll be encouraged to see stave church after stave church. Sure, they're interesting, but there's no point in spending time seeing more than a few of them. Of Norway's 28 remaining stave churches, seven are described in this book. The easiest to see are the ones that have been moved to open-air museums in Oslo and Lillehammer. But I prefer to appreciate a stave church in its original fjords-and-rolling-hills setting. My two favorites are both near Sognefjord: Borgund and Hopperstad. They are each delightfully situated, uncluttered by more recent additions, and evocative as can be. Borgund is in a pristine wooded valley, while Hopperstad is situated on a fjord. Borgund comes with the only good adjacent stave church museum. (Most stave churches on the Sognefjord are operated by the same preservation society; for more details, see www.stavechurch.com.)

Other noteworthy stave churches include the one in Lom, near the Jotunheimen Mountains, which is one of Norway's biggest, and is indeed quite impressive. The Urnes church, across from Solvorn, is technically the oldest of them all—but it's been thoroughly renovated in later ages (it is still worth considering, however, if only for its exquisite carvings and the fun excursion to get to it). The Fantoft church, just outside Bergen, burned down in 1992, and the replica built to replace it has none of the original's magic. The stave church in Undredal (see the Norway in a Nutshell chapter) advertises itself as the smallest. I think it's also the dullest.

OSLO

While Oslo is the smallest of the Scandinavian capitals, this brisk little city offers more sightseeing thrills than you might expect. As an added bonus, you'll be inspired by a city that simply has its act together.

Sights of the Viking spirit—past and present—tell an exciting story. Prowl through the remains of ancient Viking ships, and marvel at more peaceful but equally gutsy modern boats (the *Kon-Tiki*, *Ra*, and *Fram*). Dive into the traditional folk culture at the Norwegian open-air folk museum, and get stirred up by the country's heroic spirit at the Norwegian Resistance Museum.

For a look at modern Oslo, tour the striking City Hall, take a peek at sculptor Gustav Vigeland's people pillars, climb the newly rebuilt Holmenkollen Ski Jump, walk all over the Opera House, and then celebrate the world's greatest peacemakers at the Nobel Peace Center.

Situated at the head of a 60-mile-long fjord, surrounded by forests, and populated by more than a half-million people, Oslo is Norway's cultural hub. For 300 years (1624-1924), the city was called Christiania, after Danish King Christian IV. With independence, it reverted to the Old Norse name of Oslo. As an important port facing the Continent, Oslo has been one of Norway's main cities for a thousand years and the de facto capital since around 1300. Still, Oslo has always been small by European standards; in 1800, Oslo had 10,000 people, while cities such as Paris and London had 50 times as many.

Today the city sprawls out from its historic core to encompass over a million people in its metropolitan area, about one in five Norwegians. Oslo's port hums with international shipping and a sizeable cruise industry. Its waterfront, once traffic-congested and slummy, has undergone a huge change: Cars and trucks now travel in underground tunnels, upscale condos and restaurants are taking over, and the neighborhood has a splashy Opera House. Oslo is full of rich Norwegians and is, understandably, expensive. Its streets are a mix of grand Neoclassical facades and boxy 60s-style modernism. But overall, the feel of this major capital is green and pastoral—spread out, dotted with parks and lakes, and surrounded by hills and forests. For the visitor, Oslo is an all-you-can-see *smörgåsbord* of historic sights, trees, art, and Nordic fun.

Planning Your Time

Oslo offers an exciting two-day slate of sightseeing thrills. Ideally, spend two days, and leave on the night boat to Copenhagen or on the scenic "Norway in a Nutshell" train to Bergen the third morning. Spend the two days like this:

Day 1: Take my self-guided introductory walk. Tour the Akershus Fortress and the Norwegian Resistance Museum. Catch the City Hall tour. Spend the afternoon at the National Gallery and at the Holmenkollen Ski Jump and museum.

Day 2: Ferry across the harbor to Bygdøy and tour the *Fram, Kon-Tiki,* and Viking Ship museums. Spend the afternoon at the Norwegian Folk Museum. Finish the day at Frogner Park, enjoying the Vigeland statues (two recommended restaurants are nearby).

Keep in mind that the National Gallery and the Vigeland Museum (at Frogner Park) are always closed on Monday. The Nobel Peace Center and the Edvard Munch Museum are closed on Mondays in the off-season.

Orientation to Oslo

Oslo is easy to manage. Its sights cluster around the main boulevard, Karl Johans Gate (with the Royal Palace at one end and the train station at the other), and in the Bygdøy (big-doy) district, a 10-minute ferry ride across the harbor.

The monumental, homogenous city center contains most of the sights, but head out of the core to see the more colorful neighborhoods. Choose from Majorstuen and Frogner (chic boutiques, trendy restaurants), Grünerløkka (bohemian cafés, hipsters), and Grønland (multiethnic immigrants' zone).

OSLO

Greater Oslo

❶ See Bygdøy Map
❷ See Oslo Walk Map
❸ See Grünerløkka/Grønland Map

Tourist Information

Oslo has two centrally located TIs: The **Oslo Information Center** faces City Hall (June-Aug daily 9:00-19:00, shorter hours and closed Sat-Sun off-season, Fridtjof Nansens Plass 5, www.visitoslo .com). Another TI is in front of the **train station** (Mon-Fri 7:00-20:00; Sat-Sun 8:00-18:00, until 20:00 May-Sept). Go early or late to avoid lines; otherwise, grab a number as you enter and wait. They answer the phone only on weekdays from 9:00 to 16:00 (tel. 81 53 05 55). Also, a **TI kiosk** at the port opens when cruise ships arrive (Akerhusstranda 15, tel. 81 53 05 55).

At any TI, pick up these freebies: an Oslo map, the helpful public-transit map, the annual *Oslo Guide* (with plenty of details on sightseeing, shopping, and eating), the *What's On in Oslo* monthly (for the most accurate listing of museum hours and special events), and *Streetwise* magazine (an insightful, worthwhile student guide that's fun to read and full of offbeat ideas). If you're traveling on, pick up the *Bergen Guide* and information for the rest of Norway, including the useful, annual *Fjord Norway Travel Guide*. Consider buying the Oslo Pass (described below), unless you get the Oslo Package, which includes your hotel accommodation and an Oslo Pass.

Use It, a hardworking information center, is officially geared for those under age 26 but is generally happy to offer anyone its solid, money-saving, experience-enhancing advice (daily July-mid-Sept 9:00-18:00, off-season 11:00-17:00; Møllergata 3, look for *Ungdomsinformasjonen* sign, tel. 24 14 98 20, www.use-it.no). They can find you the cheapest beds in town (no booking fee), and offer free Internet access (30-minute limit, may have to wait for a computer). Their free *Streetwise* magazine—packed with articles on Norwegian culture, ideas on eating and sleeping cheap, good nightspots, the best beaches, and so on—is a must for young travelers and worthwhile for anyone curious to probe the Oslo scene.

Oslo Pass: This pass covers the city's public transit, ferry boats, and entry to nearly every major sight—all described in a useful handbook (230 kr/24 hours, 340 kr/48 hours, 430 kr/72 hours; big discounts for kids ages 4-15 and seniors age 67 and over, www.visitoslo.com/en/activities-and-attractions/oslo-pass/). Do the math before buying; add up the individual costs of the sights you want to see to determine whether an Oslo Pass will save you money. (Here are some sample charges: 8-ride transit pass-200 kr, Nobel Peace Center-80 kr, three boat museums at Bygdøy-170 kr, National Gallery-50 kr. These costs alone, which total 500 kr, more than justify buying a 48-hour pass.) Students with an ISIC card may be better off without the Oslo Pass. The TI's Oslo Package (see "Sleeping in Oslo," later) includes an Oslo Pass with your discounted hotel room.

Entertainment Listings: The periodical *What's On in Oslo* has an extensive listing of happenings every day. Pick it up free at the TI, and review the busy lineup of special events, tours, and concerts. *Streetwise* magazine is also good.

Arrival in Oslo

By Train

The central train station (Oslo Sentralstasjon, or "Oslo S" for short) is slick and helpful. You'll find Internet cafés, ATMs, and two Forex exchange desks. The station is plugged into a lively modern shopping mall called Byporten (Mon-Fri 10:00-21:00, Sat 10:00-20:00, closed Sun). You'll also find a Bit sandwich shop with seating for a cheap meal, an ICA supermarket (near west exit—follow *West Exit* signs; Mon-Fri 6:00-21:00, Sat 8:00-19:00, Sun 10:00-18:00), and a Vinmonopolet liquor store (Oslo's most central place to buy wine or liquor, sold only at Vinmonopolet stores). The TI is across the square in front of the station.

For tickets and train info, you can go to the station's ticket office located between tracks 8 and 9 (Mon-Fri 6:30-23:00, Sat 10:00-18:00, Sun 12:00-23:00) or to the helpful train office at the National Theater railway and T-bane station, which can have shorter lines (Mon-Fri 7:00-20:00, Sat 11:00-18:00, closed Sun; Ruseløkkveien, southwest of National Theater). At either ticket office, you can buy domestic and Norway in a Nutshell tickets, and pick up leaflets on the Flåm and Bergen Railway, but only the station office sells international tickets. The TIs also sell domestic train tickets (same price, likely friendlier and faster).

By Plane
Oslo Airport

Oslo Lufthavn, also called Gardermoen, is about 30 miles north of the city center and has a helpful 24-hour information center (tel. 91 50 64 00, www.osl.no).

The speedy **Flytoget** train zips travelers between the airport and the central train station in 20-25 minutes (170 kr, less for students and seniors, 4/hour, runs roughly 5:00-24:00, not covered by railpasses; buy and validate ticket before boarding, keep it to exit; tel. 81 50 07 77, www.flytoget.no). Note that Flytoget trains alternate between those that go only to the central train station, and others that also continue on through Oslo, stopping at the National Theater station (which is closer to some recommended hotels and uses the same ticket).

Local trains cost less than Flytoget trains and take only a little longer (119 kr, hourly, 40 minutes, covered by railpasses, some also serve National Theater station). You'll save about 30 kr on this trip with an Oslo Pass because the pass covers transportation within Oslo; you only need to pay the fare for the stretch between the airport and the edge of town.

To reach the Flytoget and local train counters at the airport: After you leave customs, exit right and walk all the way to the far corner; you'll see two separate ticket counters (one for Flytoget, NSB for the cheaper local trains) and separate TV screens showing the timetables for Flytoget and the "lokal-InterCity-fjerntog" trains.

Flybus airport buses stop directly outside the arrival hall and make several downtown stops, including the central train station (155 kr one-way, 4/hour, 40 minutes).

Taxis run to and from the airport (895-kr fixed rate until 17:00, 1,095-kr rate after 17:00, confirm price before you commit). **Oslo Taxi** is the most reliable (tel. 02323). I prefer the slick and faster Flytoget train, but the taxi can be a good value for families and those with lots of luggage.

Other Airports near Oslo

If you arrive at the Rygge or Sandefjord airports, catch a Flybus airport bus to downtown Oslo. If you're going from Oslo *to* either airport, note that buses depart Oslo's central bus terminal (next to the train station) about three hours before all flight departures.

Rygge Airport: Ryanair and Norwegian use this airport near the city of Moss, 40 miles south of Oslo (140 kr, buy ticket from bus driver, tel. 67 98 04 80, www.rygge-ekspressen.no). Airport info: tel. 69 23 00 00, www.en.ryg.no.

Sandefjord Airport Torp: Ryanair, WizzAir, and other discount airlines use this airport, 70 miles south of Oslo (200 kr, buy ticket from driver, tel. 67 98 04 80, www.torpekspressen.no). Airport info: tel. 33 42 70 00, www.torp.no.

By Cruise Ship

Most ships dock at a terminal beneath the Akershus Fortress, just a five-minute walk from City Hall and public transportation. A handy TI kiosk opens when ships arrive.

A few ships dock at Filipstad (near Aker Brygge waterfront development); shuttles take cruise passengers from here to the city center. Returning to Filipstad by taxi costs about 105 kr (134 kr on evenings and weekends).

Helpful Hints

Pickpocket Alert: They're a problem in Oslo, particularly in crowds on the street and in subways and buses. Always wear your money belt. To call the police, dial 112.

Street People and Drug Addicts: Oslo's street population loiters around the train station. While a bit unnerving to some travelers, locals consider this rough-looking bunch harmless. The police have pretty much corralled them to the square called Christian Frederiks Plass, south of the station.

Currency Exchange: Banks in Norway don't change money. Use ATMs or Forex exchange offices (outlets near City Hall at Fridtjof Nansens Plass 6, at train station, and at Egertorget at the crest of Karl Johans Gate; hours vary by location but generally Mon-Fri 9:00-18:00, Sat 9:00-16:00, closed Sun).

Internet Access: You have two options at the train station. **Sidewalk Express,** the budget choice, is near the Forex exchange office by the south exit—look for *South Exit* signs (29 kr/1.5 hours, open 24/7, coin-op). **@rctic Internet Café,** in the station's main hall and above track 13, is quieter but pricey (60 kr/hour, daily 8:00-23:00, sells international phone cards).

Post Office: It's in the train station.

Pharmacy: Jernbanetorgets Vitus Apotek is open 24 hours daily (across from train station on Jernbanetorget, tel. 23 35 81 00).

Laundry: Selva Laundromat is on the corner of Wessels Gate and Ullevålsveien at Ullevålsveien 15, a half-mile north of the train station (daily self-serve 8:00-21:00, full-serve 10:00-19:00, walk or catch bus #37 from station, tel. 41 64 08 33).

Bike Rental: Bikes are tough to rent in Oslo. A public system lets you grab simple, one-speed city bikes out of locked racks at various points around town (80 kr/24 hours; rent a card from TI that allows you to release bike from rack, leave credit-card number as deposit, and return the card to TI). A more expensive, conventional bike-rental company delivers bikes to your hotel (details at TI).

Getting Around Oslo

By Public Transit: Commit yourself to taking advantage of Oslo's excellent transit system, made up of buses, trams, ferries, and a subway (*Tunnelbane*, or T-bane for short). Use the TI's free public transit map to navigate. The system runs like clockwork, with schedules clearly posted and followed. Many stops have handy electronic reader boards showing the time remaining before the next tram arrives (usually less than 10 minutes). **Trafikanten,** the public-transit information center, faces the train station under the glass tower (same building as TI; Mon-Fri 7:00-20:00, Sat-Sun 8:00-20:00, tel. 177 or 81 50 01 76, www.trafikanten.no).

Individual **tickets** work on buses, trams, ferries, and T-bane for one hour (28 kr if bought at a Narvesen kiosk/convenience store, or 44 kr if bought on board). Other options include the **Reisekort** smartcard (200 kr for 8 rides; buy at Narvesen, 7-Eleven stores, or transit offices; reload at machines, not shareable with others on same ride), the 24-hour **Dagskort Tourist Ticket** (75 kr, pays for itself in three rides), and the **Oslo Pass** (gives free run of entire system; described earlier). Validate your ticket or smartcard by holding it next to the card reader when you board.

By Taxi: Taxis come with a 105-kr drop charge that covers you for three or four kilometers—about two miles (134 kr on evenings and weekends). To get a taxi, wave one down, find a taxi stand, or call 02323.

Tours in Oslo

By Boat, Bus, and Foot

Oslo Fjord Tours—A fascinating world of idyllic islands sprinkled with charming vacation cabins is minutes away from the Oslo harborfront. For locals, the fjord is a handy vacation getaway. Tourists can get a glimpse of this island world by public ferry or tour boat. Cheap ferries regularly connect the nearby islands with downtown (covered by Oslo Pass, transit tickets, and Reisekort smartcard).

Several tour boats leave regularly from pier 3 in front of City Hall. Båtservice has a relaxing and scenic 1.5-hour hop-on, hop-off service, with a live-but-boring multilanguage commentary, which departs from the City Hall dock (175 kr, daily at 9:45, 11:15, 12:45, and 14:15; tel. 23 35 68 90, www.boatsightseeing.com). They won't scream if you bring something to munch. They also offer two-hour fjord tours (245 kr, 3-4/day late April-Sept) and a "Summer Evening on the Fjord" dinner cruise (395 kr; joyride without narration that includes a "shrimp buffet"—just shrimp, bread, and butter; daily mid-June-Sept 19:00-22:00).

Bus Tours—Båtservice, which runs the harbor cruises (above), also offers three-hour bus tours of Oslo, with stops at the ski jump, Bygdøy museums, and Frogner Park (380 kr, 2/day late May-Aug, departs from ticket office on pier 3, longer tours also available, tel. 23 35 68 90, www.boatsightseeing.com). HMK also does daily city bus tours (200 kr/2 hours, 340 kr/4 hours, departs from TI across from City Hall, tel. 22 78 94 00, www.hmk.no). While there is a hop-on, hop-off bus service for Oslo (225 kr/24 hours, buy ticket from driver), the city doesn't really work well with this kind of tour bus. Again, commit yourself to public transit to save lots of time, and try the self-guided tram tour described below.

Guided Walking Tour—The local guides' union offers 1.5-hour historic "Oslo Promenade" walks (from 100 kr, free with Oslo Pass; Mon, Wed, Fri at 17:30 in summer; leaves from sea side of City Hall, confirm departures at TI, tel. 22 42 70 20, www.guide service.no).

Local Guide—To hire a private guide, call the guides' association at tel. 22 42 70 20 (1,200 kr/2 hours, www.guideservice.no). Another local guide bureau is at tel. 22 42 28 18.

Self-Guided Tram Tour

Tram #11/#12: A Hop-On, Hop-Off Introduction to Oslo

Tram #12, which becomes tram #11 halfway through its loop (at Majorstuen), circles the city from the train station, lacing together many of Oslo's main sights. Apart from the practical value of being able to hop on and off as you sightsee your way around town (trams come by at least every 10 minutes), this 40-minute trip gives you a fine look at parts of the city you wouldn't otherwise see.

The route starts at the main train station, at the traffic-island tram stop located immediately in front of the transit office tower. The route makes almost a complete circle and finishes at Stortorvet (the cathedral square), dropping you off a three-minute walk from where you began the tour. (Confirm with your driver that the particular tram #12 you're boarding becomes tram #11 and finishes at Stortorvet.) Here's what you'll see and ideas on where you might want to hop out:

From the **station,** you'll go through the old grid streets of 16th-century Christiania, King Christian IV's planned Renaissance town. After the city's 17th fire, in 1624, the king finally got fed up. He decreed that only brick and stone buildings would be permitted in the city center, with wide streets to serve as fire breaks.

You'll turn a corner at the **fortress** (Christiana Torv stop; get off here for the fortress and Norwegian Resistance Museum), then head for **City Hall** (Rådhus stop). Next comes the harbor and upscale **Aker Brygge** waterfront neighborhood (jump off at the Aker Brygge stop for the harbor and restaurant row). Passing the harbor, you'll see on the left a few old shipyard buildings that still survive. Then the tram goes uphill, past the **House of Oslo** (a mall of 20 shops highlighting Scandinavian interior design; Vikatorvet stop) and into a district of ugly 1960s buildings (when elegance was replaced by "functionality"). The tram then heads onto the street Norwegians renamed **Henrik Ibsens Gate** in 2006 to commemorate the centenary of Ibsen's death, honoring the man they claim is the greatest playwright since Shakespeare.

After Henrik Ibsens Gate, the tram follows Frognerveien through the chic **Frogner neighborhood.** Behind the fine old facades are fancy shops and spendy condos. Here and there you'll see 19th-century mansions built by aristocratic families who wanted to live near the Royal Palace; today, many of these house foreign embassies. Turning the corner, you roll along the edge of **Frogner Park,** stopping at its grand gate (hop out at the Vigelandsparken stop for Frogner Park and Vigeland statues).

Ahead on the left, a statue of 1930s ice queen Sonja Henie marks the arena where she learned to skate. Turning onto Bogstadveien, the tram becomes #11 at the Majorstuen stop. **Bogstadveien** is lined with trendy shops, restaurants, and cafés—it's a fun place to stroll and window-shop. (You could get out here and walk along this street all the way to the Royal Palace park and the top of Karl Johans Gate.) The tram veers left before the palace, passing the **National Historical Museum** and stopping at the **National Gallery** (Tullinløkka stop). As you trundle along, you may notice that lots of roads are ripped up for construction. It's too cold to fix the streets in winter, so, when possible, the work is done in summer. Jump out at **Stortorvet** (a big square filled with flower stalls and fronted by the cathedral and the big GlasMagasinet department store). From here, you're a three-minute walk from the station, where this tour began.

Self-Guided Walk

▲▲Welcome to Oslo

This stroll covers the heart of Oslo—the zone where most tourists find themselves walking—from the train station, up the main drag, and past City Hall to the harborfront. It takes a brisk 30 minutes if done nonstop.

Train Station: Start at the main entrance of Oslo's central train station (Oslo Sentralstasjon)—still marked *Østbanehallen*, or "East Train Station," from when Oslo had two stations. The statue of the tiger commemorates the 1,000th birthday of Oslo's founding, celebrated in the year 2000. The statue alludes to the town's nickname of Tigerstaden ("Tiger Town"). In the 1800s, Oslo was considered an urban tiger, leaving its mark on the soul of simple country folk who ventured into the wild and crazy New York City of Norway. (These days, the presence of so many beggars, or *tigger*, has prompted the nickname "Tiggerstaden.")

With your back to the train station, look for the glass Trafikanten tower that marks the **public transit office** (and TI); from here, trams zip to City Hall (harbor, boat to Bygdøy), and the underground subway (T-bane, or *Tunnelbane*—look for the *T* sign to your right) goes to Frogner Park (Vigeland statues) and Holmenkollen. Tram #12—featured in the self-guided tram tour described earlier—leaves from directly across the street.

The green building behind the Trafikanten tower is a shopping mall called **Byporten** (literally, "City Gate," see big sign on rooftop), built to greet those arriving from the airport on the shuttle train. Oslo's 37-floor pointed-glass **skyscraper,** the Radisson Blu Plaza Hotel, looms behind that. Its 34th-floor pub welcomes the public with air-conditioned views and pricey drinks (daily 16:00-24:00). The tower was built with reflective glass so that, from a distance, it almost disappears. The area behind the Radisson—the lively and colorful "Little Karachi," centered along a street called Grønland—is where most of Oslo's immigrant population settled. It's become a vibrant nightspot, offering a fun contrast to the predictable homogeneity of Norwegian cuisine and culture.

Oslo allows hard-drug addicts and prostitutes to mix and mingle in the station area. (While it's illegal to buy sex in Norway, those who sell it are not breaking the law.) Troubled young people come here from small towns in the countryside for anonymity and community. The two cameras near the top of the Trafikanten tower monitor drug deals. Signs warn that this is a "monitored area," but victimless crimes proceed while violence is minimized.

• *Turn your attention to Norway's main drag, called...*

Karl Johans Gate: This grand boulevard leads directly from the train station to the Royal Palace. The street is named for the

OSLO

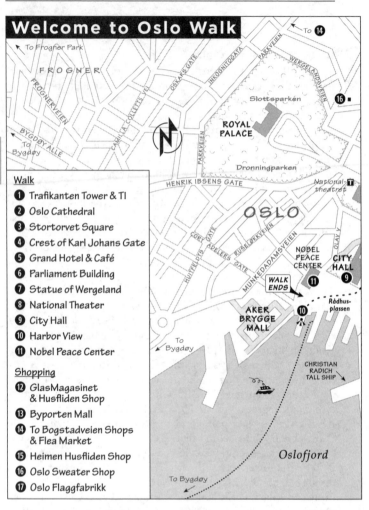

Welcome to Oslo Walk

To ⑭
To Frogner Park
FROGNER
FROGNERVEIEN
BYGDØY ALLE
To Bygdøy
OSKARS GATE
INKOGNITOGATA
PARKVEIEN
CAMILLA COLLETTS VEI
WERGELANDSVEIEN
Slottsparken
⑯ ▪
ROYAL PALACE
Dronningparken
HENRIK IBSENS GATE
National-Ⓣ theatret
O S L O
CORT ADELERS GATE
KRUSELØKKVEIEN
HUITFELDTS GATE
MUNKEDAMSVEIEN
OLAV V
NOBEL PEACE CENTER
CITY HALL
⑨
WALK ENDS
⑪
⑩
Rådhus-plassen
AKER BRYGGE MALL
To Bygdøy
CHRISTIAN RADICH TALL SHIP
Oslofjord
To Bygdøy

Walk
❶ Trafikanten Tower & TI
❷ Oslo Cathedral
❸ Stortorvet Square
❹ Crest of Karl Johans Gate
❺ Grand Hotel & Café
❻ Parliament Building
❼ Statue of Wergeland
❽ National Theater
❾ City Hall
❿ Harbor View
⓫ Nobel Peace Center

Shopping
⓬ GlasMagasinet & Husfliden Shop
⓭ Byporten Mall
⓮ To Bogstadveien Shops & Flea Market
⓯ Heimen Husfliden Shop
⓰ Oslo Sweater Shop
⓱ Oslo Flaggfabrikk

French general Jean Baptiste Bernadotte, who was given a Swedish name, established the current Swedish dynasty, and ruled as a popular king (1818-1844) during the period after Sweden took Norway from Denmark.

Walk three blocks up Karl Johans Gate. This stretch is referred to as **"Desolation Row"** by locals because it has no soul, just shops greedily looking to devour tourist dollars and euros.

• *Hook around the curved old brick structure of an old market and walk to the...*

Oslo Cathedral (Domkirke): This Lutheran church, from 1697, is where Norway celebrates and mourns its royal marriages and deaths. The steps of the church were covered in flow-

OSLO

ers following the tragic shootings and bombing of July 2011. You may still see informal memorials to the victims here.

Look for the cathedral's cornerstone (right of entrance), a thousand-year-old carving from Oslo's first and long-gone cathedral showing how the forces of good and evil tug at each of us. Step inside beneath the red, blue, and gold seal of Oslo and under an equally colorful ceiling. The box above on the right is for the royal family. Back outside, notice the tiny square windows midway up the copper cupola—once the lookout quarters of the fire watchman.

Walk behind the church. The **courtyard** is lined by a circa-1850 circular row of stalls from an old market. Rusty meat hooks now decorate the lamps of a peaceful café, which has quaint tables around a fountain. The atmospheric **Café Bacchus,** at the far left end of the arcade, serves food outside and in a classy café downstairs (light 150-kr meals, Mon-Fri 11:00-22:00, Sat 12:00-21:00, closed Sun, salads, good cakes, coffee, tel. 22 33 34 30).

• *The big square that faces the cathedral is called...*

Stortorvet: In the 17th century, when Oslo's wall was located about here, this was the point where farmers were allowed to enter and sell their goods. Today it's still lively as a flower and produce market (Mon-Fri). The statue shows Christian IV, the Danish king who ruled Norway around 1600, dramatically gesturing that-a-way. He named the city, rather immodestly, Christiania. (Oslo took back its old Norse name only in 1924.) Christian was serious about Norway. During his 60-year reign, he visited it 30 times (more than all other royal visits combined during 300 years of Danish rule). The big GlasMagasinet department store is a landmark on this square.

• *Return to Karl Johans Gate, and continue up the boulevard past street musicians, cafés, shops, and hordes of people. Kongens Gate leads left, past the 17th-century grid-plan town to the fortress. Continue hiking straight up to the crest of the hill, pausing to enjoy some of the street musicians along the way. If you're here early in the morning (Mon-Fri) you may see a commotion at #14. This is the studio of a big TV station (channel 2) where the Norwegian version of the* Today *show is taped, and as in New York, locals gather here, clamoring to get their mug on TV.*

The Crest of Karl Johans Gate: Look back at the train station. A thousand years ago, the original (pre-1624) Oslo was located at the foot of the wooded hill behind the station. Now look ahead to the Royal Palace in the distance, which was built in the 1830s "with nature and God behind it and the people at its feet." If the flag flies atop the palace, the king is in the country. Karl Johans Gate is a parade ground from here to the palace—the axis of modern Oslo. Each May 17th, Norway's Independence Day, an annual children's parade turns this street into a sea of marching student bands and costumed young flag-wavers, while the royal family watches from the palace balcony. Since 1814, Norway has preferred peace. Rather than celebrating its military on the national holiday, it celebrates its children.

King Harald V and Queen Sonja moved back into the palace in 2001, after extensive (and costly) renovations. To quell the controversy caused by this expense, the public is now allowed inside to visit each summer with a pricey one-hour guided tour (95 kr, daily English tours late June-mid-Aug at 14:00 and 14:20, Mon-Thu and Sat also at 12:00, buy tickets in advance at any post office or convenience store, or by calling 81 53 31 33, www.kongehuset.no).

From here, the *T* sign marks a stop of the T-bane (Oslo's subway). Let W. B. Samson's bakery tempt you with its pastries (and short cafeteria line; WC in back). Next to that, David Andersen's jewelry store displays traditional silver art and fine enamel work. Inside, halfway down the wall on the right (next to the free water dispenser), is a display of Norwegian folk costumes *(bunader)* with traditional jewelry—worn on big family occasions and church holidays. From here, the street called Akersgata kicks off a worthwhile stroll past the site of the July 2011 bombing, the national cemetery, and through a park-like river gorge to the trendy Grünerløkka quarter (an hour-long walk).

People-watching is great along Karl Johans Gate, but remember that if it's summer, half of the city's regular population is gone—vacationing in their cabins or farther away—and the city center is filled mostly with visitors.

Hike two blocks down Karl Johans Gate, past the big brick Parliament building (on the left). In this section, the sidewalk is heated during the frigid winter so it won't be icy. On the right is a statue of the painter Christian Krohg. Farther down Karl Johans Gate, just past the Freia shop (Norway's oldest and best chocolate), the venerable **Grand Hotel** (Oslo's celebrity hotel—Nobel Peace Prize winners sleep here) overlooks the boulevard.

• *Ask the waiter at the Grand Café if you can pop inside for a little sightseeing (he'll generally let you).*

Grand Café: This historic café was for many years the meeting place of Oslo's intellectual and creative elite (the playwright Henrik Ibsen was a regular here). Notice the photos and knick-knacks on the wall. At the back of the café, a mural shows Norway's literary and artistic clientele—from a century ago—enjoying this fine hangout. On the far left, find Ibsen, coming in as he did every day at 13:00. Edvard Munch is on the right, leaning against the window, looking pretty drugged. Names are beneath the mural.

• *For a cheap bite with prime boulevard seating, continue next door to Deli de Luca, a convenience store with a super selection of take-away food and a great people-watching perch. Across the street, a little park faces Norway's...*

Parliament Building (Stortinget): Norway's Parliament meets here (along with anyone participating in a peaceful protest outside). Built in 1866, the building seems to counter the Royal Palace at the other end of Karl Johans Gate. If the flag's flying, Parliament's in session. Today the king is a figurehead, and Norway is run by a unicameral Parliament and a prime minister.

Guided tours of the Stortinget are offered for those interested in Norwegian government (free; mid-June-Aug Mon-Fri at 10:00, 11:30, and 13:00; enter on Karl Johans Gate side, tel. 23 31 35 96, www.stortinget.no).

• *Continue walking toward the palace through the park, past the fountain, to the...*

Statue of Wergeland: The poet Henrik Wergeland helped inspire the movement for Norwegian autonomy. In the winter, the pool here is frozen and covered with children happily ice-skating. Across the street behind Wergeland stands the **National Theater** and statues of Norway's favorite playwrights: Ibsen and Bjørnstjerne Bjørnson. Across Karl Johans Gate, the pale yellow building is the first university building in Norway, dating from 1854. A block behind that is the National Gallery, with Norway's best collection of paintings.

• *Follow Roald Amundsens Gate left, to the towering brick...*

City Hall (Rådhuset): Built mostly in the 1930s with contributions from Norway's leading artists, City Hall is full of great art and is worth touring. The mayor has his office here (at the base of one of the two 200-foot towers), and every December 10, this building is where the Nobel Peace Prize is presented. For the best exterior art, circle the courtyard clockwise, studying the colorful woodcuts in the arcade. Each shows a scene from Norwegian mythology, well-explained in English: Thor with his billy-goat chariot, Ask and Embla (a kind of Norse Adam and Eve), Odin on his eight-legged horse guided by ravens, the swan maidens shedding their swan disguises, and so on. Circle around City Hall on the right to the front. The statues (especially the six laborers on the other side of the building, facing the harbor, who seem to guard the facade) celebrate the nobility of the working class.

• *Walk to the...*

Harbor: A decade ago, you would have dodged several lanes of busy traffic to get to Oslo's harborfront. But today, most cars cross underneath the city in tunnels. In addition, the city has made its town center relatively quiet and pedestrian-friendly by levying a traffic-discouraging 27-kr toll for every car entering town. (This system, like a similar one in London, subsidizes public transit and the city's infrastructure.)

At the water's edge, find the shiny metal plaque (just left of center) listing the contents of a sealed time capsule planted in 2000

Browsing

Oslo's pulse is best felt by strolling. Three good areas are along and near the central Karl Johans Gate, which runs from the train station to the palace (see my self-guided walk on page 19); in the trendy harborside Aker Brygge mall, a glass-and-chrome collection of sharp cafés, fine condos, and polished produce stalls (really lively at night, trams #10 and #12 from train station); and along Bogstadveien, a lively shopping street with no-nonsense modern commerce, lots of locals, and no tourists (T-bane to Majorstuen and follow this street back toward the palace and tourist zone). While most tourists never get out of the harbor/Karl Johans Gate district, the real, down-to-earth Oslo is better seen elsewhere, in places such as Bogstadveien. The bohemian, artsy Grünerløkka district, described on page 51, is good for a daytime wander.

out in the harbor in the little Kavringen lighthouse straight ahead (to be opened in 1,000 years). Go to the end of the stubby pier (on the right). This is the ceremonial "enter the city" point for momentous occasions. One such instance was in 1905, when Norway gained its independence from Sweden and a Danish prince sailed in from Copenhagen to become the first modern king of Norway. Another milestone event occurred at the end of World War II, when the king returned to Norway after the country was liberated from the Nazis.

• *Stand at the harbor and give it a sweeping counterclockwise look.*

Harborfront Spin-Tour: Oslofjord is a huge playground, with 40 city-owned, park-like islands. Big white cruise ships—a large part of the local tourist economy—dock just under the Akershus Fortress on the left. Just past the fort's impressive 13th-century ramparts, a statue of FDR grabs the shade. He's here in gratitude for the safe refuge the US gave to members of the royal family (including the young prince who is now Norway's king) during World War II—while the king and his government-in-exile waged Norway's fight against the Nazis from London.

Enjoy the grand view of City Hall. The yellow building farther to the left was the old West Train Station; today it houses the **Nobel Peace Center,** which celebrates the work of Nobel Peace Prize winners. The next pier is the launchpad for harbor boat tours and the shuttle boat to the Bygdøy museums. A fisherman often moors his boat here, selling shrimp from the back. At the other end of the harbor, shipyard buildings (this was the former heart of Norway's once-important shipbuilding industry) have been transformed into Aker Brygge—Oslo's thriving restaurant/shopping/nightclub zone (see "Eating in Oslo").

Oslo at a Glance

▲▲▲**City Hall** Oslo's artsy 20th-century government building, lined with huge, vibrant, municipal-themed murals, best visited with included tour. **Hours:** Daily 9:00-18:00; tours daily at 10:00, 12:00, and 14:00, tours run Wed only in winter. See page 28.

▲▲▲**National Gallery** Norway's cultural and natural essence, captured on canvas. **Hours:** Tue-Fri 10:00-18:00, Thu until 19:00, Sat-Sun 11:00-17:00, closed Mon. See page 32.

▲▲▲**Frogner Park** Sprawling park with works by Norway's greatest sculptor, Gustav Vigeland, and the studio where he created them (now a museum). **Hours:** Park—always open; Vigeland Museum—June-Aug Tue-Sun 10:00-17:00, closed Mon; Sept-May Tue-Sun 12:00-16:00, closed Mon. See page 39.

▲▲▲**Norwegian Folk Museum** Norway condensed into 150 historic buildings in a large open-air park. **Hours:** Daily mid-May-mid-Sept 10:00-18:00, off-season park open Mon-Fri 11:00-15:00, Sat-Sun 11:00-16:00, but most historical buildings closed. See page 45.

▲▲**Norwegian Resistance Museum** Gripping look at Norway's tumultuous WWII experience. **Hours:** June-Aug Mon-Sat 10:00-17:00, Sun 11:00-17:00; Sept-May Mon-Fri 10:00-16:00, Sat-Sun 11:00-16:00. See page 31.

▲▲**Viking Ship Museum** An impressive trio of ninth-century Viking ships, with exhibits on the people who built them. **Hours:** Daily May-Sept 9:00-18:00, Oct-April 10:00-16:00. See page 46.

▲▲*Fram* **Museum** Captivating exhibit on the Arctic exploration ship. **Hours:** Daily June-Aug 9:00-18:00, May and Sept 10:00-17:00, Oct-mid-Jan and mid-Feb-April 10:00-16:00, closed mid-Jan-mid-Feb. See page 47.

▲▲*Kon-Tiki* **Museum** Adventures of primitive *Kon-Tiki* and *Ra II* ships built by Thor Heyerdahl. **Hours:** Daily June-Aug 9:30-17:30, April-May and Sept 10:00-17:00, Oct-March 10:30-16:00. See page 48.

▲▲Holmenkollen Ski Jump and Ski Museum Dizzying vista and schuss through skiing history. **Hours:** Daily June-Aug 9:00-20:00, May and Sept 10:00-17:00, Oct-April 10:00-16:00. See page 49.

▲Nobel Peace Center Exhibit celebrating the ideals of the Nobel Peace Prize and the lives of those who have won it. **Hours:** Mid-May-Aug daily 10:00-18:00; Sept-mid-May Tue-Sun 10:00-18:00, closed Mon. See page 29.

▲Opera House Stunning performance center that's helping revitalize the harborfront. **Hours:** Foyer and café/restaurant open Mon-Fri 10:00-23:00, Sat 11:00-23:00, Sun 12:00-22:00. See page 30.

▲Akershus Fortress Complex and Tours Historic military base and fortified old center, with guided tours, a ho-hum castle interior, and a couple of museums (including the excellent Norwegian Resistance Museum, listed above). **Hours:** Park generally open daily 6:00-21:00; 45-minute tours of the grounds generally offered May-Aug daily at 12:00, 13:00, 15:00, and 16:00, no tours off-season. See page 30.

▲Norwegian Holocaust Center High-tech walk through rise of anti-Semitism, the Holocaust in Norway, and racism today. **Hours:** Daily mid-June-mid-Aug 10:00-18:00, mid-Aug-mid-June 11:00-16:00. See page 47.

▲Norwegian Maritime Museum Dusty cruise through Norway's rich seafaring heritage. **Hours:** Mid-May-Aug daily 10:00-18:00; Sept-mid-May Tue-Sun 10:00-15:00, closed Mon. See page 48.

▲Edvard Munch Museum Works of Norway's famous Expressionistic painter. **Hours:** June-Aug daily 10:00-18:00; Sept-May Tue-Fri 10:00-16:00, Sat-Sun 11:00-17:00, closed Mon. See page 49.

▲Grünerløkka Oslo's bohemian district, with bustling cafés and pubs. **Hours:** Always open. See page 51.

OSLO

• *From here, you can tour City Hall (cheap lunches Mon–Fri 12:30–13:30 only), visit the Nobel Peace Center, hike up to Akershus Fortress, take a harbor cruise (see "Tours in Oslo," earlier), or catch a boat across the harbor to the museums at Bygdøy (from pier 3). The sights just mentioned are described in detail in the following section.*

Sights in Oslo

Near the Harborfront

▲▲▲**City Hall (Rådhuset)**—In 1931, Oslo tore down a slum and began constructing its richly decorated City Hall. It was finally

finished—after a WWII delay—in 1950 to celebrate the city's 900th birthday. Norway's leading artists all contributed to the building, an avant-garde thrill in its day.

City halls, rather than churches, are the dominant buildings in Scandinavian capitals. The prominence of this building on the harborfront makes sense in this most humanistic, yet least churchgoing, northern end of the Continent. Up here, people pay high taxes, have high expectations, and are generally satisfied with what their governments do with their money.

At Oslo's City Hall, the six statues facing the waterfront—dating from a period of Labor Party rule in Norway—celebrate the nobility of the working class. The art implies a classless society, showing everyone working together. The theme continues inside, with 20,000 square feet of bold and colorful Social Realism murals showing town folk, country folk, and people from all walks of life working harmoniously for a better society. The huge murals take you on a voyage through the collective psyche of Norway, from its simple rural beginnings through the scar tissue of the Nazi occupation and beyond. Filled with significance and symbolism—and well-described in English—they become even more meaningful with the excellent **guided tours**.

The main hall feels like a temple to good government, with its altar-like mural celebrating "work, play, and civic administration." The mural emphasizes Oslo's youth participating in community life—and rebuilding the country after Nazi occupation. Across the bottom, the slum that once cluttered up Oslo's harborfront is being cleared out to make way for this building. Above that, scenes show Norway's pride in its innovative health care and education systems. Left of center, near the top, Mother Norway rests on a church—reminding viewers that the Lutheran

Church of Norway (the official state religion) provides a foundation for this society. On the right, four forms represent the arts; they illustrate how creativity springs from children. And in the center, the figure of Charity is surrounded by Culture, Philosophy, and Family.

The "Mural of the Occupation" lines the left side of the hall. It tells the story of Norway's WWII experience. Looking left to

right, you'll see the following: The German blitzkrieg overwhelms the country. Men head for the mountains to organize a resistance movement. Women huddle around the water well, traditionally where news is passed, while Quislings (traitors named after the Norwegian fascist who ruled the country as a Nazi puppet) listen in. While Germans bomb and occupy Norway, a family gathers in their living room. As a boy clenches his fist (showing determination) and a child holds the beloved Norwegian flag, the Gestapo steps in. Columns lie on the ground, symbolizing how Germans shut down the culture by closing newspapers and university. Two resistance soldiers are executed. A cell of resistance fighters (wearing masks and using nicknames so if tortured they can't reveal their compatriots' identities) plan a sabotage mission. Finally, prisoners are freed, the war is over, and Norway celebrates its happiest day: May 17, 1945—the first Independence Day after five years under Nazi control.

While gazing at these murals, keep in mind that the Nobel Peace Prize is awarded in this central hall each December (though the general Nobel Prize ceremony occurs in Stockholm's City Hall). You can see videos of the ceremony and acceptance speeches in the adjacent Nobel Peace Center (see next).

Cost and Hours: Free, daily 9:00-18:00, free 50-minute guided tours daily at 10:00, 12:00, and 14:00 in summer, tours run Wed only in winter, free WC, enter on Karl Johans Gate side, tel. 23 46 12 00.

Eating: A wonderful budget-lunch cafeteria is downstairs, offering a simple hot meal and salad bar at a nonprofit price; it's primarily for the building's workers, but the public is welcome (Mon-Fri 12:30-13:30 only). Fans of the explorer Fridtjof Nansen might enjoy a coffee or beer across the street at Fridtjof, an atmospheric bar filled with memorabilia from Nansen's Arctic explorations (Mon-Sat 12:00 until late, Sun 14:00-22:00, Nansens Plass 7, near Forex, tel. 93 25 22 30).

▲**Nobel Peace Center (Nobels Fredssenter)**—This thoughtful and thought-provoking museum, housed in the former West

Train Station (Vestbanen), poses the question, "What is the opposite of conflict?" It celebrates the 800-some past and present Nobel Peace Prize winners with engaging audio and video exhibits and high-tech gadgetry (all with good English explanations). Allow time for reading about past prizewinners and listening to acceptance speeches by recipients from President Carter to Mother Theresa. Check out the astonishing interactive book detailing the life and work of Alfred Nobel, the Swedish inventor of dynamite, who initiated the prizes—perhaps to assuage his conscience.

OSLO

Cost and Hours: 80 kr; mid-May-Aug daily 10:00-18:00; Sept-mid-May Tue-Sun 10:00-18:00, closed Mon; included guided tours at 12:00, 14:00, and 15:00, fewer in winter; Brynjulfs Bulls Plass 1, tel. 48 30 10 00, www.nobelpeacecenter.org.

▲**Opera House**—Opened in 2008, Oslo's striking Opera House is the talk of the town and a huge hit. The Opera House rises

from the water on the city's eastern harbor, across the highway from the train station (use the sky-bridge). Its boxy, low-slung, glass center holds a state-of-the-art, 1,400-seat main theater. The jutting white marble planes of its roof double as a public plaza. When visiting, you feel a need to walk all over it. The Opera House is part of a larger harbor-redevelopment plan that includes rerouting traffic into tunnels and turning a once-derelict industrial zone into an urban park.

Cost and Hours: Foyer and café/restaurant open Mon-Fri 10:00-23:00, Sat 11:00-23:00, Sun 12:00-22:00.

Tours: In summer, the Opera House offers guided tours of the auditorium and backstage area (100 kr, daily usually at 12:00, time can vary) and sporadic foyer concerts (50 kr, generally at 13:00). For tours, reserve by email at omvisninger@operaen.no or online at www.operaen.no (tel. 21 42 21 00).

▲Akershus Fortress Complex

This park-like complex of sights scattered over Oslo's fortified old center is still a military base. But as you dodge patrol guards and vans filled with soldiers, you'll see the castle, a prison, war memorials, the Norwegian Resistance Museum, the Armed Forces Museum, and cannon-strewn ramparts affording fine harbor views and picnic perches. There's an unimpressive changing of the guard daily at 13:30 (at the parade ground, deep in the castle complex). The park is generally open daily 6:00-21:00, but because the military is in charge here, times can change without warning. Expect bumpy cobblestone lanes and steep hills. To get here from the harbor, follow the stairs (which lead past the FDR statue) to the park.

Fortress Visitors Center: Located immediately inside the gate, the information center has an interesting exhibit tracing the story of Oslo's fortifications from medieval times through the environmental struggles of today. Stop here to pick up a castle overview booklet, quickly browse through the museum, watch the quick video, and consider catching a tour (see next; museum entry free, mid-June-mid-Aug Mon-Fri 9:00-17:00, Sat-Sun 11:00-17:00, shorter hours off-season, tel. 23 09 39 17, www.mil.no/felles/ak).

▲**Fortress Tours**—The free 45-minute English walking tours of the grounds help you make sense of the most historic piece of real estate in Oslo (generally offered May-Aug daily at 12:00, 13:00, 15:00, and 16:00; no tours off-season; depart from Fortress Visitors Center, call center at tel. 23 09 39 17 in advance to confirm times).

Akershus Castle—Although it's one of Oslo's oldest buildings (c. 1300), the castle overlooking the harbor is mediocre by European

standards; the big, empty rooms recall Norway's medieval poverty. From the old kitchen, where the ticket desk and gift shop are located, you'll follow a one-way circuit of rooms open to the public. Descend through a secret passage to the dungeon, crypt, and royal tomb. Emerge behind the altar in the chapel, then walk through echoing rooms including the Daredevil's Tower, Hall of Christian IV, and Hall of Olav I. There are terrific harbor views from the rampart just outside.

Cost and Hours: 70 kr, sparse English descriptions throughout; May-Aug Mon-Sat 10:00-16:00, Sun 12:30-16:00; Sept-April Sat-Sun 12:00-17:00 only, closed Mon-Fri; tel. 22 41 25 21.

▲▲**Norwegian Resistance Museum (Norges Hjemmefrontmuseum)**—This fascinating museum tells the story of Norway's WWII experience: appeasement, Nazi invasion (they made Akershus their headquarters), resistance, liberation, and, finally, the return of the king. It's a one-way, chronological, can't-get-lost route—enter through the 1940 door.

You'll see propaganda posters attempting to get Norwegians to join the Nazi party, and the German ultimatum to which the king gave an emphatic "No." Various displays show secret radios, transmitters, underground newspapers, crude but effective homemade weapons, and the German machine that located clandestine radio stations. Exhibits explain how the country coped with 350,000 occupying troops; how airdrops equipped a home force of 40,000 ready to coordinate with the Allies when liberation was imminent; and the happy day when peace and freedom returned to Norway.

The museum is particularly poignant because many of the patriots featured inside were executed by the Germans right out-

side the museum's front door; a stone memorial marks the spot. (At war's end, the traitor Vidkun Quisling was also executed here.) With good English descriptions, this is an inspirational look at how the national spirit can endure total occupation by a malevolent force.

Cost and Hours: 50 kr, 100-kr family ticket covers 2 adults plus up to 2 kids; June-Aug Mon-Sat 10:00-17:00, Sun 11:00-17:00; Sept-May Mon-Fri 10:00-16:00, Sat-Sun 11:00-16:00; next to castle, overlooking harbor, tel. 23 09 31 38, www.mil.no/felles/nhm.

Armed Forces Museum (Forsvarsmuseet)—Across the fortress parade ground, a too-spacious museum traces Norwegian military history from Viking days to post-World War II. The early stuff is sketchy, but the WWII story is compelling.

Cost and Hours: Free, May-Aug Mon-Fri 10:00-17:00, Sat-Sun 11:00-17:00, shorter hours off-season, tel. 23 09 35 82.

▲▲▲National Gallery (Nasjonalgalleriet)

While there are many schools of painting and sculpture displayed in Norway's National Gallery, focus on what's uniquely Norwegian. Paintings come and go in this museum (pesky curators may have even removed some of the ones listed in the self-guided tour below), but you're sure to see plenty that showcase the harsh beauty of Norway's landscape and people. A thoughtful visit here gives those heading into the mountains and fjord country a chance to pack along

a little of Norway's cultural soul. Tuck these images carefully away with your goat cheese—they'll sweeten your explorations.

The gallery also has several Picassos, a noteworthy Impressionist collection, a Van Gogh self-portrait, and some Vigeland statues. Its many raving examples of Edvard Munch's work, including one of his famous *Scream* paintings, make a trip to the Munch Museum unnecessary for most. It has about 50 Munch paintings in its collection, but only about a third are on display. Be prepared for changes, but don't worry—no matter what the curators decide to show, you won't have to scream for Munch's masterpieces.

Cost and Hours: 50 kr, free on Sun, Tue-Fri 10:00-18:00, Thu until 19:00, Sat-Sun 11:00-17:00, closed Mon, chewing gum prohibited, Universitets Gata 13, tel. 22 20 04 04, www.national museum.no.

The museum's 20-kr audioguide covers 15 paintings, has a poetic narrative with quotes from artists, and forces you to linger at each work of art—but doesn't have much more information than my self-guided tour below.

Self-Guided Tour

This easy-to-handle museum gives an effortless tour back in time and through Norway's most beautiful valleys, mountains, and fjords, with the help of its Romantic painters (especially Johan Christian Dahl). The paintings are organized roughly chronologically, from 1814 through 1950.

• *Go up the stairs but before entering the first room, look to the right at the large canvas in the stairwell.*

❶ **Christian Krohg—*Albertine to See the Police Surgeon* (c. 1885-1887):** Christian Krohg (1852-1925) is known as Edvard Munch's inspiration, but to Norwegians, he's famous in his own right for his artistry and giant personality. Krohg had a sharp interest in social justice. In this painting, Albertine, a sweet girl from the countryside, has fallen into the world of prostitution in the big city. She's the new kid on the red-light block in the 1880s, as Oslo's prostitutes are pulled into the police clinic for their regular checkup. Note her traditional dress and the disdain she gets from the more experienced girls. Krohg has buried his subject in this scene. His technique requires the viewer to find her, and that search helps humanize the prostitute.

• *We'll look at more stark Norwegian realism later. But for now, let's head somewhere more idyllic. Walk into Room Z, turn left, and enter Room L.*

Landscape Paintings and Romanticism

Landscape painting has always played an important role in Norwegian art, perhaps because Norway provides such an awesome and varied landscape to inspire artists. The style reached its peak during the Romantic period in the mid-1800s, which stressed the beauty of unspoiled nature. (This passion for landscapes sets Norway apart from Denmark and Sweden.) After 400 years of

OSLO

National Gallery—Upper Floor

To Karl Johans Gate →

ENTER BELOW

UNIVERSITETSGATA

❶ KROHG — Albertine to See the Police Surgeon

❷ DAHL — View of Fortundalen

❸ DAHL — Hellefossen near Hokksund

❹ FEARNLEY — Labro Falls near Kongsberg

❺ TIDEMAND & GUDE — The Bridal Voyage

❻ TIDEMAND — Low Church Devotion

❼ PETERSSEN — Christian II

❽ SUNDT-HANSEN — Burial at Sea

❾ KROHG — A Sick Girl

❿ SOHLBERG — Winter Night in the Mountains

⓫ MUNCH — Self-Portrait with a Cigarette

⓬ MUNCH — The Sick Child

⓭ MUNCH — Madonna

⓮ MUNCH — The Scream

⓯ MUNCH — Dance of Life

Danish rule, the soul of the country was almost snuffed out. But with semi-independence and a constitution in the early 1800s, there was a national resurgence. Romantic paintings featuring the power of Norway's natural wonders and the toughness of its salt-of-the-earth folk came into vogue.

❷ **Johan Christian Dahl**—*View of Fortundalen* (1836): This painting epitomizes the Norwegian closeness to nature. It shows a view similar to the one that 21st-century travelers enjoy on their Norway in a Nutshell excursion: mountains, rivers, and a waterfall. Painted in 1836, it's textbook Romantic style. Nature rules—the background is as detailed as the foreground, and you are sucked in.

Johan Christian Dahl (1788-1857) is considered the father of Norwegian Romanticism. Romantics such as Dahl (and Turner, Beethoven, and Lord Byron) put emotion over rationality. They reveled in the power of nature—death and pessimism ripple through their work. The birch tree—standing boldly front and center—is a standard symbol for the politically downtrodden Norwegian people: hardy, cut down, but defiantly sprouting new branches. In the mid-19th century, Norwegians were awakening to their national identity. Throughout Europe, nationalism and Romanticism went hand in hand.

Find the typical Norse farm with its haystacks looking like rune stones. It reminds us that these farmers are hardworking, independent, small landowners. There was no feudalism in medieval Norway. People were poor...but they owned their own land. You can almost taste the *geitost*.

• *Look at the other works in Rooms L and M. Dahl's paintings and those by his Norwegian contemporaries, showing heavy clouds and glaciers, repeat these same themes—drama over rationalism, nature pounding humanity. Human figures are melancholy. Norwegians, so close to nature, are fascinated by those plush, magic hours of dawn and twilight. The dusk makes us wonder: What will the future bring?*

In particular, focus on....

❸ **Dahl**—*Hellefossen near Hokksund* (1838): Another typical Dahl setting: romantic nature and an idealized scene. A fisherman checks on wooden baskets designed to catch salmon migrating up the river. In the background, a water-powered sawmill slices trees into lumber. Note another Dahl birch tree at the left, a subtle celebration of the Norwegian people and their labor.

❹ **Thomas Fearnley**—*Labro Falls near Kongsberg* (1837): Man cannot control nature or his destiny. The landscape in this painting is devoid of people—the only sign of humanity is the jumble of sawn logs in the foreground. A wary eagle perched on one log seems to be saying, "While you can cut these trees, they'll always be mine."

• *Go to the end of Room M and turn left into Room N.*

❺ **Adolph Tidemand and Hans Gude**—*The Bridal Voyage* (1848): This famous painting shows the ultimate Norwegian scene:

a wedding party with everyone decked out in traditional garb, heading for the stave church on the quintessential fjord (Hardanger). It's a studio work (not real) and a collaboration: Hans Gude painted the landscape, and Adolph Tidemand painted the people. Study their wedding finery. This work trumpets the greatness of both the landscape and Norwegian culture.

The Photographic Eye

At the end of the 19th century, Norwegian painters traded the emotions of Romanticism for more slice-of-life detail. This was the end of the Romantic period and the beginning of Realism. With the advent of photography, painters went beyond simple realism and into extreme realism.

❻ Tidemand—*Low Church Devotion* (1848): This scene shows a dissenting Lutheran church group (of which there were many in the 19th century) worshipping in a smokehouse. The light of God powers through the chimney, illuminating salt-of-the-earth people with strong faiths. Rather than accept the Norwegian king's "High Church," they worshipped in their homes in a more ascetic style. Later, many of these people emigrated to America for greater religious freedom.

❼ Eilif Peterssen—*Christian II* (1875): The Danish king signs the execution order for the man who'd killed the king's beloved mistress. With camera-like precision, the painter captures the whole story of murder, anguish, anger, and bitter revenge in the king's set jaw and steely eyes.

• *Go through Rooms O and P and into Room Q. Take time to browse the paintings.*

Vulnerability

Death, disease, and suffering were themes seen again and again in art from the late 1800s. The most serious disease during this period was tuberculosis (which killed Munch's mother and sister).

❽ Carl Sundt-Hansen—*Burial at Sea* (1890): While Monet and the Impressionists were busy abandoning the realistic style, Norwegian artists continued to embrace it. In this painting, you're invited to participate. A dead man's funeral is attended by an ethnically diverse group of sailors and passengers, but only one is a woman—the widow. Your presence completes the half-circle at the on-deck ceremony. Notice how each person in the painting has

his or her own way of confronting death. Their faces speak volumes about the life of toil here. A common thread in Norwegian art is the cycle—the tough cycle—of life. There's also an interest in everyday experiences.

❾ Krohg—*A Sick Girl* (1880): This extremely realistic painting shows a child dying of tuberculosis, as so many did in Norway in the 19th century. The girl looks directly at you. You can almost feel the cloth, with its many shades of white.

• *Continue through Room R and into Room S.*

Atmosphere

Landscape painters were often fascinated by the phenomena of nature, and the artwork in this room takes us back to this ideal from the Romantic Age. Painters were challenged by capturing atmospheric conditions at a specific moment, since it meant making quick sketches outdoors, before the weather changed yet again.

❿ Harald Sohlberg—*Winter Night in the Mountains* **(1914):** Harald Sohlberg was inspired by this image while skiing in the

mountains in the winter of 1899. Over the years, he attempted to re-create the scene that inspired this remark: "The mountains in winter reduce one to silence. One is overwhelmed, as in a mighty, vaulted church, only a thousand times more so."

• *Follow the crowds into Room T, the Munch room.*

Turmoil

Room T is filled with works by Norway's single most famous painter, Edvard Munch (see sidebar next page). Norway's long, dark winters and social isolation have produced many gloomy artists, but none gloomier than Munch. He infused his work with emotion and expression at the expense of realism. After viewing the paintings in general, take a look at these in particular (listed in clockwise order).

⓫ Edvard Munch—*Self Portrait with a Cigarette* **(1895):** In this self-portrait, Munch is spooked, haunted—an artist working, immersed in an oppressive world. Indefinable shadows inhabit the background. His hand shakes as he considers his uncertain future. (Ironic, considering he created his masterpieces during this depressed period.) After eight months in a Danish clinic, he found peace—and lost his painting power. Afterward, Munch never again painted another strong example of what we love most about his art.

⓬ Munch—*The Sick Child* **(1896):** The death of Munch's sister in 1877 due to tuberculosis likely inspired this painting. The girl's face melts into the pillow. She's becoming two-dimensional, halfway between life and death. Everything else is peripheral, even her despairing mother saying good-bye. You can see how Munch scraped and repainted the face until he got it right.

⓭ Munch—*Madonna* **(1894-1895):** Munch had a tortured relationship with women. He never married. He dreaded and struggled with love, writing that he feared if he loved too

Edvard Munch
(1863-1944)

Edvard Munch (pronounced "moonk") is Norway's most famous and influential painter. His life was rich, complex, and sad. His father was a doctor who had a nervous break-down. His mother and sister both died of tuberculosis. He knew suffering. And he gave us the enduring symbol of 20th-century pain, *The Scream*.

He was also Norway's most forward-thinking painter, a man who traveled extensively through Europe, soaking up the colors of the Post-Impressionists and the curves of Art Nouveau. He helped pioneer a new style—Expressionism—using lurid colors and wavy lines to "express" inner turmoil and the angst of the modern world.

After a nervous breakdown in late 1908, followed by eight months of rehab in a clinic, Munch emerged less troubled—but a less powerful painter. His late works were as a colorist: big, bright, less tormented...and less noticed.

much, he'd lose his painting talent. This painting is a mystery: Is she standing or lying? Is that a red halo or some devilish accessory? Munch wrote that he would strive to capture his subjects at their holiest moment. His alternative name for this work: *Woman Making Love*. What's more holy than a woman at the moment of conception?

❹ Munch—*The Scream* (1893): Munch's most famous work shows a man screaming, capturing the fright many feel as the human "race" does just that. The figure seems isolated from the

people on the bridge—locked up in himself, unable to stifle his scream. Munch made four versions of this scene, which has become *the* textbook example of Expressionism. On one, he graffitied: "This painting is the work of a madman." He explained that the painting "shows today's society, reverberating within me...making me want to scream." He's sharing his internal angst. In fact, this Expressionist masterpiece is a breakthrough painting; it's angst personified.

⑮ Munch—*Dance of Life* **(1899-1900):** In this scene of five dancing couples, we glimpse Munch's notion of femininity. To him, women were a complex mix of Madonna and whore. We see Munch's take on the cycle of women's lives: She's a virgin (discarding the sweet flower of youth), a whore (a jaded temptress in red), and a widow (having destroyed the man, she is finally alone, aging, in black). With the phallic moon rising on the lake, Munch demonizes women as they turn men into green-faced, lusty monsters.

• *Our tour is over, but there's more to see in this fine collection. Take a break from Nordic gloom and doom by visiting Rooms O and Y, with works by Impressionist and Post-Impressionist artists...even Munch got into the spirit with his Parisian painting titled* Rue Lafayette.

Near the National Gallery

National Historical Museum (Historisk Museum)—Directly behind the National Gallery and just below the palace is a fine Art Nouveau building offering an easy (if underwhelming) peek at Norway's history. The ground floor offers a walk through the local history from prehistoric times. It includes the country's top collection of Viking artifacts, displayed in low-tech, old-school exhibits with barely a word of English to give it meaning. There's also some medieval church art. The museum's highlight is upstairs: an exhibit (well-described in English) about life in the Arctic for the Sami people (previously known to outsiders as Laplanders). In this overview of the past, a few Egyptian mummies and Norwegian coins through the ages are tossed in for good measure.

Cost and Hours: 50 kr, included 45-minute Viking tours daily at noon in the summer; mid-May-mid-Sept Tue-Sun 10:00-17:00, closed Mon; mid-Sept-mid-May Tue-Sun 11:00-16:00, closed Mon; Frederiks Gate 2, tel. 22 85 99 12, www.khm.uio.no.

▲▲▲Frogner Park

This 75-acre park contains a lifetime of work by Norway's greatest sculptor, Gustav Vigeland (see sidebar on next page). In 1921, he made a deal with the city. In return for a great studio and state support, he'd spend his creative life beautifying Oslo with this sculpture garden. From 1924 to 1943 he worked on-site, designing 192 bronze and granite statue groupings—600 figures in all, each nude and unique. Vigeland even planned the landscaping. Today the park is loved and respected by the people of Oslo (no police, no fences—and no graffiti).

The garden is always open and free (buses #20 and #45, and trams #12 and #19 all stop immediately in front of the main entry; or T-bane: Majorstuen and a 5-minute walk). The Frognerbadet swimming pool is also at Frogner Park. The park is safe (cameras monitor for safety) and lit in the evening.

Gustav Vigeland
(1869-1943)

As a young man, Vigeland studied sculpture in Oslo, then supplemented his education with trips abroad to Europe's art capitals. Back home, he carved out a successful, critically acclaimed career feeding newly independent Norway's hunger for homegrown art.

During his youthful trips abroad, Vigeland had frequented the studio of Auguste Rodin, admiring Rodin's naked, restless, intertwined statues. Like Rodin, Vigeland explored the yin/yang relationship of men and women. Also like Rodin, Vigeland did not personally carve or cast his statues. Rather, he formed them in clay or plaster, to be executed by a workshop of assistants. Vigeland's sturdy humans capture universal themes of the cycle of life—birth, childhood, romance, struggle, child-rearing, growing old, and death.

Vigeland's park is more than great art: It's a city at play. Appreciate its urban Norwegian ambience. The park is huge, but this visit is a snap. Here's a quick, four-stop, straight-line, gate-to-monolith tour:

1. Enter the Park from Kirkeveien: For an illustrated guide and fine souvenir, pick up the 75-kr book in the Visitors Center (Besøkssenter) on your right as you enter. The modern cafeteria has sandwiches (indoor/outdoor seating, daily 9:00-20:30, shorter hours Sun and off-season), plus books, gifts, and WCs. Look at the statue of Gustav Vigeland (hammer and chisel in hand, drenched

in pigeon poop) and consider his messed-up life. He lived with his many models. His marriages failed. His children entangled his artistic agenda. He didn't age gracefully. He didn't name his statues, and refused to explain their meanings. While those who know his life story can read it clearly in the granite and bronze, I'd forget Gustav's troubles and see his art as observations on the bittersweet cycle of life in general—from a man who must have had a passion for living.

2. Bridge: The 300-foot-long bridge is bounded by four granite columns: Three show a man fighting a lizard, the fourth shows a woman submitting to the lizard's embrace. Hmmm. (Vigeland was familiar with medieval mythology, where dragons represent man's primal—and sinful—nature.) But enough lizard love; the 58 bronze statues along the bridge are a general study of the human body. Many deal with relationships between people. In the middle, on the right, find the circular statue of a man and woman going round and round—perhaps the eternal attraction and love between the sexes. But directly opposite, another circle feels like a prison—

man against the world, with no refuge. From the man escaping, look down at the children's playground: eight bronze infants circling a head-down fetus.

On your left, see the famous *Sinnataggen,* the hot-headed little boy. It's said Vigeland gave him chocolate and then took it away to get this reaction. The statues capture the joys of life (and, on a sunny day, so do the Norwegians filling the park around you).

3. Fountain: Continue through a rose garden to the earliest sculpture unit in the park. Six giants hold a fountain, symbolically toiling with the burden of life, as water—the source of life—cascades steadily around them. Twenty tree-of-life groups surround the fountain. Four clumps of trees (on each corner) show humanity's relationship to nature and the seasons of life: childhood, young love, adulthood, and winter.

Take a quick swing through life, starting on the right with youth. In the branches you'll see a swarm of children (Vigeland called them "geniuses"): A boy sits in a tree, boys actively climb

while most girls stand by quietly, and a girl glides through the branches wide-eyed and ready for life...and love. Circle clockwise to the next stage: love scenes. In the third corner, life becomes more complicated: a sad woman in an animal-like tree, a lonely child, a couple plummeting downward (perhaps falling out of love), and finally an angry man driving away babies. The fourth corner completes the cycle, as death melts into the branches of the tree of life and you realize new geniuses will bloom.

The 60 bronze reliefs circling the basin develop the theme further, showing man mixing with nature and geniuses giving the carousel of life yet another spin. Speaking of another spin, circle again and follow these reliefs.

The sidewalk surrounding the basin is a maze—life's long and winding road with twists, dead ends, frustrations, and, ultimately, a way out. If you have about an hour to spare, enter the labyrinth (on the side nearest the park's entrance gate, there's a single break in the black border) and follow the white granite path until (on the monolith side) you finally get out. (Tracing this path occupies older kids, affording parents a peaceful break in the park.) Or you can go straight up the steps to the monolith.

4. Monolith: The centerpiece of the park—a teeming mono- lith of life surrounded by 36 granite groups—continues Vigeland's

cycle-of-life motif. The figures are hunched and clearly earthbound, while Vigeland explores a lifetime of human relationships. At the center, 121 figures carved out of a single block of stone rocket skyward. Three stone carvers worked daily for 14 years, cut- ting Vigeland's full-size plaster model into the final 180-ton, 50-foot-tall erection.

Circle the plaza, once to trace the stages of life in the 36 statue groups, and a second time to enjoy how Norwegian kids relate to the art. The statues—both young and old—seem to speak to children.

Vigeland lived barely long enough to see his monolith raised. Covered with bodies, it seems to pick up speed as it spirals sky- ward. Some people seem to naturally rise. Others struggle not to fall. Some help others. Although the granite groups around the monolith are easy to understand, Vigeland left the meaning of the monolith itself open. Like life, it can be interpreted many different ways.

From this summit of the park, look a hundred yards farther, where four children and three adults are intertwined and spinning in the Wheel of Life. Now, look back at the entrance. If the main gate is at 12 o'clock, the studio where Vigeland lived and worked— now the Vigeland Museum—is at 2 o'clock (see the green cop- per tower poking above the trees). His ashes sit in the top of the tower in clear view of the monolith. If you liked the park, visit the Vigeland Museum (described next), a delightful five-minute walk away, for an intimate look at the art and how it was made.

▲▲Vigeland Museum—Filled with original plaster casts and well-described exhibits on his work, this palatial city-provided studio was Vigeland's home and workplace. The high south-facing windows provided just the right light.

Vigeland, who had a deeply religious upbringing, saw his art as an expression of his soul. He once said, "The road between feeling and execution should be as short as possible." Here, immersed in his work, Vigeland supervised his craftsmen like a father, from 1924 until his death in 1943.

Cost and Hours: 50 kr; June-Aug Tue-Sun 10:00-17:00, closed Mon; Sept-May Tue-Sun 12:00-16:00, closed Mon; bus #20 or #45 or tram #12 to Frogner Plass, Nobels Gate 32, tel. 23 49 37 00, www.vigeland.museum.no.

Oslo City Museum (Oslo Bymuseum)—This hard-to-be-thrilled-about little museum tells the story of Oslo. For a quick overview of the city, watch the 15-minute English video.

Cost and Hours: Free, Tue-Sun 11:00-17:00, closed Mon, borrow English description sheet, located in Frogner Park at Frogner Manor Farm across street from Vigeland Museum, tel. 23 28 41 70, www.oslomuseum.no.

▲▲Oslo's Bygdøy Neighborhood

This thought-provoking and exciting cluster of sights is on a park-like peninsula just across the harbor from downtown. It provides a busy and rewarding half-day (at a minimum) of sightseeing. Here, within a short walk, are six important sights (listed in order of importance):

• **Norwegian Folk Museum,** an open-air park with traditional log buildings from all corners of the country.

• **Viking Ship Museum,** showing off the best-preserved Viking longboats in existence.

• *Fram* **Museum,** showcasing the modern Viking spirit with the ship of arctic-exploration fame.

• *Kon-Tiki* **Museum,** starring the *Kon-Tiki* and the *Ra II,* in which Norwegian explorer Thor Heyerdahl proved that early civilizations—with their existing technologies—could have crossed the oceans.

• **Norwegian Maritime Museum,** interesting mostly to old salts, has a wonderfully scenic movie of Norway.

• **Norwegian Holocaust Center,** a high-tech look at the Holocaust in Norway and contemporary racism.

OSLO

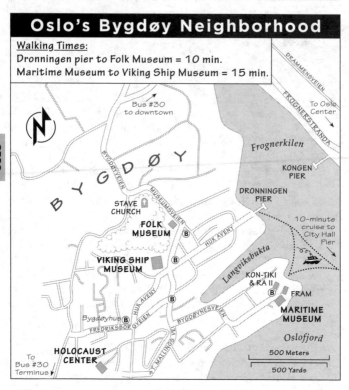

Oslo's Bygdøy Neighborhood

Walking Times:
Dronningen pier to Folk Museum = 10 min.
Maritime Museum to Viking Ship Museum = 15 min.

Getting There: Sailing from downtown to Bygdøy is fun, and it gets you in a seafaring mood. Ride the Bygdøy ferry—marked *Public Ferry Bygdøy Museums*—from pier 3 in front of City Hall (40 kr one-way; covered by Oslo Pass, transit tickets, and Reisekort smartcard; May-Sept daily 8:45-21:00, usually 3/hour; doesn't run Oct-April). Boats generally leave from downtown and from the museum dock at :05, :25, and :45 past each hour. In summer, avoid the nearby, and much more expensive, tour boats. For a less memorable approach, you can take bus #30 (from train station or National Theater, direction: Bygdøy).

Getting Around Bygdøy: The Norwegian Folk and Viking Ship museums are a 10-minute walk from the ferry's first stop (Dronningen). The other boating museums (*Fram, Kon-Tiki,* and Maritime) are at the second ferry stop (Bygdøynes). The Holocaust Center is off Fredriksborgveien, about halfway between these two museum clusters. All Bygdøy sights are within a pleasant (when sunny) 15-minute walk of each other. The walk gives you a picturesque taste of small-town Norway.

The city bus #30 connects the sights four times hourly in this order: the Norwegian Folk Museum, Viking Ship Museum,

Kon-Tiki Museum, and Norwegian Holocaust Center. (For the Holocaust Center, you'll use the Bygdøyhus stop a long block away; tell the bus driver you want the stop for the "HL-Senteret"). The bus turns around at its final stop (Huk), then passes the sights in reverse order on its way back to the city center. If you take the bus within an hour of having taken the public ferry, your ticket is still good on the bus. Note that after 17:00, bus and boat departures are sparse. If returning to Oslo by ferry, get to the dock a little early—otherwise the boat is likely to be full, and you'll have to wait for the next sailing.

Eating at Bygdøy: Lunch options near the *Kon-Tiki* are a sandwich bar (relaxing picnic spots along the grassy shoreline) and a cafeteria (with tables overlooking the harbor). The Norwegian Folk Museum has a decent cafeteria inside and a fun little farmers' market stall across the street from the entrance. The Holocaust Center has a small café on its second floor.

▲▲▲Norwegian Folk Museum (Norsk Folkemuseum)— Brought from all corners of Norway, 150 buildings have been reassembled here on 35 acres. While Stockholm's Skansen was the first museum of this kind to open to the public, this museum is a bit older, started in 1882 as the king's private collection (and the inspiration for Skansen).

Think of the visit in three parts: the park sprinkled with old buildings, the re-created old town, and the folk-art museum. In peak season, the park is lively, with craftspeople doing their traditional things and costumed guides all around. (They're paid to happily answer your questions—so ask many.) The evocative Gol stave church, at the top of a hill at the park's edge, is a mustsee (built in 1212 in Hallingdal and painstakingly reconstructed here). Across the park, the old town comes complete with apartments from various generations (including some reconstructions of actual people's homes) and offers an intimate look at lifestyles here in 1905, 1930, 1950, 1979, and even a modern-day Norwegian-Pakistani apartment.

The museum beautifully presents woody, colorfully painted folk art (ground floor), exquisite-in-a-peasant-kind-of-way folk

costumes (upstairs), and temporary exhibits. Everything is thoughtfully explained in English. Don't miss the best Sami culture exhibit I've seen in Scandinavia (across the courtyard in the green building, behind the toy exhibit).

Upon arrival, pick up the site map and review the list of activities, concerts, and guided tours on that day. In summer, guided tours go daily at 12:00 and 14:00; the Telemark Farm hosts a small daily fiddle-and-dance show on the hour; and a folk music-and-dance show is held each Sunday at 14:00. The folk museum is lively only June through mid-August, when buildings are open and staffed. Otherwise, the indoor museum is fine, but the park is just a walk past lots of locked-up log cabins. If you don't take a tour, glean information from the 10-kr guidebook and the informative attendants stationed in buildings throughout the park.

Cost and Hours: 100 kr, daily mid-May–mid-Sept 10:00-18:00, off-season park open Mon-Fri 11:00-15:00, Sat-Sun 11:00-16:00 but most historical buildings closed, free lockers, Museumsveien 10, bus #30 stops immediately in front, tel. 22 12 37 00, www.norskfolkemuseum.no.

▲▲**Viking Ship Museum (Vikingskiphuset)**—In this impressive museum, you'll gaze with admiration at two finely crafted, majestic oak Viking ships dating from the 9th and 10th centuries. Along with the well-preserved ships, you'll see remarkable artifacts that may cause you to consider these notorious raiders in a different light. Over a thousand years ago, three things drove Vikings on their far-flung raids: hard economic times in their

bleak homeland, the lure of prosperous and vulnerable communities to the south, and a mastery of the sea. There was a time when most frightened Europeans closed every prayer with, "And deliver us from the Vikings, Amen." Gazing up at the prow of one of these sleek, time-stained vessels, you can almost hear the screams and smell the armpits of those redheads on the rampage.

The *Oseberg* ship, from A.D. 834, is the first ship you see. With its ornate carving and impressive rudder, it was likely a royal pleasure craft. It seems designed for sailing on calm inland waters during festivals, but not in the open ocean.

The *Gokstad* ship, from A.D. 950, is a practical working boat, capable of sailing the high seas. A ship like this brought settlers to the west of France (Normandy was named for the Norsemen). And in such a vessel, explorers such as Eric the Red hopscotched from Norway to Iceland to Greenland and on to what they called Vinland—today's Newfoundland in Canada. Imagine 30 men hauling on long oars out at sea for weeks and months at a time. In 1892, a replica of this ship sailed from Norway to America in 44 days to celebrate the 400th anniversary of Columbus *not* discovering America.

The ships tend to steal the show, but don't miss the hall displaying **jewelry and personal items** excavated along with the ships. The ships and related artifacts survived so well because they were buried in clay as part of a gravesite. Many of the finest items were not actually Viking art, but goodies they brought home after raiding more advanced (but less tough) people. Still, there are lots of actual Viking items, such as metal and leather goods, that give insight into their culture. Highlights are the cart and sleighs, ornately carved with scenes from Viking sagas.

The museum doesn't offer tours, but it's easy to eavesdrop on the many guides leading big groups through the museum. Everything is well-described in English. You probably don't need the little museum guidebook—it repeats exactly what's already posted on the exhibits.

Cost and Hours: 60 kr, daily May-Sept 9:00-18:00, Oct-April 10:00-16:00, Huk Aveny 35, tel. 22 13 52 80, www.khm .uio.no.

▲**Norwegian Holocaust Center (HL-Senteret)**—Located in the stately former home of Nazi collaborator Vidkun Quisling, this museum and study center offers a high-tech look at the racist ideologies that fueled the Holocaust. To show the Holocaust in a Norwegian context, the first floor displays historical documents about the rise of anti-Semitism and personal effects from Holocaust victims. Downstairs, the names of 760 Norwegian Jews killed by the Nazis are listed in a bright, white room. The *Innocent Questions* glass-and-neon sculpture outside shows an old-fashioned punch card, reminding viewers of how the Norwegian puppet government collected seemingly innocuous information before deporting its Jews. The *Contemporary Reflections* video is a reminder that racism and genocide continue today.

Cost and Hours: 50 kr, ask for free English audioguide or catalog with translation of exhibit text, daily mid-June-mid-Aug 10:00-18:00, mid-Aug-mid-June 11:00-16:00, Huk Aveny 56—follow signs to *HL-Senteret*, tel. 22 84 21 00, www.hlsenteret.no.

▲▲*Fram* **Museum (Frammuseet)**—This museum holds the 125-foot, steam- and sail-powered ship that took modern-day Vikings Roald Amundsen and Fridtjof Nansen deep into the Arc-

tic and Antarctic, farther north and south than any vessel had gone before. For three years, the *Fram*—specially designed to survive the crushing pressures of a frozen-over sea—drifted, trapped in the Arctic ice. The exhibit is engrossing. Read the ground-floor displays, check out the videos below the bow of the ship, then climb the steps to the third-floor gangway to explore the *Fram*'s claustrophobic but fascinating interior. The museum also tells the chilling tales of other Arctic and Antarctic adventures undertaken beneath the Norwegian flag. The polar sloop *Gjøa*, dry-docked outside next to the ferry dock, is the ship that Amundsen and a crew of six used from 1903 to 1906 to "discover" the Northwest Passage.

Cost and Hours: 60 kr, daily June-Aug 9:00-18:00, May and Sept 10:00-17:00, Oct-mid-Jan and mid-Feb-April 10:00-16:00, closed mid-Jan-mid-Feb, Bygdøynesveien 36, tel. 23 28 29 50, www.fram.museum.no.

▲▲**Kon-Tiki Museum (*Kon-Tiki* Museet)**—Next to the *Fram* is a museum housing the *Kon-Tiki* and the *Ra II*, the ships built by Thor Heyerdahl (1914-2002). In 1947, Heyerdahl and five crewmates constructed the *Kon-Tiki* raft out of balsa wood, using only pre-modern tools and techniques. They set sail from Peru on the tiny craft, surviving for 101 days on fish, coconuts, and sweet potatoes (which were native to Peru). About 4,300 miles later, they arrived in Polynesia. The point was to show that early South Americans could have settled Polynesia. (While Heyerdahl proved they could have, anthropologists doubt they did.) The *Kon-Tiki* story became a best-selling book and award-winning documentary (and helped spawn the "Tiki" culture craze in the US). In 1970, Heyerdahl's *Ra II* made a similar 3,000-mile journey from Morocco to Barbados to prove that Africans could have populated America. Both ships are well-displayed and described in English. Various 10-minute clips from the *Kon-Tiki* movie (winner of 1951 Oscar for best documentary) play constantly in a small theater at the end of the exhibit

Cost and Hours: 50 kr, daily June-Aug 9:30-17:30, April-May and Sept 10:00-17:00, Oct-March 10:30-16:00, Bygdøynesveien 36, tel. 23 08 67 67, www.kon-tiki.no.

▲**Norwegian Maritime Museum (Norsk Sjøfartsmuseum)**— If you like the sea, this museum is a salt lick, providing a wide-ranging look at Norway's maritime heritage. Its dusty collection includes the charred remains of Norway's oldest boat (2,200 years old), artifacts from the immigration days, and a case devoted to World War II. Don't miss the movie *The Ocean: A Way of Life*, included with your admission. It's a breathtaking widescreen film swooping you scenically over Norway's dramatic sea and fishing townscapes from here all the way to North Cape in a comfy theater (20 minutes, shown at the top and bottom of the hour, follow *Supervideografen* signs).

Cost and Hours: 60 kr, kids under 16 free; mid-May-Aug daily 10:00-18:00; Sept-mid-May Tue-Sun 10:00-15:00, closed Mon; Bygdøynesveien 37, tel. 24 11 41 50, www.marmuseum.no.

Outer Oslo

▲▲**Holmenkollen Ski Jump and Ski Museum**—The site of one of the world's oldest ski jumps (from 1892), Holmenkollen has hosted many championships, including the 1952 Winter Olympics. To win the privilege of hosting the 2011 World Ski Jump Championship, Oslo built a bigger jump to match modern ones built elsewhere. This futuristic, cantilevered, Olympic-standard **ski jump** has a tilted elevator that you can ride to the top. Stand right at the starting gate, just like an athlete, and get a feel for this daredevil sport. The jump empties into a 50,000-seat amphitheater, and if you go on a sunny day, you'll see one of the best possible views of Oslo.

The **ski museum,** a must for skiers, traces the evolution of the sport, from 4,000-year-old rock paintings to crude 1,500-year-old wooden sticks to the slick and quickly evolving skis of modern times, including a fun exhibit showing the royal family on skis. You'll see gear from Roald Amundsen's famous trek to the South Pole, including the stuffed remains of Obersten (the Colonel), one of his sled dogs.

Cost and Hours: 100-kr ticket includes museum and viewing platform at top of jump; daily June-Aug 9:00-20:00, May and Sept 10:00-17:00, Oct-April 10:00-16:00; tel. 22 92 32 64, www.holmenkollen.com or www.skiforeningen.no.

Simulator: To cap your Holmenkollen experience, step into the simulator and fly down the ski jump and ski in a virtual downhill race. My legs were exhausted after the five-minute terror. This simulator (or should I say stimulator?), at the lower level of the complex, costs 55 kr (if you pay for four tickets, try getting a fifth one free).

Getting There: The T-bane gets you out of the city, through the hills, forests, and mansions that surround Oslo, and to the jump (take any westbound train—that's *tog mot vest*—to Majorstuen, then line #1 to Holmenkollen, and hike up the road 10 minutes). For an easy downhill jaunt through the Norwegian forest, with a woodsy coffee or meal break in the middle, stay on the T-bane past Holmenkollen to the end of the line (Frognerseteren) and walk 10 minutes downhill to the recommended **Frognerseteren Hovedrestaurant,** a fine traditional eatery with a sod roof, reindeer meat on the griddle, and a city view. Continue on the same road another 20 minutes downhill to the ski jump, and then to the Holmenkollen T-bane stop.

▲**Edvard Munch Museum (Munch Museet)**—The only Norwegian painter to have had a serious impact on European art, Munch (pronounced "moonk") is a surprise to many who visit this fine museum, located one mile east of Oslo's center. The emotional, disturbing, and powerfully Expressionistic work of this strange and perplexing man is arranged chronologically. You'll see an extensive collection of paintings, drawings, lithographs, and photographs. Note that Oslo's centrally located National Gallery, which also displays many Munch works, can be a good alternative if you find the Munch Museum too time-consuming to reach.

The Munch Museum was in the news in August 2004, when two Munch paintings, *Madonna* and a version of his famous *Scream,* were brazenly stolen right off the walls in broad daylight. Two men in black hoods simply entered through the museum café, waved guns at the stunned guards and tourists, ripped the paintings off the wall, and sped off in a black Audi station wagon. Happily, in 2006, the thieves were caught and the stolen paintings recovered. Today they are on display behind glass with heightened security.

Cost and Hours: 75 kr; June-Aug daily 10:00-18:00; Sept-May Tue-Fri 10:00-16:00, Sat-Sun 11:00-17:00, closed Mon; 25-kr audioguide, guided tours daily July-Aug at 13:00, T-bane or bus #20 to Tøyen, Tøyengata 53, tel. 23 49 35 00, www.munch .museum.no.

Forests, Lakes, and Beaches—Oslo is surrounded by a vast forest dotted with idyllic little lakes, huts, joggers, bikers, and sun-worshippers. Mountain-biking possibilities are endless (as you'll discover if you go exploring without a good map). Consider taking your bike on the T-bane (for the added cost of a child's ticket) to the end of line #1 (Frognerseteren, 30 minutes from National Theater) to gain the most altitude possible. Then follow the gravelly roads (mostly downhill but with some climbing) past several dreamy lakes to Sognsvann at the end of T-bane line #3. Farther east, from Maridalsvannet, a bike path follows the Akers River all the way back into town. (The TI has details.) While Oslo isn't much on bike rentals, you can rent them in summer at Skiservice, located at the Voksenkollen stop on T-bane line #1, at the high end of the woods (about 350 kr/day, tel. 22 13 95 00, www.skiservice .no). However, keep in mind that you'll need to bring your bike back here—via T-bane if you like.

For plenty of trees and none of the exercise, ride T-bane line #3 to its last stop, Sognsvann (with a beach towel rather than a bike), and join the lakeside scene. A pleasant trail leads around the lake.

Other popular beaches are located on islands in the harbor (such as Bygdøy Huk—direct boat from pier 3 in front of City Hall). The various island getaways are described in Use It's *Streetwise* magazine.

Tusenfryd—This giant amusement complex just out of town offers a world of family fun. It's sort of a combination Norwegian Disneyland/Viking Knott's Berry Farm, with more than 50 rides, plenty of entertainment, and restaurants.

Cost and Hours: Admission is based on your height: under 95 centimeters (3 feet)—free, under 1.2 meters (4 feet)—270 kr, over 1.2 meters (4 feet)—345 kr. Daily June-late Aug 10:30-19:00, closed in winter, tel. 64 97 66 99, www.tusenfryd.no.

Getting There: Bus #541 takes fun-seekers to the park from behind Oslo's train station (48 kr, 2/hour, 20-minute ride, departs Oslo 10:00-16:00, departs Tusenfryd 14:30-17:30).

Wet Fun—Oslo offers a variety of water play. In Frogner Park, the **Frognerbadet** has three outdoor pools, a waterslide, high dives, a cafeteria, and lots of young families (80 kr, students-59 kr, mid-May-late Aug Mon-Fri 7:00-19:00, Sat-Sun 10:00-18:00, last entry one hour before closing, closed late Aug-mid-May, Middelthunsgate 28, tel. 23 27 54 50).

Tøyenbadet, a modern indoor/outdoor pool complex with a 330-foot-long waterslide, also has a gym and sauna (80 kr, children-38 kr, Mon-Fri 7:00-19:30, Sat-Sun 9:00-15:00, sometimes closed mornings for school events, 10-minute walk from Edvard Munch Museum, Helgengate 90, tel. 23 30 44 70). Oslo's free botanical gardens are nearby.

From Akers River to the Grünerløkka District

Connect the dots by following the self-guided "Walk up the Akers River to Grünerløkka."

Akers River—This river, though only about five miles long, powered Oslo's early industry: flour mills in the 1300s, sawmills in the 1500s, and Norway's Industrial Revolution in the 1800s. A walk along the river not only spans Oslo's history, but also shows the contrast the city offers. The bottom of the river (where this walk doesn't go)—bordered by the high-rise Oslo Radisson Blu Plaza Hotel and the "Little Pakistan" neighborhood of Grønland—has its share of drunks and drugs, reflecting a new urban reality in Oslo. Farther up, the river valley becomes a park as it winds past decent-size waterfalls and red-brick factories. The source of the river (and Oslo's drinking water) is the pristine Lake Maridal, situated at the edge of the Nordmarka wilderness. The idyllic recreation scenes along Lake Maridal are a world apart from the rougher reality downstream.

▲Grünerløkka—The Grünerløkka district is the largest planned urban area in Oslo. It was built in the latter half of the 1800s to house the legions of workers employed at the factories powered by the Akers River. The first buildings were modeled on similar places built in Berlin. (German visitors observe that there's now more turn-of-the-20th-century Berlin here than in present-day Berlin.) While slummy in the 1980s, today it's trendy. Locals sometimes refer to it as "Oslo's Greenwich Village." Although that's way over the mark, it is a bustling area with lots of cafés, good spots for a fun meal, and few tourists.

OSLO

Grünerløkka/Grønland Area

Walk
1. Akersgata & Start of Walk
2. July 2011 Bombing Site
3. Vår Frelsers Cemetery
4. Gamle Aker Church
5. Telthusbakken Road
6. Åmotbrua (Bridge)
7. Big Waterfall
8. Fabrikkjentene Statue & Honse-Lovisas Hus
9. Thorvald Meyers Gate
10. Olaf Ryes Plass
11. Vaterlands Bridge & End of Walk

400 Meters
400 Yards

Eateries
12. Südøst Restaurant
13. Punjab Tandoori & Asylet Restaurant
14. Alibaba Restaurant
15. Dattera Til Hagen Rest.
16. Olympen Brown Pub & Pigalle Restaurant
17. Café Con Bar

Getting There: Grünerløkka can be reached from the center of town by a short ride on tram #11, #12, or #13, or by taking the short but interesting walk described next.

▲**Walk up the Akers River to Grünerløkka**—While every tourist explores the harborfront and main drag of Oslo, few venture into this neighborhood that evokes the Industrial Revolution. Once housing poor workers, it now attracts hip professionals. A hike up the Akers River, finishing in the stylish Grünerløkka district, shines a truly different light on Oslo. Allow about an hour at a brisk pace, including a fair bit of up and down. Navigate with the TI's free city map and the map in this chapter. This walk is best during daylight hours.

Begin the walk by leaving Karl Johans Gate at the top of the hill, and head right up Akersgata, which eventually becomes Ullevålsveien. **Akersgata** is Oslo's "Fleet Street" (lined with major newspaper companies) and home to some big government buildings that were the target of the July 2011 bombing (see sidebar). The site of the car bombing is one block over, on Grubbegata; Norwegians are planning to build a memorial here in the near future.

• *Due to the bombing, the next few blocks of Akersgata may be closed off. If that's the case, take this detour: From Akersgata, turn right on Grensen (a busy commercial street), walk two blocks, and turn left on Møllergata. Walk for about 10 minutes along Møllergata, crossing over a freeway. At the next intersection, you'll see a church on the right. Turn left on Hammersborg Torg, jog slightly to your left at the next street, and then turn right to take the pedestrian walkway in front of the Diechmanske Library. The next street is Akersgata; turn right at the brick church, and continue the walk as described below.*

Now you'll pass the massive brick Trefoldighets Church and St. Olav's Church before reaching the **Vår Frelsers (Our Savior's) Cemetery.** Enter the cemetery across from the Baby Shop store (where Ullevålsveien meets Wessels Gate).

Stop at the big metal map just inside the gate to chart your course through the cemetery: Go through the light-green

Æreslunden section—with the biggest plots and highest elevation—and out the opposite end (#13 on the metal map) onto Akersveien. En route, check out some of the tombstones of the illuminati and literati buried in the honorary Æreslunden section. They include Munch,

In Cold Blood

Norwegians like to think of themselves as a quiet, peaceful nation on the edge of Europe—after all, it's their legislators who award the Nobel Peace Prize. So the events of July 22, 2011—when an anti-immigration fanatic named Anders Behring Breivik set off a car bomb in Oslo, killing eight, and then traveled to a Labor Party summer camp where he shot and killed 69 young people and counselors—have had a profound effect on the country's psyche.

Unlike the US, Britain, or Spain, Norway had escaped 21st-century terrorism until Breivik's attack. When the public found out that the man behind the bombing and gunfire was a native Norwegian—dressed in a policeman's uniform—who hunted down his victims in cold blood, it became a national nightmare.

Though Norwegians are often characterized as stoic people, there was a huge outpouring of grief. Bouquets flooded the square in front of Oslo Cathedral. Permanent memorials will eventually be built at the sites of the tragedies.

Breivik, who was arrested after the shootings, was described by police as a gun-loving fundamentalist obsessed with what he saw as the "threat" of multiculturalism and immigration to Norwegian values. His targets

Ibsen, Bjørnson, and many of the painters whose works you can see in the National Gallery (all marked on a map posted at the entrance). Exiting on the far side of the cemetery, walk left 100 yards up Akersveien to the church.

The Romanesque **Gamle Aker Church** (from the 1100s), the oldest building in Oslo, is worth a look inside (free, Mon-Thu 14:00-16:00, Fri 12:00-14:00). The church, which fell into ruins and has been impressively rebuilt, is pretty bare except for a pulpit and baptismal font from the 1700s.

From the church, backtrack 20 yards, head left at the playground, and go downhill on the steep **Telthusbakken Road** toward the huge, gray former grain silos (now student housing). The cute lane is lined with colorful old wooden houses: The people who constructed these homes were too poor to meet the no-wood fire-safety building codes within the city limits, so they built in what used to be suburbs. At the bottom of Telthusbakken, cross the busy Maridalsveien and walk directly through the park to the Akers River. The lively Grünerløkka district is straight across the river from here, but if you have 20 minutes and a little energy, were the Norwegian government and politically active youths—some only 14 years old—and their counselors at an island summer camp sponsored by Norway's center-left party.

It's true that Norway has a big and growing immigrant community. More than 11 percent of today's Norwegians are not ethnic Norwegians, and a quarter of Oslo's residents are immigrants. These "new Norwegians" have provided a much-needed and generally appreciated labor force, filling jobs that wealthy Norwegians would rather not do.

But there is some resentment in a country that is disinclined to be a melting pot. There have been scuffles between Norwegian gangs and immigrant groups. Another source of friction is the tough love Norwegians feel they get from their government compared to the easy ride offered to needy immigrants: "They even get pocket money in jail!"

Horrified by Breivik's actions, many Norwegians are now going out of their way to make immigrants feel welcome. And the anti-immigrant Progress Party (which condemned the attacks) lost support in a round of local elections held shortly after the attack.

Norway seems determined not to let the July 22 massacre poison its peaceful soul. Calls for police to start carrying weapons or to reinstate the death penalty were quickly rejected. "Breivik wanted to change Norway," an Oslo resident told me. "We're determined to keep Norway the way it was."

detour upstream first and hook back down. Don't cross the river yet.

Walk along the riverside bike lane upstream through the river gorge park. Just above the first waterfall, cross **Åmotbrua,** the big white springy suspension footbridge from 1852 (moved here in 1958). Keep hiking uphill along the river. At the base of the next

big waterfall, cross over again to the large brick buildings, hiking up the stairs to the Beyer bridge (above the falls) with *Fabrikkjentene,* a statue of four women laborers. They're pondering the textile factory where they and 700 like them toiled long and hard. This gorge was once lined with the water mills that powered Oslo through its 19th-century Industrial Age boom. The tiny red house next to the bridge—the **Honse-Lovisas Hus** cultural center—makes a good rest-stop (Tue-Sun 11:00-18:00, closed Mon, coffee and cake). Cross over to the red-brick Ringnes Brewery and follow **Thorvald Meyers Gate** down-hill directly into the heart of Grünerløkka. The main square, called **Olaf Ryes Plass**, is a happening place to grab a meal or drink. Trams take you from here back to the center.

• *To continue exploring, you could keep going straight and continue walking until you reach a T-intersection with a busy road (Trondheimsveien). From there (passing the recommended Südøst Restaurant), you can catch a tram back to the center, or drop down to the riverside path and follow it downstream to Vaterlands bridge in the Grønland district. From here the train station is a five-minute walk down Stenersgata. (The last section, around Grønland, is a bit seedy and best done in daylight.)*

Near Oslo

▲**Eidsvoll Manor**—During the Napoleonic period, control of Norway went from Denmark to Sweden. This ruffled the patriotic feathers of Norway's Thomas Jeffersons and Ben Franklins, and on May 17, 1814, Norway's constitution was written and signed in this stately mansion (in the town of Eidsvoll Verk, north of Oslo). While Sweden still ruled, Norway had more autonomy than ever.

To get ready for the bicentennial of the constitution, the manor is closed until 2014 while undergoing restoration. However, a brand-new visitor's center in the nearby Wergeland House tells the history of Norway's march to independence with 21st-century high-tech touches.

Cost and Hours: 75 kr, includes English audioguide; May-Aug daily 10:00-17:00; April and Sept Tue-Fri 10:00-15:00, Sat-Sun 12:00-17:00, closed Mon; Oct-March Wed-Fri 10:00-15:00, Sat-Sun 12:00-17:00, closed Mon-Tue; tel. 63 92 22 10, www.eidsvoll1814.no.

Getting There: Eidsvoll is 45 minutes from Oslo by car (take road E6 toward Trondheim, turn right at *Eidsvolls Bygningen* sign, free parking) or bus (direct bus #854 runs hourly from Oslo Airport). You can also take the train to Eidsvoll (hourly, 45 minutes plus 15-minute walk). If you're driving from Oslo to Lillehammer and the Gudbrandsdal Valley, it's right on the way and worth a stop.

Drøbak—This delightful fjord town is just an hour from Oslo by bus (95 kr one-way, 2/hour, bus #541 or #542 from behind the train station) or ferry (70 kr one-way, sporadic departures usually Wed and Fri-Sun, check at pier 1 or ask at Oslo TI). Consider taking the 1.25-hour boat trip down, exploring the town, having dinner, and taking the bus back.

For holiday cheer year-round, stop into **Tregaarden's Jule-huset** Christmas shop, right off Drøbak's main square (generally Mon-Fri 10:00-17:00, Sat 10:00-15:00, variable hours on Sun, longer hours in Dec, closed Jan-Feb, tel. 64 93 41 78, www.julehus.no).

Then wander out past the church and cemetery on the north side of town to a pleasant park. Looking out into the fjord, you can see the old **Oscarsborg Fortress,** where Norwegian troops fired their cannons to sink Hitler's battleship, *Blücher.* The attack bought enough time for Norway's king and Parliament to escape capture and eventually set up a government-in-exile in London during the Nazi occupation of Norway (1940-1945). Nearby, a monument is dedicated to the commander of the fortress, and the *Blücher*'s anchor rests aground. (A 70-kr round-trip summer ferry shuttles visitors from the town harbor.)

OSLO

If you want to spend the night, the **TI** can recommend accommodations (June-Aug Mon-Fri 8:30-17:00, Sat-Sun 9:30-16:00; Sept-May Mon-Fri 8:30-16:00, closed Sat-Sun; tel. 64 93 50 87, www.visitdrobak.no). **Restaurant Skipperstuen** is a good option for dinner, with outdoor seating that overlooks the fjord and all the Oslo-bound boat traffic (entrées from 300 kr, Mon-Sat 11:00-21:00, closed Sun, tel. 64 93 07 03).

Shopping in Oslo

Shops in Oslo are generally open 10:00-18:00. Many close early on Saturday and all day Sunday. Shopping centers are open Monday through Friday 10:00-21:00, Saturday 9:00-18:00, and are closed Sunday. Remember, when you make a purchase of 315 kr or more, you can get the 25 percent tax refunded when you leave the country if you hang on to the paperwork.

Oslo's fanciest department store is **GlasMagasinet** (top end, near the cathedral on Stortorvet, good souvenir shop). The big, splashy **Byporten** mall, adjoining the central train station, is more youthful and hip (Mon-Fri 10:00-21:00, Sat 10:00-20:00, closed Sun). The trendiest boutiques and chic, high-quality shops lie along the street named **Bogstadveien** (running from behind the Royal Palace to Frogner Park). And on Saturday mornings, you can browse the **flea market** at Vestkanttorvet (March-Nov only, two blocks east of Frogner Park at the corner of Professor Dahl's Gate and Neubergsgate).

Sweaters and colorful Norwegian folk crafts are on many visitors' shopping lists. The **Husfliden shop,** in the basement of the GlasMagasinet department store, is much appreciated for its traditional yarn and Norsk folk items (Mon-Fri 10:00-18:00, Thu until 19:00, Sat 10:00-16:00, closed Sun, tel. 22 42 10 75). For a superb selection of sweaters and other Norwegian crafts (top quality at high prices), visit **Heimen Husfliden** (Mon-Fri 10:00-18:00, Sat 10:00-15:00, closed Sun, Rosenkrantz Gate 8, tel. 22 41 40 50). The **Oslo Sweater Shop** has good prices for sweaters (Mon-Fri 10:00-18:00, Sat 10:00-15:00, closed Sun, in Radisson Blu Scandinavia

Hotel at Tullinsgate 5, tel. 22 11 29 22). For flags (a long, skinny *vimple* dresses up a boat or cabin wonderfully), pop into **Oslo Flaggfabrikk** (Mon-Fri 9:00-17:00, Sat 10:00-15:00, closed Sun, near City Hall at Hieronymus Heyerdahlsgate 1, tel. 22 40 50 60).

Vinmonopolet stores are the only place where you can buy wine and spirits in Norway. The most convenient location is at the central train station (Mon-Thu 10:00-18:00, Fri 9:00-18:00, Sat 9:00-15:00, closed Sun). The bottles used to be kept behind the counter, but now you can actually touch the merchandise. Locals say it went from being a "jewelry store" to a "grocery store."

Sleeping in Oslo

In Oslo, the season and type of hotel dictate the best deals. The basic formula: In midsummer and on weekends, discounted business-class hotels offer the best value; otherwise, consider a cheap hotel or a hostel.

Like those in its sister Scandinavian capitals, Oslo's hotels are mostly designed for business travelers; they're expensive during the tourists' off-season (autumn through spring), full in May and June for conventions, and wide open otherwise. From July through mid-August—and weekends (Fri-Sat but not Sun) year-round—fancy business-class hotels deeply discount their rooms. At half-price (about 1,000 kr for a double), you get a huge breakfast and a lot of extra comfort for little more than the cost of a cheap hotel or hostel.

During business days (Sun-Thu) outside of summer, business hotels hold out for their inflated "rack rates," and budget travelers opt for Oslo's dumpy-for-Scandinavia (but still nice by European standards) cheapie options: doubles for about 800 kr in central "cheap" hotels, or 800 kr in private homes on the outskirts of the city. For a meet-the-Norwegians experience—but not convenience—go for a private home. For convenience and modern comfort, I like the Thon Budget Hotels (described later).

If you arrive without a reservation, the TI can try to sort through all of the confusing hotel specials and get you the best deal going on fancy hotel rooms on the push list. With the uncertain economy and "dynamic pricing," it's tough to get a hotel to give a firm rate. If booking on your own and on a budget, check hotel websites far in advance to see who's willing to offer the most aggressive discount.

The most predictable special is the TI's **Oslo Package,** which offers business-class rooms plus an Oslo Pass for 500-800 kr per person (based on double occupancy); prices vary depending on the hotel you choose. The Oslo Package is offered daily year-round. It's a good deal for couples and ideal for families with young children. Two kids under 16 sleep free, breakfast is included, and up

---

Sleep Code

(5 kr = about $1, country code: 47)
S = Single, **D** = Double/Twin, **T** = Triple, **Q** = Quad, **b** = bathroom, **s** = shower. You can assume credit cards are accepted and breakfast is included unless otherwise noted. Everyone speaks English.

To help you sort through these listings easily, I've divided the rooms into three categories, based on the price for a standard double room with bath during high season:

$$$ Higher Priced—Most rooms 1,100 kr or more.
  $$ Moderately Priced—Most rooms between 600-1,100 kr.
  $ Lower Priced—Most rooms 600 kr or less.

Prices can change without notice; verify the hotel's current rates online or by email. For other updates, see www .ricksteves.com/update.

---

to four family members get free Oslo Passes, covering admission to sights and all public transportation. These passes are valid for four days, even if you only stay one night at the hotel (allowing you to squeeze two days of sightseeing out of a one-night stay—for example, if you take an overnight train or boat out of town on your second evening). Buy the Oslo Package through your travel agent at home, ScanAm World Tours in the US (US tel. 800-545-2204), or upon arrival in Oslo at the TI. Even if you show up late in the day when prices may be deeply discounted, you still get the Oslo Pass along with your room. For details on the Oslo Package, see www.visitoslo.com.

Near the Train Station and Karl Johans Gate

These accommodations are within a 15-minute walk of the station. While evidence of an earlier shady time survives nearest the station, the hotels feel secure and comfortable. Parking in a central garage will run you about 250-300 kr per day.

Thon Hotels

This chain of business-class hotels (found in big cities throughout Norway) knows which comforts are worth paying for and which are not. They offer little character, but provide maximum comfort per krone in big, modern, conveniently located buildings. Each hotel has a cheery staff and lobby, tight but well-designed rooms, non-smoking floors, free Wi-Fi, and a big buffet breakfast.

Thon Hotels come in categories: Their "City Hotels" are a cut above their "Budget Hotels." While City Hotels are much

OSLO

Oslo Hotels & Restaurants

To ⑫

1. Thon City Hotel Stefan
2. Thon City Hotel Terminus
3. Thon City Hotel Cecil
4. Thon Budget Hotel Spectrum
5. Thon Budget Hotel Astoria
6. Thon Budget Hotel Munch
7. Thon Budget Hotel Oslo Panorama
8. Hotell Bondeheimen & Kaffistova Cafeteria
9. P-Hotel
10. Oslo Budget Hotel
11. Perminalen Hotel
12. To Cochs & Ellingsen's Pensjonats & Frogner Park Eateries
13. Anker Hostel
14. Grand Café
15. Deli de Luca
16. Brasserie 45 Restaurant
17. YaYa's Thai Beach Bungalow
18. City Hall Workers' Cafeteria
19. Aker Brygge Eateries

ROYAL PALACE   Slotts-parken

Dronningparken

HENRIK IBSENS GATE   National-theatret

To Frogner Park & Bygdøy

PARKVEIEN

CORT ADELERS GATE

HUITFELDTS GATE

RUSELØKKVEIEN

MUNKEDAMSVEIEN

OLAV V

NOBEL PEACE CENTER

Rådhusplassen

⑱

AKER BRYGGE MALL

To Bygdøy

⑲

N

Oslofjord

To Bygdøy

more expensive during business times (weekdays outside of summer), Budget Hotels have lower rates all year. That means City Hotels can be a better value in low season when they often are discounted. City Hotels generally offer free juice and coffee all day. In Budget Hotels (which have no phones or mini-fridges in the rooms), rooms with double beds are a bit bigger than twin-bedded rooms for the same price.

Thon Hotels base their prices on demand. Rates vary wildly, so the following prices are roughly the midpoint of a huge range: **Thon City Hotels**—Sb-1,525, Db-1,825 kr; **Thon Budget Hotels**—Sb-750 kr, Db-1,075 kr, higher in winter. Extra beds are 300 kr for an adult and 150 kr for a child under 17 (kids under 6 stow away for free). Book by phone or online (central booking tel. 23 08 02 00, www.thonhotels.no).

Thon Hotels generally offer a 10 percent discount for those who prepay via their website with no option to change or cancel their booking. The free Thon Membership Card offers a 10 percent discount if you stay five nights in one year (doesn't apply to summer/weekend rates). My price ratings for Thon Hotels are based on their average summer/weekend rates. Of the 14 Thon Hotels in

Oslo, I find the following most convenient:

$$$ Thon City Hotel Stefan, in a classy and central location two blocks off Karl Johans Gate, is a cut above its sisters in comfort and charm. If you want to splurge, this is the place to do it (Rosenkrantz Gate 1, entrance on Kristian Augusts Gate side, tel. 23 31 55 00, fax 23 31 55 55, www.thonhotels.no/stefan, stefan @thonhotels.no).

$$$ Thon City Hotel Terminus is similar but closer to the station (Steners Gate 10, tel. 22 05 60 00, fax 22 17 08 98, www .thonhotels.no/terminus, terminus@thonhotels.no).

$$$ Thon City Hotel Cecil is near the Parliament building a block below Karl Johans Gate (Stortingsgata 8, tel. 23 31 48 00, fax 23 31 48 50, www.thonhotels.no/cecil, cecil@thonhotels.no).

$$ Thon Budget Hotel Spectrum is four blocks from the station near the Grønland Torg shopping street. A quarter of its rooms are plagued by disco noise on weekends (leave station out north entrance toward bus terminal, go across footbridge toward tall glass Radisson Blu Plaza Hotel, and pass through Grønland Torg, Brugata 7; tel. 23 36 27 00, fax 23 36 27 50, www.thonhotels .no/spectrum, spectrum@thonhotels.no).

$$ Thon Budget Hotel Astoria has the least charm of my recommended Thon Hotels, but it's well-located and perfectly serviceable (3 blocks in front of station, 50 yards off Karl Johans Gate, Dronningens Gate 21, tel. 24 14 55 50, fax 22 42 57 65, www.thon hotels.no/astoria, astoria@thonhotels.no).

$$ Thon Budget Hotel Munch, a few blocks from the National Gallery, is like its sisters. Of all the Thon Budget hotels listed, this one has the most upscale location (Munchs Gate 5, tel. 23 21 96 00, fax 23 21 96 01, www.thonhotels.no/munch, munch @thonhotels.no).

$$ Thon Budget Hotel Oslo Panorama is a 15-story attempt at a downtown condominium building (the condos didn't work so now it's a budget hotel). While higher rooms are more expensive, even those reserving a cheap room often get bumped up. If you request anything higher than the fourth floor, you'll likely enjoy a bigger room, perhaps with a balcony (just off Dronningens Gate at Rådhusgata 7, about 6 blocks from station, tel. 23 31 08 00, fax 23 31 08 10, www.thonhotels.no/oslopanorama, oslopanorama @thonhotels.no).

More Hotels near the Train Station

$$$ Hotell Bondeheimen ("Farmer's Home") is a historic hotel run by the farmers' youth league, *Bondeungdomslaget*. It once housed the children of rural farmers attending school in Oslo. Now a Best Western, its 127 rooms have all the comforts of a modern hotel (July Db-990 kr, Aug Db-1,285 kr; higher off-season, you generally save money by booking on their website; non-smoking rooms, elevator, Rosenkrantz Gate 8, tel. 23 21 41 00, www.bondeheimen.com, booking@bondeheimen.com). This almost-100-year-old building is also home to the Kaffistova cafeteria (see "Eating in Oslo") and the Heimen Husfliden shop (see "Shopping in Oslo").

$$$ P-Hotel rents 92 comfortable rooms—some with hardwood-slick floors—for the same price every day of the year. You get a boxed breakfast delivered each morning, as well as free Internet access and Wi-Fi. Avoid late-night street noise by requesting a room high up or in the back (Sb-895 kr, Db-1,250 kr, bigger rooms add 200 kr per person up to five, some sixth-floor rooms have balconies, pay by credit card—no cash accepted, Grensen 19, T-bane: Storting, tel. 23 31 80 00, www.p-hotels.com, oslo@p-hotels.no).

$$ Oslo Budget Hotel, with a youth-hostel vibe, has clean, basic, well-worn rooms (many with bunks) in a somewhat seedy fourth-floor location handy to the train station. The hotel originated 100 years ago as a cheap place for Norwegians to sleep while they waited to sail to their new homes in America. It now serves the opposite purpose. With prices the same throughout the year, this hotel is a good value on off-season weekdays (Sun-Thu), when other hotels are at their most expensive (S-400 kr, Sb-500 kr, D-500 kr, Db-600 kr, T-600 kr, Tb-800 kr, Q-800 kr, Qb-900 kr, 10 percent discount with this book—mention when you reserve, pay by credit card—no cash accepted, breakfast-19 kr at nearby café, all non-smoking rooms, free Internet access and Wi-Fi, reception open 15:00-23:00, Prinsens Gate 6, tel. 22 41 36 10, fax 22 42 24 29, www.budgethotel.no, oslo@budgethotel.no).

$$ Perminalen Hotel, a place for military personnel on leave, is perfectly central, spartan, inexpensive, and welcoming to civvies. They have the same fair prices all year. Spliced invisibly into a giant office block on a quiet street, it has sleek woody furniture and a no-nonsense reception desk (Sb-640 kr, twin Db-860 kr, some seventh-floor rooms have balconies, entirely non-smoking, elevator, pay Internet access, free Wi-Fi in lobby, tram #12 from station to Øvre Slotts Gate 2, tel. 23 09 30 81, fax 23 41 18 58, www.perminalen.com, post.perminalen@iss.no). Single beds in shared quads segregated by sexes (with lockers and breakfast) rent for 380 kr each. Its cheap mess hall is open all day.

The West End

$$ Cochs Pensjonat has 88 characteristic rooms (20 remodeled doubles), many with kitchenettes. It's on the far side of the Royal Palace (S-460 kr, Sb-610 kr, D-660 kr, Db-760 kr, newly refurnished Db-820 kr, Q-1,020 kr, Qb-1,180 kr, breakfast-69 kr at nearby café, non-smoking rooms, elevator; T-bane to National Theater, exit to Parkveien, and 10-minute walk through park; or more-convenient trams #11, #17, or #18 to Høgskolen/Dalsbergsstien; Parkveien 25; tel. 23 33 24 00, fax 23 33 24 10, www.cochspensjonat.no, booking@cochs.no, three generations of the Skram family).

$$ Ellingsen's Pensjonat rents 18 clean, bright rooms with fluffy down comforters. It's in a residential neighborhood four blocks behind the Royal Palace (S-400 kr, Sb-480 kr, D-610 kr, Db-670 kr, extra bed-150 kr, breakfast-69 kr at nearby café, cash only, non-smoking, back rooms have less street noise, tram #19 from central station to Uranienborgveien, near Uranienborg church at Holtegata 25, tel. 22 60 03 59, fax 22 60 99 21, www.ellingsenspensjonat.no, post@ellingsenspensjonat.no).

Private Homes

The central station TI can find you an 800-kr double for a 55-kr fee (minimum two-night stay, breakfast not included, likely a tram ride out of the center).

Hostels

$ **Anker Hostel,** a huge student dorm open to travelers of any age, offers 250 of Oslo's best cheap doubles. Though it comes with the ambience of a bomb shelter, each of its rooms is spacious, simple, and clean. There are kitchens and elevators (bed in 6-bed room-220 kr, bed in quad-250 kr, Db-580 kr, sheets-50 kr, towel-20 kr, no breakfast, self-serve laundry, parking-175 kr/day; tram #12 or #13, or bus #30 or #31 from central station, bus and tram stop: Hausmannsgate; or 10-minute walk from station; Storgata 55, tel. 22 99 72 00, fax 22 99 72 20, www.ankerhostel.no, hostel@anker .oslo.no).

$ **Haraldsheim Youth Hostel (IYHF),** a huge, modern hostel open all year, comes with a grand view, laundry, self-service kitchen, 270 beds...and a long commute (2.5 miles out of town). Beds in the fancy quads with private showers and toilets are 270 kr per person (bed in simple quad with bathroom down the hall-245 kr). They also offer private rooms (S-415 kr, Sb-470 kr, bunk-bed D-540 kr, Db-625 kr; all include breakfast, members get 10 percent off, sheets-50 kr, catch bus #31 or tram #17 or T-bane lines #4 or #6 from Oslo's central train station to Sinsenkrysset, then 5-minute uphill hike to Haraldsheimveien 4, tel. 22 22 29 65, fax 22 22 10 25, www.haraldsheim.no, post@haraldsheim.oslo.no). Eurailers can train to the hostel with their railpass (2/hour, to Grefsen and walk 10 minutes).

Sleeping on the Train or Boat

Norway's trains and ferries offer ways to travel while sleeping. The eight-hour night train between Bergen and Oslo leaves at about 23:00 in each direction (nightly except Sat). Eurail hobos sleep cheap, if not well, for the cost of a 50-kr train reservation (sleep on a train ride out, cross platform, and sleep back). Overnight trains connect Oslo with Copenhagen June-August only (leaves nightly at 20:30, arrives at Malmö Central Station at 6:42 the next morning, easy transfers to Copenhagen). The overnight cruise between these Nordic capitals is a clever way to avoid a night in a hotel and to travel while you sleep, saving a day in your itinerary (see "Oslo Connections," later).

Eating in Oslo

Eating Cheaply

How do the Norwegians afford their high-priced restaurants? They don't eat out much. This is one city in which you might just settle for simple or ethnic meals—you'll save a lot and miss little. Many menus list small and large plates. Because portions tend to be large, choosing a small plate or splitting a large one makes some other-

OSLO

Oslo's One-Time Grills

Norwegians are experts at completely avoiding costly restaurants. "One-time grills," or *engangsgrill,* are the rage for locals on a budget. For about 20 kr, you get a disposable outdoor cooker consisting of an aluminum tray, easy-to-light charcoal, and a flimsy metal grill. All that's required is a sunny evening, a grassy park, and a group of friends. During balmy summer evenings, the air in Oslo's city parks is thick with the smell of disposable (and not terribly eco-friendly) grills. It's fun to

see how prices for this kind of "dining" aren't that bad in the supermarket: Norwegian beer-12 kr/bottle, potato salad-20 kr/tub, cooked shrimp-75 kr/half kilo, "ready for grill" steak-two for 110 kr, *grill polse* hot dogs-60 kr per dozen, *lomper* (Norwegian tortillas for wrapping hot dogs)-15 kr per stack, and the actual grill itself.

Bars are also too expensive for the average Norwegian. Young night owls drink at home before *(forspiel)* and after *(nachspiel)* an evening on the town, with a couple of hours, generally around midnight, when they go out for a single drink in a public setting. A beer in a bar costs about $8-10 (compared to $6 in Ireland and $2 in the Czech Republic), while they can get an entire six-pack for that price in a grocery store.

wise pricey options reasonable. You'll notice many locals just drink free tap water, even in fine restaurants. For a description of Oslo's classic (and expensive) restaurants, see the TI's *Oslo Guide* booklet.

Splurge for a hotel that includes breakfast, or pay for it if it's

optional. At 75 kr, a Norwegian breakfast fit for a Viking is a good deal. Picnic for lunch or dinner. Basements of big department stores have huge, first-class supermarkets with lots of alternatives to sandwiches for picnic dinners. The little yogurt tubs with cereal come with collapsible spoons. Wasa crackers and meat, shrimp, or cheese spread in a tube are cheap and pack well. The central station has an ICA supermarket with long hours (Mon-Fri 6:00-21:00,

Sat 8:00-19:00, Sun 10:00-18:00). Many supermarkets have take-out food that is discounted just before closing—showing up just before 20:00 to buy some roast chicken could be your cheapest meal in Oslo.

You'll save 12 percent by getting take-away food from a restaurant rather than eating inside. (The VAT on take-away food is 12 percent; restaurant food is 24 percent.) Fast-food restaurants ask if you want to take away or not before they ring up your order on the cash register. Even McDonald's has a two-tiered price list.

Oslo is awash with little budget eateries (modern, ethnic, fast food, pizza, department-store cafeterias, and so on). **Deli de Luca,** a cheery convenience store chain, notorious for having a store on every key corner in Oslo, is a step up from the similarly ubiquitous 7-Elevens. Most are open 24/7, selling sandwiches, pastries, sushi, and to-go boxes of warm pasta or Asian noodle dishes. You can fill your belly here for about 75 kr. Some outlets (such as the one at the corner of Karl Johans Gate and Rosenkrantz Gate) have seating on the street or upstairs. Beware: Because this is still a *convenience* store, not everything is well-priced. Convenience stores—while convenient—charge double what supermarkets do.

Eating on or near Karl Johans Gate

Consider the restaurants and eateries listed below. They're grouped by those that are from Karl Johans Gate and slightly to the north (between this main boulevard and the National Gallery) and to the south (between Karl Johans Gate and City Hall).

Strangely, **Karl Johans Gate** itself—the most Norwegian of boulevards—is lined with a strip of good-time American chain eateries where you can get ribs, burgers, and pizza, including T.G.I. Fridays and the Hard Rock Cafe. Egon Pizza offers a daily 100-kr all-you-can-eat pizza deal (available Tue-Sat 11:00-18:00, Sun-Mon all day). Each place comes with great sidewalk seating and essentially the same prices.

Grand Café is perhaps the most venerable place in town. At lunchtime, they set up a sandwich buffet (110-kr single sandwich, 310-kr all-you-like). Lunch plates are 150 kr, and dinner plates run about 250-300 kr. Reserve a window, and if you hit a time when there's no tour group, you're suddenly a posh Norwegian (daily 11:00-23:00, Karl Johans Gate 31, tel. 23 21 20 18).

Deli de Luca, just across from the Grand Café, offers good-value food and handy seats on Karl Johans Gate. For a fast meal with the best people-watching view in town, you may find yourself dropping by here repeatedly (daily 11:00-23:00, slightly shorter hours Sat-Sun, Karl Johans Gate 33, tel. 22 33 35 22).

Kaffistova is where my thrifty Norwegian grandparents always took me. After remaining unchanged for 30 years, it got a facelift in 2007. This alcohol-free cafeteria still serves simple, hearty, and typically Norwegian (read: bland) meals for a good price (Mon-Fri 10:00-21:00, Sat-Sun 11:00-19:00; Rosenkrantz Gate 8, tel. 23 21 42 10).

Brasserie 45, overlooking Stortingsgata and the National Theater from its second-floor perch, is a modern eatery offering decent Continental cuisine with energetic service. While larger entrées go for about 200 kr, their "wok chicken" goes for 140 kr. It's worth calling ahead to reserve a window seat with a view of Karl Johans Gate (Mon-Thu 15:00-23:00, Fri-Sat 14:00-24:00, Sun 14:00-22:00, always a veggie option, Stortingsgata 20, tel. 22 41 34 00).

YaYa's Thai Beach Bungalow is a welcome change from Norwegian bland. The tiki-bar decor is infectious, and the food is surprisingly authentic—I slurped up every morsel of my green curry pork. Don't be surprised if your dinner is accompanied hourly by the sounds and lights of a tropical thunderstorm (starters-80 kr, main dishes-150 kr, vegetarian options, daily 16:00-22:00, Fri-Sat until 23:00, between the Parliament building and City Hall at Øvre Vollgate 13, tel. 22 83 71 10).

City Hall workers' cafeteria, just steps off the harborfront, welcomes the public with the cheapest lunch I've found in Oslo. It has soup, an inexpensive salad bar measured by weight (35 kr for a meal-sized bowl), and a daily hot dish for around 50 kr (Mon-Fri 12:30-13:30 only). While City Hall workers get access to the place before 12:30 and the food can be pretty picked over, it's still a fine, handy value. From the grand harbor entrance, it's up one flight of stairs above the city info desk and WC. From the tour entrance on its inland courtyard, it's just downstairs.

Harborside Dining in Aker Brygge

The **Aker Brygge** harborfront mall is popular with businesspeople and tourists. While it isn't cheap, its inviting cafés and restaurants with outdoor, harborview tables make for a memorable waterfront meal. Before deciding where to eat, you might want to walk the entire lane (including the back side), considering both the regular places (some with second-floor view seating) and the various floating options. Nearly all are open for lunch and dinner.

Druen, the first restaurant on the strip—while not a particularly good food value—is best for people-watching. I like the balcony seats upstairs, under outside heaters and with a harbor view. They serve international dishes—spicy Asian, French, and seafood—in small plates for 175 kr, hearty salads for 155 kr, and big meals for 220-260 kr (daily from 11:00, Stranden 1, Aker Brygge, tel. 23 11 54 60).

Lekter'n, right on the water, offers the best harbor view (rather than views of strolling people). This trendy bar has a floating dining area open only when the weather is warm. It serves hamburgers, pizza, and shrimp buckets. Budget eaters can split a 160-kr pizza (all outdoors, Stranden 3, tel. 22 83 76 46).

Rorbua, the "Fisherman's Cabin," is a lively yet cozy eatery tucked into this mostly modern stretch of restaurants. Inside, it's extremely woody with a rustic charm and candlelit picnic tables surrounded by harpoons and old B&W photos. Grab a stool at one of the wooden tables, and choose from a menu of meat-and-potato dishes (150-200 kr) and seafood offerings (200-250 kr). A hearty daily special with coffee for 145 kr is one of the best restaurant deals in the city (daily 12:30-23:00, Stranden 71, tel. 22 83 53 86).

Lofoten Fiskerestaurant serves fish amid a dressy yacht-club atmosphere at the end of the strip. While it's beyond the people-watching action, it's comfortable even in cold and blustery weather because of its heated atrium, which makes a meal here practically outdoor dining. Reservations are a must, especially if you want a harborside window table (lunch-150-225 kr, dinner from 275 kr, open daily, Stranden 75, tel. 22 83 08 08).

Budget Tips: If you're on a budget, get a take-out meal from the fast-food stands and grab a bench along the boardwalk. The **ICA "Gourmet"** grocery store—in the middle of the mall a few steps behind all the fancy restaurants—has salads, warm take-away dishes, and more (turn in about midway down the boardwalk, Mon-Fri 9:00-22:00, Sat 9:00-20:00, closed Sun).

Dining near Frogner Park

Lofotstua Restaurant feels transplanted from the far northern islands it's named for. Kjell Jenssen and his son, Jan Hugo, proudly serve up fish Lofoten-style. Evangelical about fish, they will patiently explain to you the fine differences between all the local varieties, with the help of a photo-filled chart. They serve only the freshest catch, perfectly—if simply—prepared. If you want meat, they've got it—whale or seal (170-290-kr plates, Mon-Fri 15:00-22:00, generally closed in July, 5-minute walk from gate of Vigeland statue garden, tram #12, in Majorstuen at Kirkeveien 40, tel. 22 46 93 96). This place is packed daily in winter for their famous lutefisk.

Curry and Ketchup Indian Restaurant is filled with in-the-know locals enjoying tasty and hearty meals for about 100 kr. This happening place requires no reservations and feels like an Indian market. If you want a reasonable Indian meal in Oslo, this is hard to beat (daily 14:00-23:00, cash only, a 5-minute walk from gate of Vigeland statue garden, tram #12, in Majorstuen at Kirkeveien 51, tel. 22 69 05 22).

Trendy Dining at the Bottom of Grünerløkka

Südøst Restaurant, once a big bank, now fills its vault with wine (which makes sense, given Norwegian alcohol prices). Today it's popular with young Norwegian professionals as a place to see and be seen. It's a fine mix of Norwegian-chic woody ambience inside with a trendy, crossover menu, and a big riverside terrace outdoors with a more casual menu. Diners enjoy its chic setting, smart service, and Asian fusion cuisine (Mon-Sat 11:00-22:00, Sun 12:00-18:00, at bottom of Grünerløkka, tram #17 to Trondheimsveien 5, tel. 23 35 30 70).

Eating Cheap and Spicy in Grønland

The street called Grønland leads through this colorful immigrant neighborhood (a short walk behind the train station or T-bane: Grønland). After the cleanliness and orderliness of the rest of the city, the rough edges and diversity of people here can feel like a breath of fresh air. Whether you eat here or not, the street is fun to explore. In Grønland, backpackers and immigrants munch street food for dinner. Cheap and tasty *börek* (feta, spinach, mushroom) is sold hot and greasy to go for 25 kr.

Punjab Tandoori is friendly and serves hearty meals (lamb and chicken curry, tandoori specials) for 70 kr. They're open late when other places aren't. I like eating outside here with a view of the street scene (daily 11:00-23:00, Grønland 24).

Alibaba Restaurant is clean, simple, and cheap for Turkish food. They have good indoor or outdoor seating (99-kr fixed-price meal Mon-Thu only, open daily 12:30-22:30, corner of Grønlandsleiret and Tøyengata at Tøyengata 2, tel. 22 17 22 22). The 99-kr special is much cheaper than the menu items, but isn't advertised very clearly; you may need to request it.

Asylet is more expensive and feels like it was here long before Norway ever saw a Pakistani. This big, traditional eatery—like a Norwegian beer garden—has a rustic, cozy interior and a gravelly backyard filled with picnic tables (150-200-kr plates and hearty dinner salads, daily 11:00-24:00, Grønland 28, tel. 22 17 09 39).

Dattera Til Hagen feels like a college party. It's a lively scene filling a courtyard with picnic tables and benches under strings of colored lights. If it's too cold, hang out inside. Locals like it for the tapas, burgers, and salads (150-kr plates, pricey beers, Grønland 10, tel. 22 17 18 61). On weekends after 22:00, it becomes a disco.

Olympen Brown Pub is a dressy dining hall that's a blast from the past. You'll eat in a spacious woody saloon with big dark furniture, faded paintings of circa-1920 Oslo lining the walls, and huge chandeliers. It's good for solo travelers, because sharing the long dinner tables is standard practice. They serve hearty 200-kr plates and offer a huge selection of beers. The grill restaurant upstairs, called **Pigalle,** comes with music and can be more fun (daily 11:00-2:00 in the morning, Grønlandsleiret 15, tel. 22 17 28 08).

Café Con Bar is a trendy yuppie eatery on the downtown edge of Grønland. Locals consider it to have the best burgers in town (150 kr). While the tight interior seating is very noisy, the sidewalk tables are great for people-watching (open daily, kitchen closes at 23:00, bar closes late; where Grønland hits Brugata).

Roasted Rudolph Under a Thatched Roof High on the Mountain

Frognerseteren Hovedrestaurant, nestled high above Oslo (and 1,400 feet above sea level), is a classy, sod-roofed old restaurant. Its terrace, offering a commanding view of the city, is a popular stop for famous apple cake and coffee. The café is casual and less expensive, with indoor and outdoor seating (90-kr sandwiches and cold dishes, 125-kr entrées, Mon-Sat 11:00-22:00, Sun 11:00-21:00, reservations unnecessary). The elegant view restaurant is pricier (275-365-kr plates, Mon-Fri 12:00-22:00, Sat 13:00-22:00, Sun 13:00-21:00, reindeer specials, reserve for evening dining, tel. 22 92 40 40).

You can combine a trip into the forested hills surrounding the city with lunch or dinner and get a chance to see the famous Holmenkollen Ski Jump up close.

Oslo Connections

For train information, call 81 50 08 88 and press 4 for English. For international trains, dial 81 56 81 00. Even if you have a rail-pass, reservations are required for long rides (e.g., a reservation to Stockholm in first class costs 140 kr, second class for 50 kr). First class often comes with a hot meal, fruit bowl, and unlimited juice and coffee.

Be warned that international connections from Oslo are often in flux. Schedules can vary depending on the day of the week, so carefully confirm the specific train you need and purchase any required reservations in advance. Aside from the occasional direct train to Stockholm, most trips from Oslo to Copenhagen or Stockholm require a change in Sweden. From June through August only, direct night trains run from Oslo to Stockholm and to Malmö, Sweden (which is very close to Copenhagen).

From Oslo by Train to Bergen: Oslo and Bergen are linked by a spectacularly scenic train ride (3-5/day, 7 hours, overnight possible daily except Sat). Many travelers take it as part of the **Norway in a Nutshell** route, which combines train, ferry, and bus travel in an unforgettably beautiful trip.

By Train to: Lillehammer (hourly, 2.5 hours), **Kristiansand** (4/day, 4.5 hours), **Stavanger** (4/day, 8-8.5 hours, overnight possible), **Copenhagen** (2/day, 8 hours, transfer at Göteborg; for night train—which runs in summer only—sleep on the direct train to Malmö, Sweden, easy transfer for 35-minute ride to Copenhagen, www.sj.se), **Stockholm** (2/day direct InterCity trains, 6 hours; 2/day with change in Kristinehamn, 6 hours; plus a direct 9-hour night train in summer only).

By Bus to Stockholm: Taking the bus to Stockholm is cheaper but slower than the train (3/day, 8 hours, www.swebus.se).

Overnight Cruise to Copenhagen

Consider connecting Oslo and Copenhagen by cruise ship. The boat leaves daily from Oslo at 17:00 (arrives in Copenhagen at 9:30 the following morning; going the other way, it departs Copenhagen at 17:00 and arrives in Oslo at 9:30; about 16 hours sailing each way). The boat leaves Oslo from the far (non-City Hall) side of the Akershus Fortress peninsula (get there via bus #60 from the train station, 2-3/hour, get off at Vippetangen stop and follow signs to DFDS ticket office). Boarding is from 15:30 to 16:00. From Oslo, you'll sail through the Oslofjord—not as dramatic as Norway's western fjords, but impressive if you're not going to Bergen. On board are three gourmet restaurants, dinner and breakfast buffets, cafés, nightclubs, shops, a sauna, hot tub, and swimming pool. This is fun and convenient, but more expensive and not as swanky as the Stockholm-Helsinki cruise.

You can take this cruise one-way or do a round-trip from either city. Book online or by phone (from Norway, call DFDS Seaways' Denmark office at 00-45-33 42 30 10, Mon-Fri 8:00-17:00, closed Sat-Sun, www.dfdsseaways.com; in the US, call 800-533-3755, www.seaeurope.com). Book in advance for the best prices.

NORWAY in a NUTSHELL

A Scenic Journey to the Sognefjord

While Oslo and Bergen are the big draws for tourists, Norway is first and foremost a place of unforgettable natural beauty. There's a certain mystique about the "land of the midnight sun," but you'll get the most scenic travel thrills per mile, minute, and dollar by going west from Oslo rather than north.

Norway's greatest claims to scenic fame are her deep, lush fjords. Three million years ago, an ice age made this land as inhabitable as the center of Greenland. As the glaciers advanced and cut their way to the sea, they gouged out long grooves—today's fjords.

The entire west coast is slashed by stunning fjords, and the Sognefjord—Norway's longest (120 miles) and deepest (1 mile)—is tops. Anything but the Sognefjord is, at best, foreplay. The seductive Sognefjord has tiny but tough ferries, towering canyons, and isolated farms and villages marinated in the mist of countless waterfalls.

A series of well-organized and spectacular bus, train, and ferry connections—appropriately nicknamed "Norway in a Nutshell"—lays Norway's beautiful fjord country before you on a scenic platter. With the Nutshell, you'll delve into two offshoots of the Sognefjord, which make an upside-down "U" route: the Aurlandsfjord and the Nærøyfjord. You'll link the ferry ride to the rest of Norway with two trains and a bus: The main train is an express route that takes you through stark polar scenery above the tree line. To get from the express train down to the ferry, you'll catch an old-fashioned slow train one way (passing waterfalls and forests) and a bus the other way (offering fjord views and more waterfalls). All connections are designed for tourists, explained in English, convenient, and easy. At the start of the fjord, you'll go

Norway in a Nutshell

Not to Scale:
Bergen to Oslo is 300 Miles/480 KM
& 7 Hours by Rail

Atlantic

Lustrafjord

Balestrand

Sognefjord

Aurland

Gudvangen

Flåm

Stal-heim

Waterfall

BERGEN   Voss   Myrdal   OSLO

DCH

through the town of Flåm (a transit hub), then pass briefly by the workaday town of Aurland and the hamlet of Undredal (by taking the Nutshell trip segments at your own pace, you can visit the latter two fjord towns on your own; all are described in this chapter).

This region enjoys mild weather for its latitude, thanks to the warm Gulf Stream. (When it rains in Bergen, it just drizzles here.) Recently the popularity of the Nutshell route has skyrocketed. And the 2005 completion of the longest car tunnel in the world (15 miles between Flåm and Lærdal) rerouted the main E16 road between Bergen and Oslo through this idyllic fjord corner. All of this means that July and August come with a crush of crowds, dampening some of the area's magic. Unfortunately, many tourists are overcome by Nutshell tunnel-vision, and spend so much energy scurrying between boats, trains, and buses that they forget to simply enjoy the fjords. Relax—you're on vacation.

Planning Your Time

Even the blitz tourist needs a day for the Norway in a Nutshell trip. With more time, sleep in a town along the fjord, and customize your fjord experience to include sights outside the Nutshell.

Day 1: The Nutshell works well as a single day (one-way between Oslo and Bergen in either direction, or as a long day trip from either city). Those with a car and only one day should leave the car in Oslo and do the Nutshell by train, bus, and boat. If you're using public transportation and want to make efficient use of your time, organize your trip so that it ends in Bergen, or return to Oslo on a night train (sleeping through all the scenery you saw westbound).

Day 2: If you have enough time, spend the night somewhere on the Sognefjord—either along the Nutshell route itself (in Flåm or Aurland; accommodations listed later), or in another, even more appealing fjordside town (such as Balestrand or Solvorn).

With More Time: The Sognefjord deserves more than a day. If you can spare the time, venture off the Nutshell route. You can easily connect to some non-Nutshell towns (such as Balestrand) via the handy express boat. Drivers can improve on the Nutshell by taking a northern route: From Oslo, drive through the Gudbrandsdal Valley, go over the Jotunheimen Mountains, then along Lustrafjord to Balestrand; from there, you can cross the Sognefjord on a car ferry (such as Kaupanger-Gudvangen) and drive the Nutshell route on to Bergen. For more tips, see the "Beyond the Nutshell" sidebar.

Orientation to the Nutshell

The most exciting single-day trip you could make from Oslo or Bergen is this circular train/boat/bus/train jaunt through fjord country. Everybody does this famous trip...and if you're looking for a delicious slice of Norway's scenic grandeur, so should you.

Local TIs (listed throughout this chapter) are well-informed about your options, and they sell tickets for various segments of the trip. At TIs, train stations, and hotels, look for souvenir-worthy brochures with photos, descriptions, and exact times (a sidebar later in this chapter has sample schedules).

Route Overview: The route works round-trip from Oslo or Bergen, or one-way between Oslo and Bergen (going in either direction). The basic idea is this: Take a train halfway across the mountainous spine of Norway, make your way down to the Sognefjord for a boat cruise, then climb back up out of the fjord and get back on the main train line. Each of these steps is explained in the self-guided tour, below. Transportation along the Nutshell route is carefully coordinated. If any segment of the journey is delayed, your transportation for the next segment will wait (because everyone on board is catching the same connection).

When to Go: The Nutshell trip is possible all year. In the summer (late June-late Aug), the connections are most convenient, the weather is most likely to be good...and the route is at its most crowded. Outside of this time, sights close and schedules become

Beyond the Nutshell

The Sognefjord is the ultimate natural thrill Norway has to offer, and there's no doubt that the Nutshell route outlined in this chapter is the most efficient way to see it quickly. Unfortunately, its trains, buses, and boats are thronged with other visitors who have the same idea. Those who stick with the Nutshell crowd enjoy it, but—as they spend the day jostling with a United Nations of tourists for the best photo—can't shake that lemming feeling.

Travelers with a bit more time, and the willingness to chart their own course, often have a more rewarding Sognefjord experience. It's surprisingly easy to break out of the Nutshell and hit the northern part of the Sognefjord (for example, using the Bergen-Vik-Balestrand-Aurland-Flåm express boat).

In the next chapter, you'll find some tempting stopovers on the north bank of the Sognefjord, including adorable fjordside villages (such as Balestrand and Solvorn), evocative stave churches (including Hopperstad and Urnes), and a chance to get up close to a glacier (at the Nigard Glacier).

Read up on your options, then be adventurous about mixing and matching the fjordside attractions that appeal to you most. Use the Nutshell as a springboard for diving into the Back Door fjords of your travel dreams.

more challenging. Some say the Nutshell is most beautiful in winter, though schedules are severely reduced (and you can't do it as a day trip from Oslo). It's easy to confirm schedules, connections, and prices locally or online (latest info posted each May on www.ruteinfo.net).

Express Boat to Balestrand and Bergen: If you don't want to do the Nutshell route, take note of the very handy and speedy express boat connecting this area (Aurland and Flåm) with two other worthwhile destinations: Balestrand (on the Sognefjord's northern bank) and Bergen. While this boat misses the best fjord (Nærøyfjord), many travelers use it to craft their own itinerary that escapes the Nutshell rut.

Eating: Options along the route aren't great—on the Nutshell I'd consider food just as a source of nutrition and forget about fine dining. You can buy some food on the fjord cruises (50-75-kr hot dogs, burgers, and pizza) and the Oslo-Bergen train (50-100-kr hot meals, 150-kr daily specials). Depending on the timing of your layovers, Myrdal or Flåm are your best lunch-stop options (both train stations have decent cafeterias, and other eateries surround the Flåm station)—although you won't have a lot of time there if you're making the journey all in one day. Your best bet is to pack a picnic lunch. While some hotels sell a sack lunch assembled from their breakfast buffet, many will let you snag a sandwich for free if you ask politely. Or you can plan ahead and buy picnic fixings at a grocery store to bring along.

By Yourself or with a Package Deal?

If you have a railpass, or if you're a student or a senior (and therefore eligible for discounts), do the Nutshell on your own. If not, the Fjord Tours package deals (described later) will save you time and a bit of money.

On Your Own

To do the Nutshell on your own without a railpass, allow 1,300 kr for a one-way trip between Oslo and Bergen. Doing the Nutshell as a round-trip from Bergen costs only 995 kr, but doesn't include the majestic train ride between Myrdal and Oslo. Likewise, the 2,200-kr round-trip from Oslo doesn't go all the way to Bergen, but does include all the must-sees (the Voss-Bergen stretch is the least-thrilling stretch).

Railpass Discounts: If you have any railpass that includes Norway, the Oslo-Bergen train is covered (except a 50-kr reservation fee for second class; free for first-class passholders), and the Myrdal-Flåm Flåmsbana train is discounted (to 175 kr). You still have to pay full fare for the Gudvangen-Voss bus (82 kr) and the boat cruise (265 kr). Your total one-way cost between Oslo and Bergen: about 450 kr with a first-class pass, 500 kr with a second-class pass.

Buying Tickets: You can get Nutshell train tickets, including the Myrdal-Flåm segment, at the train station in Oslo or Bergen. In summer it's smart to reserve the Oslo-Myrdal segment in advance (see below). Purchase your fjord-cruise ticket on the boat or from the TI in Flåm (or reserve a day ahead in peak season; see below), and buy the tickets for the Gudvangen bus on board from the driver. If you're a student or senior, always ask about discounts.

Reservations: At the busiest part of peak season (July-Aug), the Oslo-Bergen train—especially the segment between Oslo and Myrdal—can fill up well in advance: *It's very important to reserve a seat at least a week ahead.* Do it as soon as your itinerary is set: Dial 81 50 08 88 or 23 15 15 15 (from the US, call 011-47-81-50-08-88 or 011-47-23-15-15-15), press 4 for English, and book with a credit card. It can be difficult to get through to this number in peak season—keep trying. Once connected, you can buy a ticket (which includes a seat reservation) or, if you have a railpass, you can make just a seat reservation. You can also buy tickets online at www.nsb.no (but railpass-holders cannot make

Sample Norway in a Nutshell Schedules

Here are several one-day options for doing the Nutshell in the summer (late June-late Aug). Confirm specific times before your trip (www.ruteinfo.net).

Oslo-Bergen: Train departs Oslo-8:11, arrives Myrdal-12:53; Flåmsbana train departs Myrdal-13:02, arrives Flåm-14:00; boat departs Flåm-15:10, arrives Gudvangen-17:00; bus departs Gudvangen upon arrival, arrives Voss-19:05; train departs Voss-19:20, arrives Bergen-20:34. (Several departures allow you to stop over in Voss.)

Bergen-Oslo: Train departs Bergen-8:40, arrives Voss-9:53; bus departs Voss-10:00, arrives Gudvangen-11:10; boat departs Gudvangen-11:30, arrives Flåm-13:40; Flåmsbana train departs Flåm-16:05, arrives Myrdal-17:03; train departs Myrdal-17:52, arrives Oslo-22:32.

Day Trip from Oslo: Train departs Oslo-6:33, arrives Myrdal-11:41; Flåmsbana train departs Myrdal-12:11, arrives Flåm-13:05; boat departs Flåm-13:20, arrives Gudvangen-15:30; bus departs Gudvangen-15:40, arrives Voss-16:55; train departs Voss-17:10, arrives Oslo-22:32.

Day Trip from Bergen: Train departs Bergen-8:40, arrives Voss-9:53; bus departs Voss-10:00, arrives Gudvangen-11:10; boat departs Gudvangen-11:30, arrives Flåm-13:40; Flåmsbana train departs Flåm-14:50, arrives Myrdal-15:47; train departs Myrdal-15:56, arrives Bergen-17:52.

Variations: If you spend a night (or more) on the fjords, you have many options other than the speedy itineraries outlined above. One popular variation is to take the express boat from Bergen to Balestrand for an overnight, then plunge into the Nutshell the next day (or vice versa—do the Nutshell partway, then boat to Bergen).

NORWAY IN A NUTSHELL

seat reservations). Note that some credit cards are only accepted by phone. Ask about cancellation policies before you book.

It's possible to reserve ahead for the Flåm-Gudvangen fjord cruise, but it rarely fills up. Although you can't make a reservation for the Myrdal-Flåm train or the Gudvangen-Voss bus, this won't pose a problem for you.

Package Deals

Fjord Tours sells the Nutshell package and other package trips at all Norwegian State Railways stations, including Oslo and Bergen, or through their customer-service line in Norway (tel. 81 56 82 22, www.fjordtours.no).

The costs of the Nutshell packages are as follows:

- One-way from Bergen or Oslo-1,370 kr
- Round-trip from Oslo via Voss (but not Bergen)-1,895 kr
- Round-trip from Oslo via Bergen-2,160 kr
- Round-trip from Bergen via Myrdal (but not Oslo)-995 kr

They also sell a "Sognefjord in a Nutshell" tour, which takes an express boat from Bergen to Flåm, then picks up the Nutshell route from there (round-trip back to Bergen-1,190 kr; one-way to Oslo-1,565 kr). Note that the trip only goes once daily in winter (Oct-April).

Self-Guided Tour

▲▲▲Norway in a Nutshell

If you only have one day for this region, it'll be a thrilling day. The following segments of the Nutshell route are narrated from Oslo to Bergen. If you're going the other way, hold the book upside down.

▲▲Oslo-Bergen Train

This is simply the most spectacular train ride in northern Europe. The scenery crescendos as you climb over Norway's mountainous spine. After a mild three hours of deep woods and lakes, you're into the barren, windswept heaths and glaciers. These tracks were begun in 1894 to link Stockholm and Bergen, but Norway won its independence from Sweden in 1905, so the line served to link the two main cities in the new country—Oslo and Bergen. The entire railway, an amazing engineering feat completed in 1909, is 300 miles long; peaks at 4,266 feet, which, at this Alaskan latitude, is far above the tree line; goes under 18 miles of snow sheds; trundles over 300 bridges; and passes through 200 tunnels in just under seven hours.

Here's what you'll see traveling westward from Oslo: Leaving Oslo, you pass through a six-mile-long tunnel and stop in Drammen, Norway's fifth-largest town. The scenery stays low-key and woodsy up Hallingdal Valley until you reach Geilo, a popular ski resort. Then you enter a land of big views and tough little cabins. Finse, at about 4,000 feet, is the highest stop on the line. From here, you enter the longest high-mountain stretch of railway in Europe. Much of the line is protected by snow tunnels. The scenery gets more dramatic as you approach Myrdal (MEER-doll). Just before Myrdal, look to the right and down into the Flåm Valley (Flåmsdalen), where the branch line winds its way down to the fjord. Nutshell travelers get off at Myrdal.

Cost: Note that the Nutshell route includes only part of this train ride (as a day trip from Oslo, for instance, you take the Oslo-Myrdal and Voss-Oslo segments). Here are the one-way fares for various segments: Oslo-Bergen-788 kr, Oslo-Myrdal-623 kr, Myrdal-Voss-108 kr, Myrdal-Bergen-266 kr, Voss-Bergen-176 kr. You can save money on these fares if you book in advance at www.nsb.no.

Remember, second-class railpass-holders pay just 50 kr to reserve, and first-class passholders pay nothing.

Anyone can pay 90 kr for a reservation and upgrade to "Komfort" class, with more legroom, reclining seats, free coffee and tea, and an electrical socket for your laptop (reserve ahead or ask the conductor when you board).

The Facts on Fjords

The process that created the majestic Sognefjord began during an ice age about three million years ago. A glacier up to 6,500 feet thick slid downhill at an inch an hour, following a former river valley on its way to the sea. Rocks embedded in the glacier gouged out a steep, U-shaped valley, displacing enough rock material to form a mountain 13 miles high. When the climate warmed up, the ice age came to an end. The melting glaciers retreated and the sea level rose nearly 300 feet, flooding the valley now known as the Sognefjord. The fjord is more than a mile deep, flanked by 3,000-foot mountains—for a total relief of 9,300 feet. Waterfalls spill down the cliffs, fed by runoff from today's glaciers. Powdery sediment tinges the fjords a cloudy green, the distinct color of glacier melt.

Why are there fjords on the west coast of Norway, but not, for instance, on the east coast of Sweden? The creation of a fjord requires a setting of coastal mountains, a good source of moisture, and a climate cold enough for glaciers to form and advance. Due to the earth's rotation, the prevailing winds in higher latitudes blow from west to east, so chances of glaciation are ideal where there is an ocean to the west of land with coastal mountains. When the winds blow east over the water, they pick up a lot of moisture, then bump up against the coastal mountain range, and dump their moisture in the form of snow—which feeds the glaciers that carve valleys down to the sea.

You can find fjords along the northwest coast of Europe—including western Norway and Sweden, Denmark's Faroe Islands, Scotland's Shetland Islands, Iceland, and Greenland; the northwest coast of North America (from Puget Sound in Washington state north to Alaska); the southwest coast of South America (Chile); the west coast of New Zealand's South Island; and on the continent of Antarctica.

As you travel through Scandinavia, bear in mind that, while we English-speakers use the word "fjord" to mean only glacier-cut inlets, Scandinavians often use it in a more general sense to include bays, lakes, and lagoons that weren't formed by glacial action.

Schedule: This train runs three to five times per day (over-night possible daily except Sat). The segment from Oslo to Myrdal takes 4.75-5.5 hours; going all the way to Bergen takes 7-7.5 hours.

Reservations: In peak season, get reservations for this train at least a week in advance.

▲▲Myrdal-Flåm Train (Flåmsbana)

The little 12-mile spur line leaves the Oslo-Bergen line at Myrdal (2,800 feet), which is nothing but a scenic high-altitude train junction with a decent cafeteria. From Myrdal, the train winds down

to Flåm (sea level) through 20 tunnels (more than three miles' worth) in 55 thrilling minutes. It's party time on board, and the engineer even stops the train for photos at the best water-fall, Kjosfossen. According to a Norwegian legend, a temptress lives behind these falls and tries to lure men to the rocks with her singing...look out for her.

The train line is an even more impressive feat of engineering when you realize it's not a cogwheel train—it's held to the tracks only by steel wheels, though it does have five separate braking systems. Before boarding, pick up the free, multilingual souvenir pamphlet with lots of info on the trip (or see www.flaams bana.no).

Cost: 250 kr one-way (railpass-holders pay 175 kr), 350 kr round-trip. You can buy tickets at the ticket desk in the Flåmsbana stations in Myrdal or Flåm, at local TIs, or—if you're in a rush to make a tight connection—buy them on board.

Schedule: The train departs in each direction nearly hourly.

Reservations: Reservations are not possible—you can buy your ticket ahead (at any train station in Norway), but that won't guarantee you a seat on a particular train. (Ticket-sellers assure me it's exceedingly rare not to get on the train you want.)

▲▲▲Flåm-Gudvangen Fjord Cruise

The Flåmsbana train deposits you at **Flåm,** a scenic, functional transit hub at the far end of the Aurlandsfjord. If you're doing the Nutshell route nonstop, follow the crowds and hop on the sightseeing boat that'll take you to **Gudvangen** (listen for the train conductor to announce which pier number to go to). With minimal English narration, the boat takes you close to the goats, sheep, waterfalls, and awesome cliffs.

You'll cruise up the lovely **Aurlandsfjord,** motoring by the town of **Aurland** (a good home base, but your boat may not stop here unless you ask), pass **Undredal,** and hang a left at the stunning **Nærøyfjord** ("Narrow Fjord"). The cruise ends at the apex of the Nærøyfjord, in **Gudvangen.**

The trip is breathtaking in any weather. For the last hour, as you sail down the Nærøyfjord, camera-clicking tourists scurry around the drool-stained deck like nervous roosters, scratching fitfully for a photo that will catch the magic. Waterfalls turn the black cliffs into bridal veils, and you can nearly reach out and touch the cliffs of the Nærøyfjord. It's the world's narrowest fjord: six miles long and as little as 820 feet wide and 40 feet deep. On a sunny day, the ride is one of those fine times—like when you're high on the tip of an Alp—when a warm camaraderie spontaneously combusts between the strangers who've come together for the experience.

Cost: For the whole route (Flåm-Gudvangen), you'll pay 265 kr one-way (133 kr for students with ISIC cards; 370 kr round-trip). Taking the boat for just the 20-minute hop between Flåm and Aurland costs 85 kr (more than twice as expensive and twice as slow as the bus). There are no railpass discounts.

Schedule: From late June through late August, boats leave Flåm daily at 9:00, 11:00, 13:20, and 15:10; and leave Gudvangen daily at 10:30, 11:30, 13:20, and 16:00. Frequency drops off-season (3/day early June and late Aug-mid-Sept; 2/day May and late Sept; only 1/day Oct-April).

Reservations: It's possible to reserve, but boats rarely fill up, even in the very peak of the season (July-mid-Aug). To reserve, email booking@fjord1.no, book online at www.fjord1.no, or call 55 90 70 70 by 14:00 one business day before.

Other Ways to Cruise Nærøyfjord: While most visitors thunder onto the state-run ferry described above, consider taking a trip on a Sognefjorden Cruise ship, or a thrilling ride on little inflatable FjordSafari speedboats.

▲Gudvangen-Voss Bus

Gudvangen is little more than a boat dock and giant tourist kiosk. Nutshellers get off the boat at Gudvangen and take the one-hour bus to Voss (buses meet each ferry—but confirm this in advance if you plan to take the last boat of the day, which arrives in Gudvangen at about 20:00—the ferry crew can call ahead to be sure the bus waits for you). Most buses take the extra-scenic route via Stalheim (described below). If you're a waterfall junkie, sit on the right.

First the bus takes you up the **Nærøydal.** After crossing a river, the bus climbs up a corkscrew series of switchbacks flanked by a pair of dramatic waterfalls. With its 18 percent grade, it's the steepest road in Norway. At the top, most buses stop at the landmark **Stalheim Hotel** for a last grand view back into fjord country. Though this hotel dates from 1885, there's been an inn here since about 1700, where the royal mailmen would change horses. The hotel is geared for tour groups (genuine trolls sew the pewter buttons on the sweaters), but the priceless view from the backyard is free. Stop in the living room to survey the art showing this perch in the 19th century.

The bus rejoins the main road and heads through pastoral countryside to Voss. Just before Voss, look to the right for the wide and tumbling **Tvindefossen waterfall.** Drivers will find the grassy meadow and flat rocks at its base ideal for letting the mist fog their glasses and enjoying a drink or snack (be discreet, as "picnics are forbidden").

Cost: 82 kr, pay on board, no railpass discounts.

Reservations: Not possible or necessary.

Voss

The Nutshell bus from Gudvangen drops you at the Voss train station, which is on the Oslo-Bergen train line. Drivers should zip right through, and Nutshellers should catch the next train out. A plain town in a lovely lake-and-mountain setting, Voss lacks the striking fjordside scenery of Flåm, Aurland, or Undredal, and is basically a home base for summer or winter sports (Norway's Winter Olympics teams often practice here).

Voss has a **TI** across from the train station (June-Aug Mon-Fri 8:00-19:00, Sat 9:00-19:00, Sun 12:00-19:00; Sept-May Mon-Fri 8:30-15:30, closed Sat-Sun; in the center of town at Evangervegen 6, tel. 56 51 94 90), a 13th-century church, and little else. Fans of American football will want to see the humble monument to player and coach Knute Rockne, who was born in Voss in 1888; look for the metal memorial plaque on a rock near

the train station. Two miles outside town, the Mølstertunet Folk
Museum has 16 buildings showing off farm life in the 17th and
18th centuries (55 kr; mid-May–mid-Sept daily 10:00-17:00; mid-
Sept–mid-May Mon-Fri 10:00-15:00, Sun 12:00-15:00, closed Sat;
Mølstervegen 143, tel. 56 51 15 11, www.vossfolkemuseum.no).

▲Voss-Bergen Train

The least exciting segment of the trip—but still pleasantly scenic—
this train chugs along the valley between the midsize town of Voss
(described above) and Bergen. For the best scenery, sit on the right
side of the train if coming from Oslo/Voss, or the left side if coming from Bergen. Between Voss and Dale, you'll pass several scenic lakes; near Bergen, you'll go along the Veafjord.

Cost: The train costs 176 kr between Voss and Bergen and is
fully covered by railpasses that include Norway.

Schedule and Reservations: Unlike the long-distance Oslo-
Bergen journey, this line is also served by more frequent com-
muter trains (about hourly, 1-1.25 hours), and reservations aren't
necessary.

Voss-Oslo Train: Note that if you're doing the Nutshell
round-trip from Oslo, you can catch the train from Voss (rather
than Bergen) back to Oslo. The trip takes 5.5-6 hours and costs
704 kr; reservations are strongly recommended in peak season.

Flåm

Flåm (sometimes spelled Flaam, pronounced "flome")—where the
boat and Flåmsbana train meet, at the head of the Aurlandsfjord—
feels more like a transit junction than a village. But its striking
setting, easy transportation connections, and touristy bustle make
it appealing as a home base for exploring the nearby area.

Orientation to Flåm

Most of Flåm's services are inside the train station, including the
TI (see below), train ticket desk, several Internet terminals, post
office, public WC, cafeteria, and souvenir shops hawking overpriced reindeer pelts (cheaper in Bergen). Just outside the station,
the little red shed at the head of the tracks serves as a left-lug-
gage desk (25 kr, daily 8:00-19:45, on your right as you depart the
train, ring bell if nobody's there), and displays a chart of the services you'll find in the station. The boat dock for fjord cruises is
just beyond the end of the tracks. Surrounding the station are a
grocery store (Mon-Thu 9:00-17:00, Fri-Sun 9:00-20:00, shorter

hours and closed Sun off-season) and a smattering of hotels, hostels, travel agencies, and touristy restaurants. Aside from a few scattered farmhouses and some homes lining the road, there's not much of a town here. (The old town center—where tourists rarely venture, and which you'll pass on the Flåm-Myrdal train—is a few miles up the river, in the valley.)

Tourist Information

At the TI inside the train station, you can purchase your boat tickets and load up on handy brochures (daily May-Sept 8:15-16:00, June-Aug also 16:30-20:00, closed Oct-April, pay Wi-Fi, tel. 57 63 21 06, www.visitflam.com or www.alr.no, very helpful Vladimir). Answers to most of your questions can be found posted on the walls and from staff at the counter. Bus schedules, boat and train timetables, maps, and more are photocopied and available for your convenience.

Sights near Flåm

Flåm's village activities are all on the pier. There's a free historic train museum next to track 1, a fjord "panorama" movie (50 kr, 23 minutes), and the Aegir Bryggeri, a micro-brewery offering tastes of its five beers (75 kr) in a great woody brew-pub setting. But the main reason people come to Flåm is to leave it. If you want to linger, consider renting a rowboat or kayak to go out on the usually calm, peaceful waters of the fjord. You can paddle near the walls of the fjord and really get a sense of the immensity of these mountains.

Because Aurland and Flåm are close together (10 minutes away by car or bus, or 20 minutes by boat), I've also listed attractions "Near Aurland," later.

▲▲▲Cruising Nærøyfjord

The most scenic fjord I've seen anywhere in Norway is about an hour from Flåm (basically the last half of the 2-hour Flåm-Gudvangen trip). There are several ways to cruise it: You can take the state-run ferry, described above as part of the Norway in a Nutshell trip (4-hour round-trips departing Flåm at 9:00, 11:00, and 13:20, 370 kr; these should also stop in Aurland—make sure the crew knows if you want to get off, and the cruise ends in Gudvangen). Two other Flåm-based options follow:

Sognefjorden Cruise/Bus Tour—This private company runs trips from Flåm to Gudvangen and back to Flåm; you'll go one way on the boat and the other on a bus (300 kr, children-150 kr; daily mid-June-Aug at 10:00, 11:00, 12:00, or 13:30 with an optional 45-minute stop in Undredal; tel. 57 66 00 55).

▲▲**FjordSafari to Nærøyfjord**—FjordSafari takes little groups out onto the fjord in small, open Zodiac-type boats with an English-speaking guide. Participants wear full-body weather suits, furry hats, and spacey goggles (making everyone on the boat look like crash-test dummies). As the boat rockets across the water, you'll be thankful for the gear, no matter what the weather. You'll get the same scant information and stops as on the slow ferry, except that Safari boats stop right under a towering rock cliff—a magnificent experience. Their two-hour Flåm-Gudvangen-Flåm tour focuses on the Nærøyfjord, and gets you all the fjord magnificence you can imagine (580 kr). Their three-hour tour (690 kr) is the same as the two-hour tour, except that it includes a stop in Undredal, where you can see goat cheese being made and wander that sleepy village. They run several departures daily from June through August (fewer off-season, kids get discounts, tel. 99 09 08 60, www.fjordsafari.no, Johanna). They also offer a 1.5-hour "mini" tour that costs 480 kr and misses the Nærøyfjord...so what's the point?

▲Flåm Valley Bike Ride or Hike

For the best single-day, non-fjord activity from Flåm, take the train to Myrdal, then hike or mountain-bike along the road (part gravel but mostly paved) back down to Flåm (2-3 hours by bike, gorgeous waterfalls, great mountain scenery, and a cute church with an evocative graveyard, but no fjord views). The Flåm TI rents mountain bikes (50 kr/hour, 250 kr/day) as does the local youth hostel. It costs 90 kr to take a bike to Myrdal on the train. You can hike just the best two hours from Myrdal to Berekvam, where you can catch the train into the valley. Pick up the helpful map with this and other hiking options (easy to strenuous) at the Flåm TI.

▲▲Otternes Farms

This humble but magical cluster of four centuries-old farms, realistically accessible only to drivers, is perched high on a ridge, up a twisty gravel road midway between Flåm and Aurland. Laila Kvellestad runs this low-key sight, valiantly working to save and share traditional life as it was back when butter was the farmers' gold. (That was before emigration decimated the work-force, coinage replaced barter, and industrialized margarine became more popular than butter, leaving farmers to eke out a living relying only on their goats and the cheese they produce.) Until 1919 the only road between Aurland and Flåm passed between this huddle of 27 buildings, high above the fjord. First settled in 1522, farmers lived here until the 1990s. Laila gives 45-minute English tours through several time-warp houses and barns at 10:00, 12:00, 14:00, and 16:00 (50-kr entry plus 30-kr for guided tour, June-mid-Sept daily 10:00-17:00, tel. 48 12 51 38, www.otternes.no). It's wise to call first to confirm tour times and that it's open. For an additional 50 kr, Laila serves a traditional snack with your tour (pancakes with coffee or tea), but you must book in advance.

Over (or Under) the Mountains, to Lærdal and Borgund

To reach these sights, you'll first head along the fjord to Aurland. Of the sights below, the Lærdal Tunnel, Stegastein viewpoint, and Aurlandsvegen "Snow Road" are best for drivers. The Borgund Stave Church can be reached by car, or by bus from Flåm or Aurland.

For more specifics on driving through the Lærdal Tunnel or on the Aurlandsvegen "Snow Road," see below.

Lærdal Tunnel

Drivers find that this tunnel makes connecting Flåm and Lærdal a snap. It's the world's longest road-vehicle tunnel, stretching 15 miles between Aurland and Lærdal as part of the E16 highway. It also makes the wonderful Borgund Stave Church (described below) less than an hour's drive from Aurland. The downside to the tunnel is that it goes beneath my favorite scenic drive in Norway (the Aurlandsvegen "Snow Road," described next). But with a little more than an hour, you can drive through the tunnel to Lærdal and then return via the "Snow Road," with the Stegastein viewpoint as a finale, before dropping back into Aurland.

▲▲Stegastein Viewpoint and Aurlandsvegen "Snow Road"

With a car and clear weather, consider twisting up the mountain behind Aurland on route 243 for about 20 minutes for a fine view

over the Aurlandsfjord. A new viewpoint called Stegastein—which looks like a giant, wooden, inverted number "7"—provides a platform from which you can enjoy stunning views across the fjords. Immediately beyond the viewpoint, you leave the fjord views and enter the mountaintop world of the Aurlandsvegen "Snow Road." When you finally hit civilization on the other side, you're a mile from the Lærdal tunnel entrance and about 30 minutes from the fine Borgund Stave Church.

▲▲Borgund Stave Church

About 16 miles east of Lærdal, in the village of Borgund, is Norway's most-visited and one of its best-preserved stave churches. It's been closed for renovation but should reopen before summer of 2012.

Borgund's church comes with one of Norway's best stave-church history museums, which beautifully explains these icons of medieval Norway. Dating from around 1180, the interior features only a few later additions, including a 16th-century pulpit, 17th-century stone altar, painted decorations, and crossbeam reinforcements.

The oldest and most authentic item in the church is the stone baptismal font. In medieval times, priests conducting baptisms would go outside to shoo away the evil spirits from an infant before bringing it inside the church for the ritual. (If infants died before being baptized, they couldn't be buried in the churchyard, so parents would put their bodies in little coffins and hide them under the church's floorboards to get them as close as possible to God.)

Explore the dimly lit interior, illuminated only by the original, small, circular windows up high. Notice the X-shaped crosses of St. Andrew (the church's patron), carvings of dragons, and medieval runes.

Cost and Hours: 75 kr, buy tickets in museum across street, daily mid-June-mid-Aug 8:00-20:00, May-mid-June and mid-Aug-Sept 10:00-17:00, closed Oct-April. The museum has a shop and a fine little cafeteria serving filling and tasty lunches (70-kr soup with bread, tel. 57 66 81 09, www.stavechurch.com).

Getting There: It's about a 30-minute **drive** east of Lærdal, on E16 (the road to Oslo—if coming from Aurland or Flåm, consider taking the scenic route via the Stegastein viewpoint, described above). There's also a convenient **bus** connection: The bus departs Flåm and Aurland around midday (direction: Lillehammer) and heads for the church, with a return bus departing Borgund in mid-afternoon (240-kr round-trip, get ticket from driver, about 1 hour each way with about 1 hour at the church, bus runs daily May-Sept, tell driver you want to get off at the church).

Sleeping and Eating in Flåm

My recommended accommodations are away from the tacky train-station bustle, but a close enough walk to be convenient. The first two places are located along the waterfront a quarter-mile from the station: Walk around the little harbor (with the water on your left) for about 10 minutes. It's more enjoyable to follow the level, waterfront dock than to hike up the main road.

Dining options beyond your hotel's dining room or kitchenette are sparse. The cafeteria section of Furukroa Restaurant in the station complex has reasonably priced food (daily 9:00-18:00, Fri-Sat until 19:00).

$$$ Flåm Marina and Apartments, perched right on the fjord, is ideal for families and longer stays. They offer 10 new-feeling, self-catering apartments that sleep 2-5 people each. All units offer views of the fjord with a balcony, kitchenette, and small dining area (Db-1,195 kr June-late Sept, less off-season, 320 kr more for each additional adult, check online or ask about specials for longer stays, no breakfast, boat rental, laundry facilities, next to the guest harbor just below Heimly Pensjonat—see next, tel. 57 63 35 55, fax 57 63 35 44, www.flammarina.no, booking@flammarina.no).

$$ Heimly Pensjonat, with 23 straightforward rooms, is clean, efficient, and the best small hotel in town. Sit on the porch with new friends and watch the clouds roll down the fjord (Sb-895 kr, Db-995 kr, view Db costs 100 kr more in summer, extra bed-325 kr for adult or 225 kr for child, includes breakfast, cheaper

---

Sleep Code

(5 kr = about $1, country code: 47)
S = Single, **D** = Double/Twin, **T** = Triple, **Q** = Quad, **b** = bathroom, **s** = shower. You can assume that staff speak English, breakfast is included, and credit cards are accepted unless otherwise noted.

To help you sort easily through these listings, I've divided the accommodations into three categories, based on the price for a standard double room with bath during high season:

   $$$ Higher Priced—Most rooms 1,000 kr or more.
    $$ Moderately Priced—Most rooms 600-1,000 kr.
     $ Lower Priced—Most rooms 600 kr or less.

Note that the season is boom or bust here. It can be dead in June and packed in July and August. Prices can change without notice; verify the hotel's current rates online or by email. For other updates, see www.ricksteves.com/update.

Oct-May, Db rooms are mostly twins, try to reserve a room with a view at the standard price, bike and car rental, tel. 57 63 23 00, fax 57 63 23 40, www.heimly.no, post@heimly.no). The budget annex out back has more rooms that share bathrooms (D-510 kr, sheets and towels-100 kr/person, breakfast-95 kr).

$-$$ Flåm Youth Hostel and Camping Bungalows, voted Scandinavia's most beautiful campground, is run by the friendly Håland family, who rent the cheapest beds in the area (hostel: bunk in 4-bed room-200 kr, S-330 kr, D-470-570 kr; newer, fancier building: bunk in 4-bed room-270 kr, Db-755 kr; cabins-650-1,100 kr; sheets and towels-60 kr, showers-10 kr, 10 percent discount for members, no meals but kitchen access, laundry, apple grove, tel. 57 63 21 21, www.flaam-camping.no, camping@flaam-camping.no). It's a five-minute walk toward the valley from the train station: Cross the bridge and turn left up the main road; then look for the hostel on the right.

Aurland

A few miles north of Flåm, Aurland is more of a real town and less of a tourist depot. While it's nothing exciting (Balestrand

is more lively and appealing, and Solvorn is cuter), it's a good, easygoing fjordside home base. And thanks to its location—on the main road and boat lines, near Flåm—it's relatively handy for those taking public transportation.

Getting There: Aurland is an easy 10-minute drive or bus trip from Flåm. If you want to stay overnight in Aurland, note that every train (except the late-night one) arriving in Flåm connects with a bus or boat to Aurland. Eleven buses and at least four ferries link the towns daily in summer (bus-33 kr, 10 minutes; boat-85 kr, 20 minutes). The Flåm-Gudvangen boat usually stops at Aurland en route, so it's possible to continue the Nutshell route from Aurland without backtracking to Flåm, but make sure the boat crew knows you want to get off at Aurland. Boat tickets bought at the Aurland TI come with a reservation (helpful on the busiest days in July and August, when the boats can fill up in Flåm). The Bergen-Balestrand-Flåm express boat stops in Aurland.

Orientation to Aurland

From Aurland's dingy boat dock area, walk one block up the paved street into the heart of town. On your right are the ICA and Spar supermarkets (handy for picnic supplies) and Aurlandskafeen, the best restaurant in town (at the bridge). To your left is the Vangsgården Guest House and, behind it, Aurland Fjordhotel. To reach the TI, go straight ahead and bear right, then look behind the white church (800 years old and worth a peek). The bus stop, with buses to Flåm, is in front of the TI.

Tourist Information

The TI stocks English-language brochures about hikes and day trips from the area, offers free Internet terminals, and hosts a small history exhibit (mid-June-Aug Mon-Fri 9:00-18:00, Sat 10:00-17:00, closed Sun; Sept-mid-June Mon-Fri 8:30-15:30, closed Sat-Sun; behind the white church—look for green-and-white *i* sign; tel. 57 63 33 13, www.alr.no).

Sleeping in Aurland

(5kr = about $1, country code: 47)

$$$ Aurland Fjordhotel is big, modern, and centrally located. While it has a business-hotel vibe, most of its 30 rooms come with gorgeous fjord-view balconies (Sb-985 kr, Db-1,370 kr, Tb-1,785, prices lower off-season, check website for deals, includes breakfast, free Wi-Fi, tel. 57 63 35 05, fax 57 63 36 22, www.aurland -fjordhotel.com, post@aurland-fjordhotel.com, Steinar and Dorte Kjerstein).

$$ Vangsgården Guest House, closest to the boat landing, is a complex of old buildings dominating the old center of Aurland and run from one reception desk (free Wi-Fi in main building, tel. 57 63 35 80, www.vangsgaarden.no, vangsgaarden @alb.no, open all year, Astrid). The main building is a simple, old guesthouse offering basic rooms, a large self-serve kitchen, and a fine old-timey living room (Sb-600 kr, Db-1,025 kr). Their old-fashioned **Aabelheim Pension** is Aurland's best *koselig* (cozy)-like-a-farmhouse place (same prices). And lining the waterfront are their six adorable, woody cabins, each with a kitchen, bathroom, and two bedrooms (1,250 kr for 2-6 people, sheets-65 kr/person, book 2 months in advance). The optional 75-kr breakfast is served in a delightfully homey dining room. The owners also run the Duehuset Pub (see "Eating in Aurland," next page) and rent bikes for 200 kr/day.

Near Aurland

$$ Skahjem Gard is an active farm run by Aurland's former deputy mayor, Nils Tore. They've converted their old sheep barn into seven spick-and-span family apartments with private bathrooms and kitchenettes, each sleeping up to four people (650 kr for studio, 750 kr with separate bedroom; rustic, cozy fishing cottage with a separate bathroom-450 kr; sheets and towels-70 kr/ person, free Wi-Fi, two miles up the valley—road #50, follow *Hol* signs, tel. 57 63 33 29, mobile 95 17 25 67, www.skahjemgard.com, nskahjem@online.no). It's a 25-minute walk from town, but Nils will pick up and drop off travelers at the ferry. This is best for families and foursomes with cars.

$ Winjum Huts, about a half-mile from Aurland's dock, rents 14 basic cabins on a peaceful perch overlooking the majestic fjord. The washhouse/kitchen is where you'll find the toilets and showers. Follow the road uphill past the Aurland Fjordhotel; the huts are after the first hairpin curve (400-500 kr for up to 4 people, 2-bed apartment-1,100 kr, sheets-50 kr/person, showers-10 kr/5 minutes, no food available—just beer, tel. 57 63 34 61 or 41 47 47 51).

Eating in Aurland

Aurlandskafeen is a basic little café/diner serving the best-value food in town from its inviting cafeteria line. It's a block from the main square, at the bridge over the river. Sit upstairs or on its riverside terrace (95-kr daily plates, open daily 10:00-21:00—provided there are customers, shorter hours off-season, tel. 57 63 36 66).

Duehuset Pub ("The Dove's House"), run by Vangsgården Guest House, serves up decent food in the center of town (190-240-kr pizzas big enough for four, 155-240-kr main dishes; June-Sept daily 15:00-23:00; Oct-May Fri-Sun 18:00-23:00, closed Mon-Thu).

The **Aurland Fjordhotel** is your only alternative for splurges (195-kr main dishes, 65-kr starters, 240-295-kr dinner buffet, daily 19:00-22:00, shorter hours off-season, bar open later, tel. 57 63 35 05).

For cheap eats on dockside benches, gather a picnic at the **Spar** or **ICA** supermarkets (both open Mon-Fri 9:00-20:00, Sat 9:00-18:00, closed Sun).

Undredal

This almost impossibly remote community is home to about 75 people (and 400 goats). A huge percentage of the town's former

population (300 people) emigrated to the US between 1850 and 1925. Undredal was accessible only by boat until 1988, when the road from Flåm opened. There's not much in the town, which is famous for its church and its goat cheese, but I'll never forget the picnic I had on the ferry wharf. While appealing, Undredal is quiet (some say better from the boat) and difficult to reach—you'll have to be patient to connect to other towns. For more information on the town, see www.undredal.no.

Undredal has Norway's smallest still-used **church,** seating 40 people for services every fourth Sunday. The original church was built in 1147 (look for the four original stave pillars inside). It was later expanded, pews added, and the interior painted in the 16th century in a way that resembles the traditional Norwegian *rosemaling* style (which came later). It is undergoing renovation until early summer 2012; you could check with the Undredal Overnatting guesthouse (listed below) to make sure it's reopened. You can get in only with an overpriced 15-minute tour (60 kr, mid-June-mid-Aug daily 9:30-18:30, less in shoulder season, closed Oct-April).

Undredal's farms exist for cheese. The beloved local cheese comes in two versions: brown and white. The brown version is unaged and slightly sweet, while the white cheese has been aged and is mild and a bit salty. For samples, visit the Undredalsbui grocery store at the harbor (Mon-Fri 9:00-17:00, Sat 9:00-15:00, Sun 12:00-16:00, shorter hours and closed Sun off-season).

The 15-minute drive from Flåm is mostly through a tunnel. By sea, you'll sail past Undredal on the Flåm-Gudvangen boat (you can request a stop). To get the ferry to pick you up in Undredal, turn on the blinking light (though some express boats will not stop).

This sleepy town can accommodate about eight visitors a night. **$$ Undredal Overnatting** rents four modern, woody, comfortable rooms and two apartments. The reception is at the café on the harbor, while the accommodations are at the top of town (Db-740 kr, apartments start at 990 kr, sheets-60 kr/person, breakfast-90 kr, tel. 57 63 30 80 or 57 63 31 00, visit@undredal.no).

MORE ON THE SOGNEFJORD

Balestrand • The Lustrafjord • Scenic Drives

Norway's world of fjords is decorated with medieval stave churches, fishing boats, cascading waterfalls, dramatic glaciers, and brightly painted shiplap villages. Travelers in a hurry zip through the fjords on the Norway in a Nutshell route. Their heads spin from all the scenery, and most wish they had more time on the Sognefjord. If you can linger in fjord country, this chapter is for you.

Snuggle into the fjordside village of Balestrand, which has a variety of walking and biking options and a fun local arts scene. Balestrand is also a handy jumping-off spot for adventures great and small, including a day trip up the Fjærlandsfjord to gaze at a receding tongue of the Jostedal Glacier, or across the Sognefjord to the truly medieval-feeling Hopperstad Stave Church. Farther east is the Lustrafjord, a tranquil branch of the Sognefjord offering drivers an appealing concentration of visit-worthy sights. On the Lustrafjord, you'll enjoy enchanting hamlets with pristine fjord views (such as Solvorn), historic churches (including Norway's oldest stave church at Urnes and the humble village Dale Church in Luster), an opportunity to touch and even hike on a glacier (the Nigard), and more stunning fjord views.

This region is important to the people of Norway. After four centuries under Danish rule, the soul of the country was nearly lost. With semi-independence and a constitution in the early 1800s, the country experienced a resurgence of national pride. Urban Norwegians headed for the fjord country here in the west. Norway's first Romantic painters and writers were drawn to Balestrand, inspired by the unusual light and dramatic views of mountains plunging into the fjords. The Sognefjord, with its many branches, is featured in more Romantic paintings than any other fjord.

Planning Your Time

If you can spare a day or two off the Norway in a Nutshell route, spend it here. Balestrand is the best home base, especially if you're relying on public transportation (it's well-connected by express boat both to the Nutshell scene and to Bergen). If you have a car, consider staying in the heart of the Lustrafjord region in sweet little Solvorn (easy ferry connection to the Urnes Stave Church and a short drive to the Nigard Glacier). As fjord home bases go, Balestrand and Solvorn are both better—but less convenient— than Flåm or Aurland on the Nutshell route.

With one night in this area, you'll have to blitz the sights on the way between destinations; with two nights, you can slow your pace (and your pulse) to enjoy the fjord scenery and plenty of day-trip possibilities.

Balestrand

The pleasant fjord town of Balestrand (pop. 2,000) has a long history of hosting tourists, thanks to its landmark Kviknes Hotel.

But it also feels real and lived-in, making Balestrand a nice mix of cuteness and convenience. The town is near, but not *too* near, the Nutshell bustle across the fjord— and yet it's an easy express-boat trip away if you'd like to dive into the Nuttiness. In short, consider Balestrand a worthwhile detour from the typical fjord visit—allowing you to dig deeper into the Sognefjord, just like the glaciers did during the last ice age.

With two nights, you can relax and consider some day trips: Cruise up the nearby Fjærlandsfjord for a peek at a distant tongue of the ever-less-mighty Jostedal Glacier, or head across the Sognefjord to the beautiful Hopperstad Stave Church in Vik. Balestrand also has outdoor activities for everyone, from dreamy

Sognefjord Overview

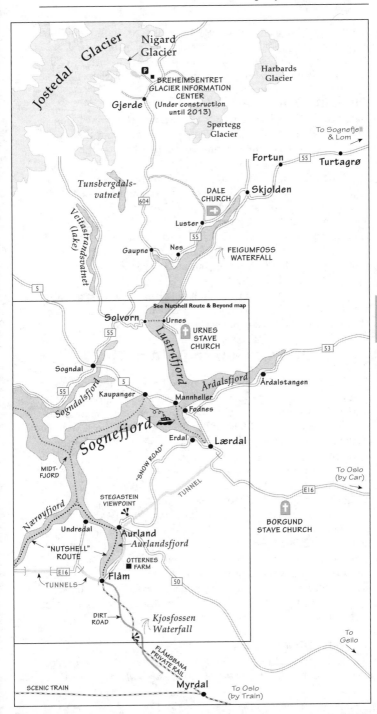

fjordside strolls and strenuous mountain hikes to wildly scenic bike rides. For dinner, splurge on the memorable *smörgåsbord*-style *store koldt bord* dinner in the Kviknes Hotel dining room, then sip coffee from its balcony as you watch the sun set (or not) over the fjord.

Planning Your Time

Balestrand's key advantage is its easy express-boat connection to Bergen, offering an alternative route to the fjord from the typical Nutshell train-bus combo. Consider zipping here on the Bergen boat, then continuing on via the Nutshell route.

One night is enough to get a taste of Balestrand. But two nights buy you some time for day trips. Note that the first flurry of day trips departs early, around 7:30-8:05 (includes the boat to Vik/Hopperstad Stave Church or the full-day Fjærlandsfjord glacier excursion), and the next batch departs around noon (the half-day Fjærlandsfjord glacier excursion and the boat to Flåm). If you wait until after 12:00 to make your choice, you'll miss the boat... literally.

Balestrand pretty much shuts down from mid-September through mid-May—when most of the activities, sights, hotels, and restaurants listed here are likely closed.

Orientation to Balestrand

Most travelers arrive in Balestrand on the express boat from Bergen or Flåm. The tidy harbor area has a TI, two grocery stores, a couple of galleries, a town history museum, and a small aquarium devoted to marine life found in the fjord. The historic wooden Kviknes Hotel and its ugly modern annex dominate Balestrand's waterfront.

Even during tourist season, Balestrand is quiet. How quiet? The police station closes on weekends. And it's tiny—from the harbor to the Balestrand Hotel is a five-minute stroll, and you can walk from the aquarium to the Kviknes Hotel in less than that.

Balestrand became accessible to the wider world in 1858 when an activist minister (from the church you see across the fjord from town) brought in the first steamer service. That put Balestrand on the Grand Tour map of the Romantic Age. Even the German Kaiser chose to summer here. Today, people from around the world come here to feel the grandeur of the fjord country and connect with the essence of Norway.

Tourist Information

At the TI, located next to the Joker supermarket at the harbor, pick up the free, helpful *Outdoor Activities in Balestrand* brochure.

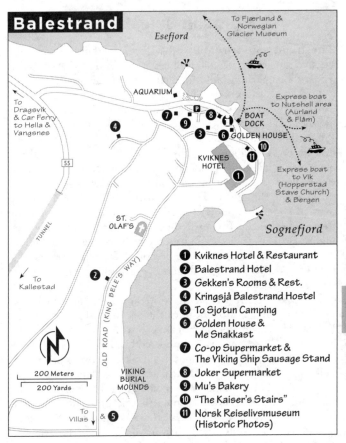

Balestrand

Esefjord

To Fjærland & Norwegian Glacier Museum

AQUARIUM

To Dragsvik & Car Ferry to Hella & Vangsnes

55

Express boat to Nutshell area (Aurland & Flåm)

BOAT DOCK

GOLDEN HOUSE

KVIKNES HOTEL

Express boat to Vik (Hopperstad Stave Church) & Bergen

TUNNEL

To Kallestad

ST. OLAF'S

Sognefjord

OLD ROAD (KING BELE'S WAY)

200 Meters
200 Yards

VIKING BURIAL MOUNDS

To Villas

1 Kviknes Hotel & Restaurant
2 Balestrand Hotel
3 Gekken's Rooms & Rest.
4 Kringsjå Balestrand Hostel
5 To Sjøtun Camping
6 Golden House & Me Snakkast
7 Co-op Supermarket & The Viking Ship Sausage Stand
8 Joker Supermarket
9 Mu's Bakery
10 "The Kaiser's Stairs"
11 Norsk Reiselivsmuseum (Historic Photos)

MORE ON THE SOGNEFJORD

If you're planning on a longer hike, consider buying the good 70-kr hiking map. The TI has numerous brochures about the Sognefjord area and detailed information on the more challenging hikes. It offers terminals with Internet access (1 kr/minute) and free Wi-Fi, rents bikes (50 kr/hour, 250 kr/day), sells day-trip excursions to the glacier, and more (late June-late Aug Mon-Sat 7:30-18:00, Sun 10:00-17:30, shorter hours in spring and fall, closed Oct-April, tel. 57 69 12 55—answered all year).

Local Guide: Bjørg Bjøberg, who runs the Golden House art gallery, knows the town well and is happy to show visitors around (500 kr/1.5 hours, tel. 91 56 28 42).

Car Rental: The Kviknes Hotel can arrange a one-day car rental for you (tel. 57 69 42 00), or contact the Balholm Car Rental agency (tel. 41 24 82 53, www.rentacarbalholm.com).

Sights in Balestrand

Balestrand Harborfront Stroll—The tiny harbor stretches from the aquarium to the big, old Kviknes Hotel. Stroll its length, starting at the aquarium (described later) and little marina. Across the street, at The Viking Ship shack, a German woman named Carola sells German sausages with an evangelical zeal (see "Eating in Balestrand," later). Next door, the Spindelvev ("Spider's Web") shop sells handicrafts made by people with physical and mental disabilities. A local home for the disabled was closed in the 1980s, but many of its former residents stayed in Balestrand because the government gave them pensions and houses in town.

Then, in the ugly modern strip mall, you'll find the TI, supermarket, and a community bulletin board with the schedule for the summer cinema (the little theater, 800 yards away, runs films nightly in their original language). On the corner is the Golden House art gallery and museum (described later). Just beyond that is the dock where the big Bergen-Sognefjord express catamaran ties up.

Across the street is a cute white house (at #8), which used to stand at the harborfront until the big Joker supermarket and Kviknes Hotel, with its modern annex, partnered to ruin the town center. This little house was considered historic enough to be airlifted 100 yards to this new spot. It's flanked by two other historic buildings, housing a gallery and an artisans' workshop.

Farther along, find the rust-red building that was the waiting room for the 19th-century steamer that first brought tourism to town. Today it houses the Norsk Reiselivsmuseum (Norwegian Travel Museum). It's filled with historic photos, described in English, that show this part of Norway over the last 150 years (free and open daily). In a few years Balestrand is hoping to build a much larger museum and visitors center; it may be under construction during your visit.

Walk a few steps farther, and stop at the tall stone monument erected to celebrate the North Bergen Steamship Company. Its boats first connected Balestrand to the rest of the world in 1858. In front of the monument, some nondescript concrete steps lead into the water. These are "The Kaiser's Stairs," built for the German emperor, Kaiser Wilhelm II, who made his first summer visit (complete with navy convoy) in 1899 and kept returning until the outbreak of World War I.

Behind the monument stands one of the largest old wooden buildings in Norway, the Kviknes Hotel. It was built in the 1870s and faces the rare little island in the fjord, which helped give the town its name: "Balestrand" means the strand or promenade in front of an island. (The island is now connected to the hotel's

front yard and is part of a playground for its guests.) Hike up the
black driveway that leads from the monument to the hotel's modern lobby. Go inside and find (to your left) the plush old lounge,
a virtual painting gallery. All the pieces are by artists from this
area, celebrating the natural wonder of the fjord country—part
of the trend that helped 19th-century Norway reconnect with its
heritage. (While you're here, consider making a reservation and
choosing a table for a *smörgåsbord* dinner tonight.) Leave the hotel
lobby (from the door opposite to the one you entered), and head up
to St. Olaf's Church (300 yards, described next). To continue this
stroll, take King Bele's Way (described later) up the fjord.

St. Olaf's Church—This distinctive wooden church was built in
1897. Construction was started by Margaret Sophia Kvikne, the

wife of Knut Kvikne (of the Kviknes Hotel
family; her portrait is in the rear of the nave),
but she died in 1894, before the church
was finished. This devout Englishwoman
wanted a church in Balestrand where
English services were held...and to this day,
bells ring to announce services by British
clergy. St. Olaf, who brought Christianity
to Norway in the 11th century, was the
country's patron saint in Catholic times.
The church was built in a "Neo-stave" style,
with lots of light from its windows and
an altar painting inspired by the famous
Risen Christ statue in Copenhagen's Cathedral of Our Lady. Here,
Christ is flanked by fields of daisies (called "Priests' Collars" in
Norwegian) and peace lilies. From the door of the church, enjoy a
good view of the island in the fjord.

Cost and Hours: Free, open daily, services in English every
Sun from late May through August.

Golden House (Det Gylne Hus)—This golden-colored house

facing the ferry landing was built as a
general store in 1928. Today it houses
an art gallery and a quirky museum created by local watercolorist and historian
Bjørg Bjøberg, and her Scottish hus-
band, Arthur Adamson.

On the ground floor, you'll find
Bjørg's gallery, with her watercolors
celebrating the beauty of Norway, and
Arthur's paintings, celebrating the
beauty of women. Upstairs is a free
exhibit of historical knickknacks, contributed by locals wanting to preserve

treasures from their own families' past. You'll see a medicine cabinet stocked with old-fashioned pills, an antiquated tourist map, lots of skis, and WWII-era mementos. A wheel in the wall once powered a crane that could winch up goods from the fjord below (before today's embankment was built, when this store was right on the waterfront). While there are no written English explanations, Bjørg is happy to explain things.

Unable to contain her creative spirit, Bjørg has paired an eccentric wonderland experience with her private tour of the Golden House's hidden rooms. The tour includes a 30-minute movie, either about her art and local nature, or about Balestrand in winter. Bjørg and Arthur also run the recommended on-site café, Me Snakkast.

Cost and Hours: Free entry; optional private one-hour tour-50/kr person, 100-kr minimum, 200-kr maximum; May-Aug daily 10:00-22:00, shorter hours late April and Sept, tel. 91 56 28 42).

Strolling King Bele's Way up the Fjord—For a delightful walk (or bike ride), head west out of town up the "old road"—once the main road from the harbor—for

about a mile. It follows the fjord's edge, passing numerous "villas" from the late 1800s. At the time, this Swiss style was popular with some locals, who hoped to introduce a dose of Romanticism into Norwegian architecture. Look for the dragons' heads (copied from Viking-age stave churches) decorating the gables. Along the walk, you'll pass a swimming area, a campground, and two burial mounds from the Viking age, marked by a ponderous statue of the Viking King Bele. Check out the wooden shelters for the mailboxes; some give the elevation (*m.o.h.* stands for "meters over *havet*"—the sea)—not too high, are they? The walk is described in the *Outdoor Activities in Balestrand* brochure (free at the TI or your hotel).

Aquarium—The tiny aquarium gives you a good look at marine life in the Sognefjord. For descriptions, borrow the English booklet at the front desk. While not thrilling, the well-explained place is a decent rainy-day option. A 15-minute slide show starts at the top and bottom of each hour. The last room is filled with wood carvings depicting traditional everyday life in the fjordside village of Munken. The fish-filled tanks on the dock outside are also worth a look.

Cost and Hours: 70 kr, June-Aug daily 9:30-17:00, closed Sept-May, tel. 57 69 13 03.

Biking—You can cycle around town, or go farther by circling the scenic Esefjord (north of town, en route to the ferry landing at

Dragsvik—about 6 miles each way). Or pedal scenically west up Sognefjord along King Bele's Way (described above). The roads here are relatively flat. Rental bikes are available at the TI.

Near Balestrand

These two side-trips are possible only if you've got the better part of a day in Balestrand. With a car, you can see Hopperstad Stave Church on the drive to Bergen.

▲▲Hopperstad Stave Church (Hopperstad Stavkyrkje) in Vik

The most accessible stave church in the area—and perhaps the most scenically situated in all Norway—is located just a 15-minute

express-boat ride across the Sognefjord, in the town of Vik. Hopperstad Stave Church boasts a breathtaking exterior, with several tiers of dragon heads overlooking rolling fields between fjord cliffs. The interior is notable for its emptiness. Instead of being crammed full of later additions, the church is blissfully uncluttered, as it was when built in the mid-12th century.

Cost and Hours: 60 kr, good 30-kr color booklet in English, daily mid-May–mid-Sept 10:00-17:00, mid-June–mid-Aug until 18:00, closed mid-Sept–mid-May, tel. 57 69 52 70, www.stavechurch.com.

Tours: The attendant will give you a free tour at your request, provided she's not too busy. (Ask where the medieval graffiti is, and she'll grab her flashlight and show you.)

Location: The church is a 20-minute walk up the valley from Vik's harbor. From the boat landing, walk up the main street from the harbor about 200 yards (past the TI, a grocery store, and hotel). Take a right at the sign for *Hopperstad Stavkyrkje*, walk 10 minutes, and you'll see the church perched on a small hill in the distance.

Getting There: Pedestrians can ride the express passenger boat between Balestrand and Vik (72 kr each way, 15 minutes). The only way to get to the church and back in one day (only possible Mon-Sat) is to take the 7:50 departure from Balestrand, then return on the 11:30 departure from Vik, arriving back in Balestrand at 11:50—just in time to join a 12:00 glacier excursion (described below). A new company (Tide) takes over the express-boat service in spring of 2012, so be sure to double-check these times at the TI or www.tide.no. Since cars can't go on this express boat, **drivers** must go around the small Esefjord to the town of Dragsvik, then catch the ferry across the Sognefjord to Vangsnes (a 20-minute drive from Vik and the church).

Touring the Church: Originally built around 1140 and retaining most of its original wood, Hopperstad was thoroughly restored and taken back to basics in the 1880s by renowned architect Peter Blix. Unlike the famous stave church at Urnes (described later), whose interior has been re-jiggered by centuries of engineers and filled with altars and pews, the Hopperstad church looks close to the way it did when it was

built. You'll see only a few non-original features, including the beautifully painted canopy that once covered a side altar (probably dating from around 1300), and a tombstone from 1738. There are only a few colorful illustrations and some very scant medieval "graffiti" carvings and runic inscriptions. Notice the intact chancel screen (the only one surviving in Norway), which separates the altar area from the congregation. As with the iconostasis (panel of icons) in today's Orthodox faith, this screen gave priests privacy to do the spiritual heavy lifting. Because Hopperstad's interior lacks the typical adornments, you can really grasp the fundamentally vertical nature of stave church architecture, leading your gaze to the heavens. Follow that impulse and look up to appreciate the Viking-ship rafters. Imagine the comfort this ceiling brought the church's original parishioners, whose seafaring ancestors had sought refuge under overturned boats. For a unique angle on this graceful structure, lay your camera on the floor and shoot the ceiling.

▲Excursion to Fjærland and the Jostedal Glacier

From Balestrand, cruise up the Fjærlandsfjord to visit the Norwegian Glacier Museum in Fjærland and to see a receding tongue of the Jostedal Glacier (Jostedalbreen). Half-day and full-day (620 kr for either tour) excursions are sold by Balestrand's TI or on board the boat. Reservations are smart (tours offered daily May-Sept only, tel. 55 23 87 00, www.tide.no, booking@tide.no).

While the museum and the glacier's tongue are underwhelming, it's a pleasant excursion with a dreamy fjord cruise (80 minutes each way). To take the all-day trip, catch the 8:05 ferry; for the shorter trip, hop on the noon boat. They both return on the same boat, getting you back in Balestrand at 16:55 (in time to catch the fast boat back to Bergen). Both tours offer the same fjord ride, museum visit, and trip to the glacier. The all-day version, however, gives you a second glacier viewing point and 2.5 hours to hang out

in the town of Fjærland. (This sleepy village, famous for its sec-
ondhand book shops, is about as exciting as Walter Mondale, the
vice president whose ancestors came from here.)

The ferry ride (no stops, no narration) is just a scenic glide
with the gulls. Bring a picnic, as there's almost no food sold on
board, and some bread to toss to the gulls (they do acrobatics to
catch whatever you loft into the air). You'll be met at the ferry
dock (labeled *Mundal*) by a bus—and your guide, who reads
a script about the glacier as you drive up the valley for about
15 minutes. You'll stop for an hour at the **Norwegian Glacier
Museum** (Norsk Bremuseum). After watching an 18-minute
aerial tour of the dramatic Jostedal Glacier in the theater, you'll
learn how glaciers were formed, experiment with your own hunk
of glacier, weigh evidence of the woolly mammoth's existence in
Norway, and learn about the effect of global climate change on
the fjords (way overpriced at 120 kr, included in excursion price,
daily June-Aug 9:00-19:00, April-May and Sept-Oct 10:00-
16:00, closed Nov-March, tel. 57 69 32 88, www.bre.museum
.no). From the museum, the bus runs you up to a café near a
lake, at a spot that gives you a good look at the Boyabreen, a
tongue of the Jostedal Glacier. Marvel at how far the glacier
has retreated—10 years ago, the visit was more dramatic. With
global warming, glacier excursions like this become more sad
than majestic. I wonder how long they'll even be able to bill this
as a "glacier visit."

Considering that the fjord trip is the highlight of this journey, you could save time and money by just riding the ferry up and
back (8:05-11:30). At 350 kr for the round-trip boat ride, it's much
cheaper than the 620-kr tour.

Note that if you're into glaciers, a nearby arm of the Jostedal,
called the **Nigard Glacier,** is a more dramatic and boots-on experience. It's easy for drivers to reach.

Sleeping in Balestrand

$$$ Kviknes Hotel is the classy grande dame of Balestrand,
dominating the town and packed with tour groups. The pictur-

esque wooden hotel—and
five generations of the Kvikne
family—have welcomed tour-
ists to Balestrand since the late
19th century. The hotel has
two parts: a new wing, and the
historic wooden section, with
17 older, classic rooms, and
no elevator. All rooms come

Sleep Code

(5 kr = about $1, country code: 47)
S = Single, **D** = Double/Twin, **T** = Triple, **Q** = Quad, **b** = bathroom,
s = shower. Unless otherwise noted, these accommodations accept credit cards.

To help you sort easily through these listings, I've divided the accommodations into three categories, based on the price for a standard double room with bath during high season:

$$$ **Higher Priced**—Most rooms 1,000 kr or more.
$$ **Moderately Priced**—Most rooms between 500-1,000 kr.
$ **Lower Priced**—Most rooms 500 kr or less.

Prices can change without notice; verify the hotel's current rates online or by email. For other updates, see www.ricksteves.com/update.

with balconies. The elegant Old World public spaces in the old section make you want to just sit there and sip tea all afternoon (Db-1,660 kr in new building, Db-2,210 kr in old building, about 400 kr more with view, includes breakfast, mostly non-smoking, pay Wi-Fi, family rooms available, closed Oct-April, tel. 57 69 42 00, fax 57 69 42 01, www.kviknes.no, booking@kviknes.no). Part of the Kviknes ritual is gorging on the *store koldt bord* buffet dinner—open to non-guests, and a nice way to soak in the hotel's old-time elegance without splurging on an overnight (see "Eating in Balestrand," later; cheaper if you stay at the hotel for 2 or more nights).

$$ Balestrand Hotel, family-run by Unni-Marie Kvikne, her California-born husband Eric Palmer, and their three children, is your best fjordside home. Open mid-May through early September, this cozy, welcoming place has 30 well-appointed, comfortable, quiet rooms; a large, modern common area with lots of English paperbacks; laundry service, free Wi-Fi, balconies (in some rooms), and outdoor benches for soaking in the scenery. The waterfront yard has inviting lounge chairs and a mesmerizing view. When reserving, let them know your arrival time, and they'll pick you up at the harborfront (non-view Sb-670 kr, view Sb-820 kr, non-view Db-990 kr, view Db-1,290 kr, includes breakfast, 5-minute walk from dock, past St. Olaf's Church—or free pick-up, tel. 57 69 11 38, www.balestrand.com, info@balestrand.com).

$$ At Gekken's Rooms, Geir rents four homey rooms above his restaurant in the town center (D-600 kr, small D-450 kr, extra bed-150 kr, shared kitchen and WC, open May-Aug only, tel. 57 69 14 14, mobile 97 51 29 26, baleson2004@yahoo.com).

$-$$ Kringsjå Balestrand Hostel, a camp school for sixth-graders, rents beds and rooms to budget travelers from mid-June to mid-August. Half of their 58 beds are in doubles. All the four-bed rooms have private bathrooms and view balconies (bunk in 4-bed dorm-265 kr, Sb-600 kr, Db-820 kr, extra bed-100 kr, includes breakfast, discount for hostel members, sheets/towels-50 kr/person, free Wi-Fi, tel. 57 69 13 03, www.kringsja.no, kringsja @kringsja.no).

$ Sjotun Camping rents the cheapest beds around, in rustic huts (4-person hut-270 kr, sheets-50 kr/person, no breakfast, a mile west of town, tel. 57 69 12 23, www.sjotun.com).

Eating in Balestrand

Balestrand's dining options are limited, but good.

Kviknes Hotel offers a splendid, spendy *store koldt bord* buffet dinner in a massive yet stately old dining room. For a

memorable fjordside *smörgås-bord* experience, it doesn't get any better than this. Don't rush. Consider taking a preview tour—surveying the reindeer meat, lingonberries, and fjord-caught seafood—before you dive in, so you can budget your stomach space. Get a new plate with each course and save room for dessert. Each dish is labeled in English (500 kr/person, May-Sept daily 19:00-21:00, closed Oct-April). After dinner, head into the rich lounge to pick up your cup of coffee or tea (included), which you'll sip sitting on classy old-fashioned furniture and basking in fjord views.

Me Snakkast ("Let's Talk"), inside the Golden House at the harbor, dishes up Norwegian home cooking and a variety of salads. Sit outside—or indoors, in a dining area built to resemble a traditional Norwegian kitchen. The restaurant upstairs shows off part of owner Bjørg's antique collection. They serve 100-130-kr lunches and pricier meals for dinner, such as 150-220-kr meat and fish dishes (May-Sept daily 14:00-21:30, closed Oct-April, tel. 91 56 28 42).

Gekken's is an informal summer restaurant serving good-value meat, fish, and vegetarian dishes, along with burgers, fish-and-chips, and other fried fare. Sit in the simply decorated interior, or out on the shaded little terrace. Geir Arne "Gekken" Bale can trace his family's roots back 400 years in Balestrand. He has filled his walls with fascinating historic photos and paintings, making his dining hall an art gallery of sorts (light dishes-60-100 kr, daily dinner plates-100-150 kr, May-Aug daily 12:00-22:00, closed Sept-April, above and behind the TI from the harbor, tel. 57 69 14 14).

The Viking Ship, the hot-dog stand facing the harbor, is proudly run by Carola. A bratwurst missionary from Germany, she claims it took her years to get Norwegians to accept the tastier bratwurst over their beloved *pølser* weenies. Eat at her picnic tables or across the street on the harbor park (fine sausages, fish-and-chips, May-Sept daily 11:00-20:00, closed Oct-April).

Picnic: The delightful waterfront park next to the aquarium has benches and million-dollar fjord views. The Co-op and Joker **supermarkets** at the harbor have basic grocery supplies, including bread, meats, cheeses, and drinks. Co-op is bigger and has a wider selection (both open Mon-Fri 9:00-18:00—until 20:00 in summer, Sat 9:00-15:00, closed Sun). **Mu's Bakery** heats up baked goodies trucked here all the way from Germany (Mon-Sat 9:30-18:00, Sun 9:30-15:00, closed mid-Sept-early May, between Co-op and Joker supermarkets).

Balestrand Connections

Because Balestrand is separated from the Lustrafjord by the long Fjærlandsfjord, most Balestrand connections involve a boat trip.

By Express Passenger Boat

The easiest way to reach Balestrand is on the handy express boat, which connects to **Bergen, Vik** (near Hopperstad Stave Church), **Aurland,** and **Flåm** (see sidebar on opposite page for schedules). Note that you can also use this boat to join the Nutshell trip mid-fjord (transferring at Midtfjord—literally from boat to boat, in the middle of the fjord—to the Kaupanger-Gudvangen ferry; possible only June-Aug). From here, continue on the Nutshell boat down the Nærøyfjord to Gudvangen, where you'll join the crowd onward to Voss, then Bergen or Oslo. As you're making schedule and sightseeing decisions, consider that the Balestrand-Flåm boat skips the Nærøyfjord, the most dramatic arm of the Sognefjord.

By Car Ferry

Balestrand's main car-ferry dock is at the village of **Dragsvik,** a six-mile, 15-minute drive around the adorable little Eselfjord. From Dragsvik, a car ferry makes the short crossing east to **Hella** (a 30-minute drive from Sogndal and the Lustrafjord), then crosses the Sognefjord south to **Vangsnes** (a 20-minute drive to Hopperstad Stave Church and onward to Bergen). The ferry goes at least once per hour (2/hour in peak times, fewer boats Sun, 79 kr for car and driver).

Express Boat Between Bergen and the Sognefjord

The made-for-tourists express boat makes it a snap to connect Bergen with Balestrand and other Sognefjord towns (for foot passengers only—no cars). In summer, the boat goes twice each day in both directions, linking up Bergen, Vik, Balestrand, Aurland, and Flåm. You can also use this boat to connect towns on the Sognefjord, such as zipping from quiet Balestrand to busy Flåm, in the heart of the Nutshell action (reservations are smart—call 55 23 87 00, email booking@tide.no, or visit www.tide.no; discounts for students and seniors, tickets also sold on boat and at TI). Tide took over the express-boat contract in spring of 2012—confirm the following times and prices locally.

Between Bergen and the Sognefjord: The boat trip between Bergen and **Balestrand** takes four hours (500 kr,

departs Bergen May-Sept daily at 8:00, also Mon-Fri at 16:30, Sat at 14:15, some Sun at 16:30—but not mid-June-late Aug; Oct-April Mon-Fri at 8:00, Sun-Fri at 16:30, Sat at 14:15; departs Balestrand May-Sept daily at 16:55, Mon-Sat also at 7:50, some Sun at 11:30—but not mid-June-late Aug; Oct-April Mon-Sat at 7:50, Sun at 15:55). In summer, the 8:00 boat from Bergen continues to **Flåm** (685 kr).

Between Flåm and Balestrand: Going by boat between Flåm and Balestrand takes about 1.5 hours (230 kr, departs Flåm May-Sept daily at 15:30, stops at Aurland, arrives in Balestrand at 16:55; second boat sometimes runs from Flåm Mon-Fri at 6:00, arrives Balestrand at 8:00; departs Balestrand daily at 11:50 arriving Flåm at 13:25; a different boat departs Balestrand Mon-Fri at 8:30 in July-early Aug; no express boats between Flåm and Balestrand Oct-April).

From Oslo to Balestrand via the Nutshell: This variation on the standard Norway in a Nutshell route is called "Sognefjord in a Nutshell" (Oslo-Myrdal-Flåm-Balestrand-Bergen). From **Oslo,** you can take an early train to Flåm (no later than the 8:11 train as part of the Norway in a Nutshell route—see previous chapter), then catch the 15:30 express boat to Balestrand. After your visit, you can continue on the express boat to Bergen, or return to the Nutshell route by taking the express boat to Midtfjord (a meeting point for the two boats in the middle of the fjord), and transferring to the next boat to Gudvangen (June-Aug only, otherwise transfer in Flåm).

Note that you can also drive through Sogndal to catch the **Kaupanger-Gudvangen** or **Mannheller-Fodnes** ferries (described under "Lustrafjord Connections," near the end of this chapter).

By Bus

A local bus links Balestrand to **Sogndal** (Mon-Fri 3/day, none Sat-Sun, 1.25 hours, includes ride on Dragsvik-Hella ferry, get details at TI).

The Lustrafjord

This arm of the Sognefjord is rugged country—only 2 percent of the land is fit to build or farm on. The Lustrafjord is ringed with tiny villages where farmers sell cherries and giant raspberries. A few interesting attractions lie along the Lustrafjord: the village Dale Church at Luster; the impressive Nigard Glacier (a 45-minute drive up a valley); the postcard-pretty village of Solvorn; and, across the

fjord, Norway's oldest stave church at Urnes. While a bit trickier to explore by public transportation, this beautiful region is easy by car, but still feels remote. There are no ATMs between Lom and Gaupne—that's how remote this region is.

Suggested Route for Drivers

The Lustrafjord can be seen either coming from the north (over the Sognefjell pass from the Jotunheimen region) or from the south (from Balestrand or the Norway in a Nutshell route). Note that public buses between Lom and Sogndal follow this same route (see "Lustrafjord Connections," later).

Here's what you'll see if you're driving from the north (if you're coming from the south, read this section backwards): Descending from Sognefjell, you'll hit the fjord at the village of Skjolden (decent TI in big community center, tel. 97 60 04 43). Follow Route 55 along the west bank of the fjord. In the town of Luster, consider visiting the beautifully decorated Dale Church (described next). Farther along, near the hamlet of Nes, you'll have views across the fjord of the towering Feigumfoss waterfall. Drops and dribbles come from miles around for this 650-foot tumble. Soon Route 55 veers along an inlet to the town of Gaupne, where you can choose to detour about an hour to the Nigard Glacier (up Route 604; described under "Sights on the Lustrafjord," next). After Gaupne, Route 55 enters a tunnel and cuts inland, emerging at a long, fjord-like lake at the town of Hafslo. Just beyond is the turnoff for Solvorn, a fine home-base town with the ferry across to Urnes and its stave church (Solvorn and Urnes Stave Church both described under "Sights on the Lustrafjord," next). Route 55 continues to Sogndal, where you can choose to turn off for the Kaupanger and Mannheller ferries across the Sognefjord, or continue on Route 55 to Hella and the boat across to either Dragsvik (near Balestrand) or Vangsnes (across the Sognefjord, near Vik and Hopperstad Stave Church).

Route Timings: If you're approaching from Lom in the Gudbrandsdal Valley, figure about 1.5 hours over Sognefjell to the start of the Lustrafjord at Skjolden, then another 30 minutes to Gaupne (with the optional glacier detour: 2 hours to see it, 4 hours to hike on it). From Gaupne, figure 30 minutes to Solvorn or 40 minutes to Sogndal. Solvorn to Sogndal is about 30 minutes. Sogndal to Hella, and its boat to Balestrand, takes about 40 minutes. These estimated times are conservative, but they don't include photo stops.

Sights on the Lustrafjord

These attractions are listed as you'll reach them driving from north to south along the fjordside Route 55. If you're sleeping in this area, you could visit all four sights in a single day (but it'd be a busy, somewhat rushed day). If you're passing through, Dale Church and Solvorn are easy, but the other two involve major detours—choose one or skip them both.

▲Dale Church (Dale Kyrkje) in Luster

The namesake town of Luster, on the west bank of the Lustrafjord, boasts a unique 13th-century Gothic church. In a land of wooden

stave churches, this stone church, with its richly decorated interior, is worth a quick stop as you pass through town.

The soapstone core of the church dates from about 1250, but the wooden bell tower and entry porch were likely built around 1600. As you enter, on the left you'll see a tall, elevated platform with seating, surrounded by a wooden grill. Nicknamed a "birdcage" for the feathery fashions worn by the ladies of the time, this high-profile pew—three steps higher than the pulpit—was built in the late-17th century by a wealthy parishioner. The beautifully painted pulpit, decorated with faded images of the four evangelists, dates from the 13th century. In the chancel (altar area), restorers have uncovered frescoes from three different time periods: the 14th, 16th, and 17th centuries. Most of the ones you see here were likely created around the year 1500. The crucifix high over the pews, carved around 1200, predates the church, as does the old bench (with lots of runic carvings)—making them more than eight centuries old.

Cost and Hours: Free entry but donation requested, daily 10:00-20:00 but often closed for services and off-season, good posted English info inside, 5-kr English brochure, just off the main road—look for red steeple, WC in graveyard, fresh goodies at bakery across the street.

▲▲Jostedal's Nigard Glacier

The Nigard Glacier (Nigardsbreen) is the most accessible branch of mainland Europe's largest glacier (the Jostedalsbreen, 185 square miles). Hiking to or on this glacier offers Norway's best easy opportunity for a hands-on glacier experience. It's a 45-minute detour from the Lustrafjord up Jostedal Valley. Visiting a glacier is a quintessential Norwegian experience, bringing you face-to-face with the majesty of nature. If

you can spare the time, it's worth the detour (even if you don't do a guided hike). But if glaciers don't give you tingles and you're feeling pressed, skip it.

Getting There: It's straightforward for **drivers.** When the main Route 55 along the Lustrafjord reaches Gaupne, turn onto Route 604, which you'll follow for 25 miles up the Jostedal Valley to the Breheimsenteret glacier information center. Access to the glacier itself is down the toll road past the information center (all described below).

In July and August, a **Glacier Bus** connects the Nigard Glacier to various home-base towns around the region (leaves Sogndal at 8:35, passes through Solvorn en route, arrives at the glacier around 10:00; departs glacier at 15:15, arrives back in Sogndal around 17:05; buses or boats from other towns—including Flåm and Aurland—coordinate to meet this bus in Sogndal; combo-tickets include various glacier visits and hikes; no bus Sept-June; for complete timetable, see www.jostedal.com). While handy, the bus is designed for those spending the entire day at the glacier.

Breheimsenteret Glacier Information Center—The national park's information center (with an info desk/gift shop and WCs) is housed in temporary quarters while a new center is being built (may open by summer of 2013) to replace its predecessor, which burned down in July of 2011. It's worth dropping by the temporary quarters even just to confirm your glacier plans—likely with Peter, who runs the place. When the new center is complete, it'll show a relaxing 20-minute film with highlights of the glacier and region, and offer a gallery of glacier-related exhibits that use models and illustrations to explain these giant, slow-moving walls of ice (daily mid-June-mid-Aug 9:00-19:00, May-mid-June and mid-Aug-Sept 10:00-17:00, closed Oct-April, tel. 57 68 32 50, www.jostedal.com).

Visiting the Glacier—The best quick visit is to walk to, but not on, the glacier. (If you want to walk *on* it, see "Hikes on the Glacier," next.) From the information center, a 30-kr toll road continues two miles to a lake facing the actual tongue of the glacier. About 75 years ago, the glacier reached all the way to today's parking lot. (It's named for the ninth farm—*ni gard*—where it finally stopped, after crushing eight farms higher up the valley.) From the lot, you can hike all the way to the edge of today's glacier (about 45 minutes each way); or, to save about 20 minutes of walking, take a special boat to a spot that's a 20-minute hike from the glacier (20 kr each way, 10-minute boat trip, 4/hour, mid-June-mid-Sept 10:00-18:00).

The walk is uneven but well-marked—follow the red *T*'s and take your time. You'll hike on stone polished smooth by the glacier, and scramble over and around boulders big and small that were deposited by it. The path takes you right up to the face of the Nigardsbreen. Respect the glacier. It's a powerful river of ice, and fatal accidents do happen. If you want to walk on the glacier, read the next listing first.

Hikes on the Glacier—If you want to actually walk on top of the

glacier, don't attempt it by yourself. The Breheimsenteret glacier information center offers guided family-friendly walks that include about one hour on the ice (250 kr, 100 kr for kids, minimum age 5, I'd rate the walks PG-13 myself, about 4/day, generally between 11:30-15:00, no need to reserve—

just call glacier center to find out time and show up). Leave the information center one hour before your tour, then meet the group on the ice, where you'll pay and receive your clamp-on crampons. One hour roped up with your group gives you the essential experience. You'll find yourself marveling at how well your strap-on crampons work on the 5,000-year-old-ice. Even if it's hot, wear long pants, a jacket, and your sturdiest shoes. (Think ahead. It's awkward to empty your bladder after you're roped up.)

Longer, more challenging, and much more expensive hikes get you higher views, more exercise, and real crampons (starting at 445 kr, includes boots, mid-May-mid-Sept daily at 11:45, also June-Aug daily at 12:45, 4 hours including 2 hours on the ice, book by phone the day before—tel. 57 68 32 50, arrive at the information center 45 minutes early to pay for tickets and pick up your gear). If you're adventurous, ask about even longer hikes and glacier kayaking. While it's legal to go on the glacier on your own, it's dangerous and crazy to do so without crampons.

▲▲Solvorn

On the west bank of the Lustrafjord, 10 miles northeast of Sogndal, idyllic Solvorn is a sleepy little Victorian town with colorful wooden sheds lining its waterfront. My

favorite town on the Lustrafjord is tidy and quaint, well away from the bustle of the Nutshell action. Its tiny ferry crosses the fjord regularly to Urnes and its famous stave church (see below). While not worth going far out of your way for, Solvorn is a mellow and surprisingly appealing place to kill some time waiting for the ferry...or just munching a picnic while looking across the fjord. A pensive stroll or photo shoot through the village's back lanes is a joy (look for plaques that explain historic buildings in English). Best of all, Solvorn also has a pair of excellent accommodations: a splurge (Hotel Walaker) and a budget place (Eplet Bed & Apple), described later under "Sleeping on the Lustrafjord."

Getting There: Solvorn is a steep five-minute **drive** down a switchback road from the main Route 55. The main road into town leads right to the Urnes ferry (see below) and dead-ends into a handy parking lot (free, 2-hour posted—but unmonitored—limit). It's a 30-minute drive or bus trip into Sogndal, where you can transfer to other **buses** (2-3 buses/day between Solvorn and Sogndal, including the Glacier Bus to the Nigard Glacier—described earlier).

▲▲Urnes Stave Church

The hamlet of Urnes (sometimes spelled "Ornes") has Norway's oldest surviving stave church, dating from 1129. While not easy to reach (it's across the Lustrafjord from other attractions), it's worth the scenic ferry ride. The exterior is smaller and simpler than most stave churches, but its interior—modified in fits and starts over the centuries—is uniquely eclectic. If you want to pack along a bike (rentable in Solvorn), see "Bring a Bike?" at the end of this listing.

Cost and Hours: 60 kr, includes 25-minute English tour (departs at :40 past most hours, to coincide with ferry arrival—described below); June-Sept daily 10:30-17:45; closed Oct-May, tel. 57 68 39 45, www.stavechurch.com.

Services: A little café/restaurant is at the farm called Urnes Gard, across from the church (same hours as church, homemade apple cakes, tel. 57 68 39 44).

Getting There: Urnes is perched on the east bank of the Lustrafjord (across the fjord from Route 55 and Solvorn). Ferries running between Solvorn and Urnes depart Solvorn at the top of most hours and Urnes at the bottom of most hours (31 kr one-way passenger fare, 85 kr one-way for car and driver, no round-trip discount, 15-minute ride, tel. 91 79 42 11, www.urnesferry.com). You can either drive or walk onto the boat—but, since you can't drive all the way up to the church, you might as well leave your car in Solvorn. Once across, it's about a five-minute uphill walk to the main road and parking lot (where drivers must leave their cars; parking lot at the church only for disabled visitors). From here, it's a steep 15-minute walk up a switchback road to the church (follow signs for *Urnes*).

Planning Your Time: Don't dawdle on your way up to the church, as the tour is scheduled to depart at :40 past most hours, about 25 minutes after the ferry arrives (giving most visitors just enough time to make it up the hill to the church). The first boat of the day departs Solvorn at 10:00; the last boat departs Solvorn at 16:00 (last tour at 16:40); and the last boat back to Solvorn departs Urnes at 18:00. Confirm the "last boat" time, and keep an eye on your watch to avoid getting stranded in Urnes.

❍ Self-Guided Tour: Most visitors to the church take the included 25-minute tour (scheduled to begin soon after the ferry arrives—described above). Here are some highlights:

Buy your ticket in the white house across from the church.

Visit the little museum here after you see the church, so you don't miss the tour.

Many changes were made to the exterior to modernize the church after the Reformation (the colonnaded gallery was replaced, the bell tower was added, and modern square windows were cut into the walls). Go around the left side of the church, toward the cemetery. This is the third church on this spot, but the carved doorway embedded in the wall here was inherited from the second church. Notice the two mysterious beasts—a warm-blooded predator (standing) and a cold-blooded dragon—weaving and twisting around each other, one entwining the other. Yet, as they bite each other on the neck, it's impossible to tell which one is "winning"...perhaps symbolizing the everlasting struggle of human existence. The door you see in the middle, however, has a very different message: the harmony of symmetrical figure-eights, an appropriately calming theme for those entering the church.

Now go around to the real entry door (with a wrought-iron lock and handle probably dating from the first church) and head inside. While it feels ancient and creaky, a lot of what you see in here is actually "new" compared to the 12th-century core of the church. The exquisitely carved, voluptuous, column-topping capitals are remarkably well-preserved originals. The interior initially was stark (no pews) and dark—lit not by windows (which were added much later), but by candles laid on the floor in the shape of a cross. Looking straight ahead, you see a cross with Mary on the left (where the women stood) and John the Baptist on the right (with the men). When they finally added seating, they kept things segregated: Notice the pews carved with hearts for women, crowns for men.

When a 17th-century wealthy family wanted to build a special pew for themselves, they simply sawed off some of the pinecone-topped columns to make way for it. When the church began to lean, it was reinforced with the clumsy, off-center X-shaped supports. Churchgoers learned their lesson, and never cut anything again.

The ceiling, added in the late 17th century, prevents visitors from enjoying the Viking-ship roof beams. But all of these additions have stories to tell. Experts can read various cultural influences into the church decorations, including Irish (some of the carvings) and Romanesque (the rounded arches).

Bring a Bike? To give your Lustrafjord excursion more dimension, take a bike on the ferry to Urnes (free passage, rentable for 150 kr/day with helmets from Eplet Bed & Apple hostel in Solvorn, where you can park your car for free). From the stave church, bike the super-scenic fjordside road (4.5 miles—with almost no traffic—to big Feigumfossen waterfall and back).

Sleeping on the Lustrafjord

(5kr = about $1, country code: 47)
These accommodations are along the Lustrafjord, listed from north to south.

In Nes

$$ Nes Gard Farmhouse B&B rents 15 homey rooms, offering lots of comfort in a grand 19th-century farmhouse for a good price (D-750 kr, Db-920 kr, rooms in main building more traditional, family apartment, tel. 95 23 26 94 or 61 36 23 45, www.nesgard .no, post@nesgard.no, Manum family). Mari and Asbjorn serve a three-course dinner for 300 kr.

$ Viki Fjord Camping has great fjordside huts—many directly on the water, with fjord views and balconies—located directly across from the Feigumfossen waterfall (230-450 kr without a private bathroom, 380-850 kr with bathroom, price depends on size and season, sheets-70 kr, tel. 57 68 64 20, mobile 99 53 97 30, www.vikicamping.no, host@vikicamping.no, Berit and Svein).

In Solvorn

For more on this delightful little fjordside town—my favorite home base on the Lustrafjord—see the description earlier in this chapter. While it lacks the handy boat connections of Flåm, Aurland, or Balestrand, that's part of Solvorn's charm.

$$$ Walaker Hotel, a former inn and coach station, has been run by the Walaker family since 1690 (that's a lot of pressure on eighth-generation owner Ole Henrik). The hotel, set right on the Lustrafjord (with a garden perfect for relaxing and, if necessary, even convalescing), is open May through September. In the main house, the halls and living rooms are filled with tradition. Notice the patriotic hymns on the piano. The 22 rooms are divided into two types: nicely appointed standard rooms in the modern annex (big Sb-1,500 kr, Db-1,800 kr); or recently renovated "historic" rooms with all the modern conveniences in two different old buildings: rooms with Old World elegance in the main house, and brightly painted rooms with countryside charm in the Tingstova house next door (Db-2,800 kr, 500 kr more for larger #20 and #23; all prices include breakfast, non-smoking, free Wi-Fi, sea kayak rental, tel. 57 68 20 80, fax 57 68 20 81, www.walaker.com, hotel @walaker.com). They serve excellent four-course dinners (575 kr plus drinks, nightly at 19:30, savor your dessert with fjordside set-ting on the balcony). Their impressive gallery of Norwegian art is in a restored, historic farmhouse out back (free for guests; Ole Henrik leads one-hour tours of the collection, peppered with some family history, nightly after dinner).

$-$$ Eplet Bed & Apple is my kind of hostel: innovative and friendly. It's creatively run by Trond, whose entrepreneurial spirit and positive attitude attract enjoyable guests. With welcom-ing public spaces and 22 beds in seven rooms (all with views, some with decks), this place is worth considering even if you don't nor-mally sleep at hostels (open May-Sept only; camping space-100 kr, bunk in 7-bed dorm-180 kr, S-500 kr, D-600 kr, T-800 kr, S/D/T cost 50 kr less for 2 nights or more, laundry-50 kr, kitchen, free Internet access and Wi-Fi, free loaner bikes for guests, tel. 41 64 94 69, www.eplet.net, trondhenrik@eplet.net). It's about 300 yards uphill from the boat dock—look for the white house with a giant red apple painted on it. It's surrounded by a raspberry and apple farm (they make and sell tasty juices from both). The hostel rents bikes and helmets to non-guests for 150 kr/day. If you plan to bike along the fjord from Urnes, consider that if you stay at the hostel, the free bikes will save you 300 kr (for two people).

Eating in Solvorn: Sleepy Solvorn is blessed with the cheery **Linahagen Kafé,** next door to Walaker Hotel, where delightful Signe and her family serve up good meals (120-kr dinner salads, 140-kr dinner plates, June-Aug daily 12:30-19:30, closed Sept-May, tel. 57 68 18 00).

In Sogndal

Sogndal is the only sizeable town in this region. While it lacks the charm of Solvorn and Balestrand, it's big enough to have a busy shopping street and a helpful **TI** (mid-June-mid-Aug Mon-Fri 9:00-18:00, Sat 10:00-16:00, closed Sun; shorter hours in May and Sept, closed in winter; in the Kulturhus at Hovevegen 2, tel. 97 60 04 43).

$$ Loftesnes Pensjonat, with 12 rooms, houses travelers mid-June through mid-August, and mostly students—reserving four rooms for travelers—during the school year (S-400 kr, Sb-420 kr, D-600 kr, Db-650 kr, no breakfast, kitchen, above a Chinese restaurant near the water, tel. & fax 57 67 15 77, mobile 90 93 51 71, loftesnes.pensjonat@gmail.com).

$-$$ Sogndal Youth Hostel rents good, cheap beds (bunk in 4-bed room-225 kr, S-310 kr, D-520 kr, Db-725 kr, 10 percent less for members, breakfast-70 kr, sheets-70 kr, towel-40 kr, members' kitchen—B.Y.O. pots, mid-June-mid-Aug only, closed 10:00-17:00, at fork in the road as you enter town, tel. 57 62 75 75, mobile 90 93 51 71, fax 57 62 75 70, www.vandrerhjem.no, sogndal@hihostels.no).

Lustrafjord Connections

Sogndal is the transit hub for the Lustrafjord region.

From Sogndal by Bus

Buses go to **Lom** over the Sognefjell pass (2/day late June-Aug only, road closed off-season, 3.25 hours), **Solvorn** (3/day in summer, 2/day in winter, fewer Sat-Sun, 30 minutes), **Balestrand** (3/day, fewer Sat-Sun, 1.25 hours, includes ride on Hella-Dragsvik ferry), **Nigard Glacier** via the Glacier Bus (1/day, 1.5 hours, departs Sogndal daily at 8:35, returns to Sogndal in the afternoon, also stops at Solvorn in each direction, July-Aug only). Most buses run less (or not at all) on weekends—check the latest at www .ruteinfo.net.

By Boat

Car ferries cost roughly $5 per hour for walk-ons and $20 per hour for a car and driver. Reservations are generally not necessary, and on many short rides, aren't even possible (for info and free and easy reservations for longer rides, call 55 90 70 70). Confirm schedules at www.ruteinfo.net. From near Sogndal, various boats fan out to towns around the Sognefjord. Most leave from two towns at the southern end of the Lustrafjord: **Kaupanger** (a 15-minute drive from Sogndal) and **Mannheller** (a 5-minute drive beyond Kaupanger, 20 min from Sogndal).

From Kaupanger: While Kaupanger is little more than a ferry landing, the small stave-type church at the edge of town merits a look. Boats go from Kaupanger all the way down the gorgeous Nærøyfjord to **Gudvangen,** which is on the Norway in a Nutshell route (where you catch the bus to Voss). Taking this boat allows you to see the best part of the Nutshell fjord scenery (the Nærøyfjord), but misses the other half of that cruise (Aurlandsfjord). The boat leaves Kaupanger daily in summer at 9:30, 12:00, 14:40, and 16:00 for the two-hour trip (these times are for June-Aug, only goes 1/day in May and Aug-mid-Sept departing Kaupanger at 9:30 and Gudvangen at 12:00, none mid-Sept-April; car and driver-625 kr, adult passenger-250 kr; reserve at least one day in advance—or longer in July-Aug, especially for the popular 12:00 departure; tel. 55 90 70 70, www.fjord1.no). Prices are high because this route is mainly taken by tourists, not locals. Boats also connect Kaupanger to **Lærdal,** but the crossing from Mannheller to Fodnes is easier (described next).

From Mannheller: Ferries frequently make the speedy 15-minute crossing to **Fodnes** (67 kr for a car and driver, 3/hour, no reservations possible). From Fodnes, drive through the five-mile-long tunnel to Lærdal and the main E16 highway (near Borgund

Stave Church, the long tunnel to Aurland, and the scenic overland road to the Stegastein fjord viewpoint).

To Balestrand: To reach Balestrand from the Lustrafjord, you'll take a short ferry trip (Hella-Dragsvik). For information on the car ferries to and from Balestrand, see "Balestrand Connections," earlier.

Scenic Drives from the Sognefjord

If you'll be doing a lot of driving, pick up a good local map. The 1:335,000-scale *Sør-Norge nord* map by Cappelens Kart is excellent (about 100 kr, available at local TIs and bookstores).

▲▲From the Lustrafjord to Aurland

The drive to the pleasant fjordside town of Aurland takes you either through the world's longest car tunnel, or over an incred-

ible mountain pass. If you aren't going as far as Lom and Jotunheimen, consider taking the pass, as the scenery here rivals the famous Sognefjell pass drive.

From Sogndal, drive 20 minutes to the Mannheller-Fodnes ferry (described under "Lustrafjord Connections," earlier), float across the Sognefjord, then drive from Fodnes to Lærdal. From Lærdal, you have two options to Aurland: The speedy route is on E16 through the new 15-mile-long **tunnel** from Lærdal, or the Aurlandsvegen **"Snow Road"** over the pass.

The tunnel is free, and impressively nonchalant—it's signed as if it were just another of Norway's countless tunnels. But driving it is a bizarre experience: A few miles in, as you find yourself trying not to be hypnotized by the monotony, it suddenly dawns on you what it means to be driving under a mountain for 15 miles. To keep people awake, three rest chambers, each illuminated by a differently colored light, break up the drive visually. Stop and get out—if no cars are coming, test the acoustics from the center.

The second, immeasurably more scenic, route is a breathtaking one-hour, 30-mile drive that winds over a pass into Aurland, crest-ing at over 4,000 feet and offering classic aerial fjord views (it's worth the messy pants). From the Mannheller-Fodnes ferry, take the first road to the right (to Erdal), then leave E68 at Erdal (just west of Lærdal) for the Aurlandsvegen. This road, while well-maintained, is open only in summer, and narrow and dangerous during snowstorms (which can hit with a moment's notice, even in warm weather). You'll enjoy vast and terrifying views of lakes, snowfields, and remote mountain huts and farmsteads on what feels like the top of Norway. As you begin the 12-hairpin zigzag descent to Aurland, you'll reach the new "7"-shaped **Stegastein viewpoint**—well worth a stop.

▲From the Lustrafjord to Bergen, via the Nutshell Route (Nærøyfjord and Gudvangen)

Car ferries take tourists between Kaupanger and the Nutshell town of Gudvangen through an arm and elbow of the Sognefjord, including the staggering Nærøyfjord (for details on the ferry, see "Lustrafjord Connections," earlier). From Gudvangen, it's a 90-mile drive to Bergen, via Voss (figure about one hour to Voss, then another two hours into Bergen). This follows essentially the same route as the Norway in a Nutshell (Gudvangen-Voss bus, Voss-Bergen train).

Get off the ferry in Gudvangen and drive up the Nærøy valley past a river. You'll see the two giant falls just before the road marked *Stalheimskleiva*. Follow the sign (exiting left) to the little Stalheimskleiva road. This incredible road doggedly worms its way up into the ozone. My car overheated in a few minutes. Take it easy. (The main road gets you there more easily—through a tunnel and about a mile back up a smaller road—but you miss the twisty road and views.) As you wind up, you can view the falls from several turnouts. At the top, stop for a break at the touristy Stalheim Hotel.

The road rejoins E16 and continues into a mellower beauty, past lakes and farms, toward Voss. Soon before you reach Voss itself, watch the right side of the road for Tvindefossen, a waterfall with a handy campground/WC/kiosk picnic area that's worth a stop. Highway E16 takes you through Voss and into Bergen. If you plan to visit Edvard Grieg's Home and the nearby Fantoft Stave Church, now is the ideal time, since you'll be driving near them and they're a headache to reach from downtown. Both are worth a detour if you're not rushed, and open until 18:00 in summer.

▲▲From Balestrand to Bergen, via Vik

If you're based in Balestrand and driving to Bergen, you have two options: Take the Dragsvik-Hella ferry, drive an hour to Kaupanger (via Sogndal), and drive the route described above; or, take the following slower, twistier, more remote, and more scenic route, with a stop at the beautiful Hopperstad Stave Church. This route is slightly longer, with more time on mountain roads and less time on the boat. Figure 20 minutes from Vangsnes to Vik, then about 1.5 hours to Voss, then another 2 hours into Bergen.

From Vagsnes, head into Vik on the main Route 13. In Vik, follow signs from the main road to Hopperstad Stave Church

(described earlier in this chapter). Then backtrack to Route 13 and follow it south, to Voss. You'll soon begin a series of switchbacks that wind you up and out of the valley. The best views are from the Storesvingen Fjellstove restaurant (on the left). Soon after, you'll crest the ridge, go through a tunnel, and find yourself on top of the world, in a desolate and harshly scenic landscape of scrubby mountaintops, snow banks, lakes, and no trees, scattered with vacation cabins. After cruising atop the plateau for a while, the road twists its way down (next to a waterfall) into a very steep valley, which it meanders through the rest of the way to Voss. This is an hour-long, middle-of-nowhere journey, with few road signs—you might feel lost, but keep driving toward Voss. When Route 13 dead-ends into E16, turn right (toward Voss and Bergen) and re-enter civilization. From here, the route follows the same roads described in the Lustrafjord-Bergen drive described above (including the Tvindefossen waterfall).

GUDBRANDSDAL VALLEY and JOTUNHEIMEN MOUNTAINS

Norway in a Nutshell is a great day trip, but with more time and a car, consider a scenic meander from Oslo to Bergen. You'll arc up the Gudbrandsdal Valley and over the Jotunheimen Mountains, then travel along the Lustrafjord.

After an introductory stop in Lillehammer, with its fine folk museum, you might spend the night in a log-and-sod farmstead-turned-hotel, tucked in a quiet valley under Norway's highest peaks. Next, Norway's highest pass takes you on an exhilarating roller-coaster ride through the heart of the myth-inspiring Jotunheimen, bristling with Norway's biggest mountains. Then the road hairpins down into fjord country.

Planning Your Time

While you could spend five or six days in this area on a three-week Scandinavian rampage, this slice of the region is worth three days. By car, I'd spend them like this:

Day 1: Leave Oslo early, and spend midday at Lillehammer's Maihaugen Open-Air Folk Museum for a tour and picnic. Drive up the Gudbrandsdal Valley, stopping at the stave church in Lom. Stay overnight in the Jotunheimen countryside.

Day 2: Drive the Sognefjell road over the mountains, then down along the Lustrafjord, stopping to visit the Dale Church and the Nigard Glacier. Sleep in your choice of fjord towns.

Day 3: Cruise the Aurland and/or Nærøy fjords and try to visit another stave church or two (such as Urnes, Hopperstad, or Borgund) before carrying on to Bergen.

This plan can be condensed into two days if you skip the Nigard Glacier side-trip.

Lillehammer and the Gudbrandsdal Valley

The Gudbrandsdal Valley is the tradition-steeped country of Peer Gynt, the Norwegian Huck Finn. This romantic valley of time-worn hills, log cabins, and velvet farms has connected northern and southern Norway since ancient times. While not as striking as other parts of the Norwegian countryside, Gudbrandsdal offers a suitable first taste of the natural wonders that crescendo farther north and west (in Jotunheimen and the Sognefjord). Throughout this region, the government subsidizes small farms to keep the countryside populated and healthy. (These subsidies would not be permitted if Norway were a member of the European Union.)

Orientation to Lillehammer

The de facto capital of Gudbrandsdal, Lillehammer, is a pleasant winter and summer resort town of 25,000. While famous for its brush with Olympic greatness (as host of the 1994 Winter Olympiad), Lillehammer is a bit disappointing—worthwhile only for its excellent Maihaugen Open-Air Folk Museum, or to break up the long drive between Oslo and the Jotunheimen region. If you do wind up here, Lillehammer has happy, old, woody pedestrian zones (Gågata and Storgata).

Tourist Information

Lillehammer's TI is inside the train station (mid-June-mid-Aug Mon-Fri 8:00-18:00, Sat-Sun 10:00-17:00; mid-Aug-mid-June Mon-Fri 8:00-16:00, Sat 10:00-14:00, closed Sun; Jernbanetorget 2, tel. 61 28 98 00, www.lillehammer.com).

Sights in Lillehammer

Lillehammer's two most worthwhile sights are up the hill behind the center of town. It's a fairly steep 15-minute walk from the train station to either sight and a 10-minute, mostly level walk between the two (follow the busy main road that connects them). Because the walk from the station is uphill (and not very well-signed), consider catching the bus from in front of the train station (bus #003 to Olympics Museum, 2/hour; bus #006 to Maihaugen, 1/hour; 30 kr one-way for either bus).

▲▲**Maihaugen Open-Air Folk Museum (Maihaugen**

Gudbrandsdal Valley & Jotunheimen Mountains

1 Røisheim Hotel
2 Elvesæter Hotel
3 Bøverdalen Youth Hostel
4 Strind Gård
5 Spiterstulen Lodge
6 Juvasshytta Lodge
7 Leirvassbu Lodge

GUDBRANDSDAL

Friluftsmuseet)—This idyllic park, full of old farmhouses and pickled slices of folk culture, provides a good introduction to what you'll see as you drive through the Gudbrandsdal Valley. Anders Sandvig, a "visionary dentist," started the collection in 1887. You'll divide your time between the fine indoor museum at the entrance and the sprawling exterior exhibits.

Upon arrival, ask about special events, crafts, or musical performances. A TV monitor shows what's going on in the park. Summer is busy with crafts in action and people reenacting life in the past, à la Colonial Williamsburg. There are no tours, so it's up to you to initiate conversations with the "residents." Off-season it's pretty dead, with no live crafts and most buildings locked up.

Cost and Hours: 150 kr in summer, 110 kr off-season; 170-kr combo-ticket with Norwegian Olympics Museum; June-Aug daily 10:00-17:00; Sept-May Tue-Sun 11:00-16:00, closed Mon; paid parking.

Information: Because English descriptions are scant, the 95-kr English guidebook is worth considering. Tel. 61 28 89 00, www.maihaugen.no.

Touring the Museum: The outdoor section, with 200 buildings from the Gudbrandsdal region, is divided into three areas: the "Rural Collection," with old sod-roof log houses and a stave church; the "Town Collection," with reconstructed bits of old-time Lillehammer; and the "Residential Area," with 20th-century houses that look like most homes in today's Norway. The time trip can be jarring: In the 1980s house, a bubble-gum-chewing girl enthused about her new, "wireless" TV remote and played ABBA tunes from a cassette-tape player.

The museum's excellent "We Won the Land" exhibit (at the entry) sweeps you through Norwegian history from the Ice Age to the Space Age. The Gudbrandsdal art section shows village life at its best. And you can walk through Dr. Sandvig's old dental office and the original shops of various crafts- and tradespeople.

Though the museum welcomes picnickers and has a simple cafeteria, Lillehammer's town center (a 15-minute walk below the museum), with lots of fun eateries, is better for lunch (see "Eating in the Gudbrandsdal Valley," later).

Norwegian Olympics Museum (Norges Olympiske Museum)—This cute museum is housed in the huge Olympic ice-hockey arena, Håkon Hall. With brief English explanations, an emphasis on Norwegians and Swedes, and an endearingly gung-ho Olympic spirit, it's worth a visit on a rainy day or for sports fans. The ground-floor exhibit traces the ancient history of the Olympics, then devotes one wall panel to each of the summer and winter Olympiads of the modern era (with special treatment for the 1952 Oslo games). Upstairs, walk the entire concourse, circling the arena seating while reviewing the highlights (and lowlights) of the 1994 games (remember Tonya Harding?). While you're up there, check out the gallery of great Norwegian athletes and the giant egg used in the Lillehammer opening ceremony. With more time, see the 13-minute film on the 1994 Lillehammer Olympiad (included in museum ticket, 2/

hour, usually in English, near ticket desk).

Cost and Hours: 110 kr, 170-kr combo-ticket with Maihaugen Open-Air Folk Museum; June-Aug daily 10:00-17:00; Sept-May Tue-Sun 11:00-16:00, closed Mon; tel. 61 25 21 00, www.mai haugen.no.

Nearby: On the hillside above Håkon Hall (a 30-minute hike or quick drive) are two ski jumps that host more Olympics sights, including a ski lift, the ski jump tower, and a bobsled ride (www .olympiaparken.no). In the summer, ski jumpers practice on the ski jumps, which are sprayed with water.

In the Gudbrandsdal Valley

If you're driving from Oslo to the Gudbrandsdal Valley, you'll go right past the historic Eidsvoll Manor.

Scenic Drives—The main E6 road north of Lillehammer (en route to Otta and Lom) passes through a bucolic valley with fine but unremarkable scenery. Along this road, a pair of toll-road side-trips (Gynt Veien and Peer Gynt Seterveien) loop off the E6

road. While they sound romantic, they're basically windy, curvy dirt roads over high, desolate heath and scrub-brush plateaus with fine mountain views. They're scenic, but pale in comparison to the Sognefjell road between Lom and the Lustrafjord (described later in this chapter).

Sleeping in the Gudbrandsdal Valley

I prefer sleeping in the more scenic and Norwegian-feeling Jotunheimen area (described later). But if you're sleeping here, Lillehammer and the surrounding valley offer several good options. My choices for Lillehammer are near the train station; the accommodations in Kvam provide a convenient stopping point in the valley.

In Lillehammer

$$$ Mølla Hotell, true to its name, is situated in an old mill along the little stream running through Lillehammer. The 58 rooms blend Old World charm with modern touches. It's more cutesy-cozy and less businesslike than other Lillehammer hotels in this price range (Db-1,250-1,450 kr depending on demand, elevator, free Internet access and Wi-Fi, a block below Gågata at Elvegata 12, tel. 61 05 70 80, fax 61 05 70 81, www.mollahotell.no, post@molla hotell.no).

Sleep Code

(5 kr = about $1, country code: 47)

S = Single, **D** = Double/Twin, **T** = Triple, **Q** = Quad, **b** = bathroom, **s** = shower. You can assume staff speak English, breakfast is included, and credit cards are accepted unless otherwise noted.

To help you sort easily through these listings, I've divided the accommodations into three categories, based on the price for a standard double room with bath during high season:

$$$ Higher Priced—Most rooms 1,000 kr or more.
 $$ Moderately Priced—Most rooms between 500-1,000 kr.
  $ Lower Priced—Most rooms 500 kr or less.

Prices can change without notice; verify the hotel's current rates online or by email. For other updates, see www.ricksteves.com/update.

$$ First Hotel Breiseth is a business-class hotel with 89 rooms in a handy location directly across from the train station (Sb-1,100 kr, Db-1,300 kr, free Wi-Fi, free parking, Jernbanegaten 1-5, tel. 61 24 77 77, www.firsthotels.no/breiseth, breiseth@first hotels.no).

$ Vandrerhjem Stasjonen, Lillehammer's youth hostel, is actually upstairs inside the train station. With 75 beds in 28 institutional but new-feeling rooms—including 18 almost hotel-like doubles—it's a winner (330-kr bunk in a 3- to 4-bed dorm, Sb-700 kr, Db-850 kr, 15 percent cheaper for members, includes sheets and breakfast, elevator, free Wi-Fi, Jernbanetorget 2, tel. 61 26 00 24, www.stasjonen.no, post@stasjonen.no).

In Kvam

This is a popular vacation valley for Norwegians, and you'll find loads of reasonable small hotels and campgrounds with huts for those who aren't quite campers (*hytter* means "bungalows," *rom* is "private room," and *ledig* means "vacancy"). These huts normally cost about 400-600 kr, depending on size and amenities, and can hold from four to six people. Although they are simple, you'll have a kitchenette and access to a good WC and shower. When available, sheets rent for around 60 kr per person. Here are a couple of listings in the town of Kvam, located midway between Lillehammer and Lom.

$$ Sinclair Vertshuset Motel has a quirky Scottish-Norwegian ambience. The 15 fine rooms are in old-fashioned motel wings, while the main building houses an inexpensive cafeteria, described below (Sb-890 kr, Db-1,090 kr, family deals, free Internet access and Wi-Fi, tel. 61 29 54 50, fax 61 29 54 51, www .vertshuset-sinclair.no, post@vertshuset-sinclair.no). The motel was named after a Scotsman who led a band of adventurers into this valley, attempting to set up their own Scottish kingdom. They failed. All were kilt.

$-$$ Kirketeigen Ungdomssenter ("Church Youth Center"), behind the town church, welcomes travelers year-round (camping spots-120 kr/tent; small cabins without water-400 kr; cabins with kitchen and bath-800 kr, sleeps up to 5 people; simple 4-bed rooms in the main building-450 kr for 2-4 people with sheets; sheets and blankets-90 kr, Wi-Fi, tel. 61 21 60 90, www.kirketeigen.no, post@kirketeigen.no).

Eating in the Gudbrandsdal Valley

In Lillehammer: Good restaurants are scattered around the city center, but for the widest selection, head to where the main pedestrian drag (Gågata) crosses the little stream running down-hill through town. Poke a block or two up and down **Elvegata,** which stretches along the river and hosts a wide range of tempting eateries—from pubs (both rowdy and upscale) to pizza and cheap sandwich stands.

In the Valley: Sinclair Vertshuset, described above, has a cafeteria handy for a quick and filling bite on the road between Lillehammer and Lom (50-70-kr sandwiches, 100-180-kr meals, daily 7:00-24:00).

GUDBRANDSDAL

Jotunheimen Mountains

Norway's Jotunheimen Mountains ("Giants' Home") feature the country's highest peaks and some of its best hikes and drives. This national park stretches from the fjords to the glaciers. You can play roller-coaster with mountain passes, take rugged hikes, wind up scenic toll roads, get up close to a giant stave church...and sleep in a time-passed rural valley. The gateway to the mountains is the unassuming town of Lom.

Lom

Pleasant Lom—the main town between Lillehammer and Sogndal—feels like a modern ski resort village. It's home to one of Norway's most impressive stave churches. While Lom has little else to offer, the church causes the closest thing to a tour-bus traffic jam this neck of the Norwegian woods will ever see.

Orientation to Lom

Park by the stave church—you'll see its dark spire just over the bridge. The church shares a parking lot with a gift shop/church museum and some public WCs. Across the street is the TI. If you're heading over the mountains, Lom's bank (at the Kommune building) has the last ATM until Gaupne.

Tourist Information

Lom's TI is an excellent source of information for hikes and drives in the Jotunheimen Mountains (mid-June-mid-Aug Mon-Sat 9:00-19:00, Sun 10:00-17:00; May-mid-June and mid-Aug-Sept Mon-Fri 9:00-16:00, Sat-Sun 10:00-15:00; Oct-April Mon-Fri 10:00-15:00, closed Sat-Sun; in the sod-roofed building across the busy road from the stave church parking lot, tel. 61 21 29 90, www .visitjotunheimen.com).

The TI also serves as a national park office and hosts a worth-while **Mountain Museum** (Norsk Fjellmuseum), tracing the history of the people who have lived off the land in Jotunheimen from the Stone Age to today. This is one of the better exhibits in fjord country. Its theater shows a 10-minute montage of images backed by Kenny G-type music, and the displays are well-presented with plenty of actual historic artifacts (50 kr, same hours as TI). The museum also has a computer with free Internet access for travelers.

Sights in Lom

▲▲Lom Stave Church (Lom Stavkyrkje)

Despite extensive renovations, Lom's church (from 1158) remains a striking example of a Nordic stave church.

Cost and Hours: Church-55 kr, daily mid-June-mid-Aug 9:00-19:00, May-mid-June and mid-Aug-Sept 9:00-17:00, closed in winter and during funerals, fine 15-kr leaflet; museum-15 kr, mid-July-mid-Aug daily 9:00-20:00, progressively shorter hours in shoulder season, in winter Mon-Sat 10:00-15:00, closed Sun, tel. 61 21 19 05.

Tours: Try to tag along with a guided tour of the church—or, if it's not too busy, a docent can give you a quick private tour (included in ticket). Even outside of opening times—including winter—small groups can arrange a tour (45 kr/person, 300-kr minimum, call 97 07 53 97 in summer or 61 21 73 00 in winter).

❷ Self-Guided Tour: Buy your ticket and go inside to take in the humble **interior** (still used by locals for services—notice the posted hymnal numbers). Men sat on the right, women on the left, and prisoners sat with the sheriff in the caged area in the rear. Standing in the middle of the nave, look overhead to see the earliest surviving parts of the church, such as the circle of X-shaped St. Andrew crosses and the Romanesque arches above them. High above the door (impossible to see without a flashlight—ask a docent to show you) is an old painting of a dragon- or lion-like creature—likely an old Viking symbol, possibly drawn here to smooth the forced conversion local pagans made to Christianity. When King Olav II (later to become St. Olav) swept through this valley in 1021, he gave locals an option: convert or be burned out of house and home.

On the white town flag, notice the spoon—a symbol of Lom. Because of its position nestled in the mountains, Lom gets less rainfall than other towns, so large spoons were traditionally used to spread water over the fields. The apse (behind the altar) was added in 1240, when trendy new Gothic cathedrals made an apse a must-have accessory for churches across Europe. Lepers came to the grilled window in the apse for a blessing. When the Reformation hit in 1536, the old paintings were whitewashed over. The church has changed over the years: Transepts, pews, and windows were added in the 17th century. And the circa-1720 paintings were done by a local priest's son.

JOTUNHEIMEN

Drop into the **gift shop/church museum** in the big black building in the parking lot. Its one-room exhibit celebrates 1,000 years of the stave church—interesting if you follow the loaner English descriptions. Inside you'll find a pair of beautiful model churches, headstones and other artifacts, and the only surviving stave-church dragon-head "steeple." In the display case near the early-1900s organ, find the little pencil-size stick carved with runes, dating from around 1350. It's actually a love letter from a would-be suitor. The woman rejected him, but she saved them both from embarrassment by hiding the stick under the church floorboards beneath a pew...where it was found in 1973. (Docents inside the church like to show off a replica of this stick.)

Before or after your church visit, explore the tidy, thought-provoking **graveyard** surrounding the church. Also, check out the precarious-looking little footbridge over the waterfall (the best view is from the modern road bridge into town).

Sleeping near Lom

(5 kr = about $1, country code: 47)
Lom itself has a handful of hotels, but the most appealing way to overnight in this area is at a rural rest stop in the countryside. All of these are on Route 55 south of Lom, toward Sognefjord—Strind Gård first, then Bøverdalen, Røisheim, and finally Elvesæter (all within 20 minutes of Lom).

$$$ Røisheim, in a marvelously remote mountain setting, is an extremely expensive storybook hotel composed of a cluster of centuries-old, sod-roofed log farmhouses. Its posh and generous living rooms are filled with antiques. Each of the 20 rooms (in eight different buildings) is rustic but elegant, with fun "barrel bathtubs" and four-poster or canopy beds. Some rooms are in old, wooden farm buildings—*stab-burs*—with low ceilings and heavy beams. The deluxe rooms are larger, with king beds and fireplaces. Call ahead so they'll be prepared for your arrival (open mid-May-Sept; standard Db-3,600 kr, deluxe Db-3,950 kr; includes breakfast, packed lunch, and an over-the-top four-course traditional dinner served at 19:30; non-smoking, free Wi-Fi, 10 miles south of Lom on Route 55, tel. 61 21 20 31, fax 61 21 21 51, www.roisheim .no, booking@roisheim.dvgl.no, Haavard Lunde).

$$$ Elvesæter Hotel has its own share of Old World romance, but is bigger, cheaper, and more modest. Delightful public spaces bunny-hop through its traditional shell, while its 200 beds sprawl through nine buildings. The Elvesæter family has done a great job of retaining the historic character of their medieval farm, even though the place is big enough to handle large tour groups. The renovated "superior" rooms are new-feeling, but have sterile modern furniture; the older, cheaper "standard" rooms are well-worn but more characteristic (open May-Sept, standard Db-1,150 kr, superior Db-1,550 kr, extra bed-450 kr, family deals, includes breakfast, good 325-kr three-course dinners, strictly non-smoking, free Wi-Fi, swimming pool, farther up Route 55, just past Bøverdal, tel. 61 21 99 00, fax 61 21 99 01, www.elveseter .no, post@elveseter.no). Even if you're not staying here, stop by to wander through the public spaces and pick up a flier explaining the towering Sagasøyla (Saga Column). It was started in 1926 to celebrate the Norwegian constitution, and was to stand in front of Oslo's Parliament Building—but the project stalled after World War II (thanks to the artist's affinity for things German and membership in Norway's fascist party). It was eventually finished and erected here in 1992.

$ Bøverdalen Youth Hostel offers 32 cheap-but-comfortable beds and a far more rugged clientele—real hikers rather than car hikers. While a bit institutional, it's well-priced and well-run (open late May-Sept, bunk in 4- to 6-bed room-180 kr, D-450 kr; 4-person cabins-700 kr with shower and toilet, 500 kr with toilet but no shower; 10 percent discount for members, sheets-65 kr, breakfast-70 kr, free Wi-Fi, kitchen, hot meals, self-serve café, tel. & fax 61 21 20 64, www.hihostels.no, boverdalen@hihostels.no, Anna Berit). It's in the center of the little community of Bøverdal (store, campground, and toll road up to Galdhøpiggen area).

$ Strind Gård is your very rustic option if you can't spring for Røisheim or Elvesæter, but still want the countryside-farm experience. This 150-year-old farmhouse, situated by a soothing waterfall, rents two rooms and one apartment, plus four sod-roofed log huts. The catch: Many of the buildings have no running water, so you'll use the shared facilities at the main building. While not everyone's cup of tea, this place will appeal to romantics who always wanted to sleep in a humble log cabin in the Norwegian mountains—it's downright idyllic for those who like to rough it (2-person huts: without bathroom-250-450 kr depending on size, beautiful private hut with bathroom-700 kr; rooms in main house: D-350-450 kr depending on size, apartment for 4-6 with private bath-700 kr; sheets and towels-70 kr, no breakfast, free Wi-Fi, low ceilings, farm smells, valley views, 2 miles south of Lom on Route 55, tel. 61 21 12 37, www.strind-gard.no, post@strind-gard .no, Anne Jorunn and Trond Dalsegg).

Drives and Hikes in the Jotunheimen Mountains

Route 55, which runs between Lom and the Sognefjord to the south, is the sightseeing spine of this region. From this main (and already scenic) drag, other roads spin upwards into the mountains—offering even better views and exciting drives and hikes. Many of these get you up close to Norway's highest mountain, Galdhøpiggen (8,100 feet). I've listed these attractions from north to south, as you'll reach them driving from Lom to the Sognefjord; except for the first, they all branch off from Route 55. Another great high-mountain experience nearby is the hike to the Nigard Glacier near Lustrafjord.

Remember that the TI in Lom acts as a national park office, offering excellent maps and advice for drivers and hikers—a stop here is obligatory if you're planning a jaunt into the mountains (see "Orientation to Lom," earlier).

Besseggen

This trail offers an incredible opportunity to walk between two lakes separated by a narrow ridge and a 1,000-foot cliff. It's one of Norway's most beloved hikes, which can make it crowded in the summer. To get to the trailhead, drivers detour down Route 51 after Otta south to Maurvangen. Turn right to Gjendesheim to park your car. From Gjendesheim, catch the boat to Memurubu, where the path starts at the boat dock. Hike along the ridge—with a blue lake (Bessvatnet) on one side and a green lake (Gjende) on the other—and keep your balance. The six-hour trail loops back to Gjendesheim. Because the boat runs sporadically, time your visit to catch one (120 kr for 20-minute ride, 3 morning departures daily, latest schedules at www.gjende.no, tel. 61 23 85 09). This is a thrilling but potentially hazardous hike, and it's a major detour: Gjendesheim is about 1.5 hours and 50 miles from Lom.

Spiterstulen

From Røisheim, this 11-mile toll road (50 kr) takes you from Route 55 to the Spiterstulen mountain hotel/lodge in about 30 minutes (3,600 feet). This is the best destination for serious all-day hikes to Norway's two mightiest mountains, Glittertinden and Galdhøpiggen (a 5-hour hike up and a 3-hour hike down, doable without a guide). Or consider a guided, two-hour glacier walk (tel. 61 21 94 00, www.spiterstulen.no).

Juvasshytta

This toll road, starting from Bøverdal, takes you in about 40 minutes to the highest you can drive and the closest you can get to Galdhøpiggen by car (6,050 feet). At the end of the 85-kr toll road, daily, guided, six-hour hikes go across the glacier to the summit and back (200 kr, late June-late Sept daily at 10:00, July-mid-Aug also daily at 11:30, check in 30 minutes before, strict age limit—no kids under age 7, 4 miles each way, easy ascent but very dangerous without a guide, hiking boots required—possible to rent from nearby ski resort). You can sleep in the newly updated **$$ Juvasshytta lodge** (Db-1,100 kr with sheets, D without sheets-860 kr, sheets-100 kr, includes breakfast, dinner-330 kr, open June-Sept, tel. 61 21 15 50, www.juvasshytta.no).

Leirvassbu

This 11-mile, 50-kr toll road (about 30 minutes one-way from Bøverkinnhalsen, south of Elvesæter) is most scenic for car hikers. It takes you to a lodge at 4,600 feet with great views and easy walks. A serious (5-hour round-trip) hike goes to the lone peak, Kyrkja—"The Cathedral," which looms like a sanded-down mini-Matterhorn on the horizon (6,660 feet).

▲▲Sognefjell Drive to the Sognefjord

Norway's highest pass (at 4,600 feet, the highest road in northern

Europe) is a thrilling drive through a cancan line of mountains, from Jotunheimen's Bøverdal Valley to the Lustrafjord (an arm of the Sognefjord). Centuries ago, the farmers of Gudbrandsdal took their horse caravans over this difficult mountain pass on treks to Bergen. Today, the road (Route 55) is still narrow, windy, and otherworldly (and usually closed mid-Oct-May).

As you begin to ascend just beyond Elvesæter, notice the viewpoint on the left for the Leirdalen Valley—capped at the end with the Kyrkja peak (described earlier). Then you'll twist up into a lake-filled valley, then through a mild canyon with grand waterfalls. Before long, as you corkscrew up more switchbacks, you're above the tree line, enjoying a "top of the world" feeling. The best views (to the south) are of the cut-glass range called Hurrungane ("Noisy Children"). The 10 hairpin turns between Turtagrø and Fortun are exciting. Be sure to stop, get out, look around, and enjoy the lavish views. Treat each turn as if it were your last.

Just before you descend to the fjord, the terrain changes, and you reach a pullout on the right, next to a hilltop viewpoint—offering your first glimpse of the fjord. The Lustrafjord village of Skjolden is just around the bend (and down several more switchbacks). Entering Skjolden, continue following Route 55, which now traces the west bank of the Lustrafjord.

Gudbrandsdal and Jotunheimen Connections

Cars are better, but if you're without wheels: **Oslo to Lillehammer** (trains almost hourly, 2.5 hours, just 2 hours from Oslo airport), **Lillehammer to Otta** (6 trains/day, 1.5 hours); a bus meets some trains (confirm schedule at the train station in Oslo) for travelers heading on to **Lom** (2 buses/day, 1 hour) and onward from **Lom to Sogndal** (2 buses/day late June-Aug only, road closed off-season, 3.25 hours).

Route Tips for Drivers

Use low gears and lots of patience both up (to keep the engine cool) and down (to save your brakes). Uphill traffic gets the right-of-way, but drivers, up or down, dive for the nearest fat part of the road whenever they meet. Ask backseat drivers not to scream until you've actually been hit or have left the road.

From Oslo to Jotunheimen: It's 2.5 hours from Oslo to Lillehammer and 3 hours after that to Lom. Wind out of Oslo following signs for *E6* (not to *Drammen*, but for *Stockholm* and then to *Trondheim*). In a few minutes, you're in the wide-open pastoral countryside of eastern Norway. Norway's Constitution Hall—Eidsvoll Manor—is a five-minute detour off E6, several miles south of Eidsvoll in Eidsvoll Verk (follow the signs to *Eidsvoll Bygningen*). Then E6 takes you along Norway's largest lake (Mjøsa), through the town of Hamar, and past more lake scenery into Lillehammer. Signs direct you uphill from downtown Lillehammer to the Maihaugen Open-Air Folk Museum. From Lillehammer, signs to *E6/Trondheim* take you up the valley of Gudbrandsdal. At Otta, exit for Lom. Halfway to Lom, on the left, look for the long suspension bridge spanning the milky-blue river—a good opportunity to stretch your legs, and a scenic spot to enjoy a picnic.

BERGEN

Bergen is permanently salted with robust cobbles and a rich sea-trading heritage. Norway's capital in the 12th and 13th centuries, Bergen's wealth and importance came thanks to its membership in the heavyweight medieval trading club of merchant cities called the Hanseatic League. Bergen still wears her rich maritime heritage proudly.

Bergen gets an average of 80 inches of rain annually (compared to 30 inches in Oslo). A good year has 60 days of sunshine. The natives aren't apologetic about their famously lousy weather. In fact, they seem to wear it as a badge of pride. "Well, that's Bergen," they'll say matter-of-factly as they wring out their raincoats. When I complained about an all-day downpour, one resident cheerfully informed me, "There's no such thing as bad weather—just inappropriate clothing"...a local mantra that rhymes in Norwegian.

With 250,000 people, Bergen has big-city parking problems and high prices, but visitors sticking to the old center find it charming. Enjoy Bergen's salty market, then stroll the easy-on-foot old quarter, with cute lanes of delicate old wooden houses. From downtown Bergen, a funicular zips you up a little mountain for a bird's-eye view of this sailors' town.

Planning Your Time

Bergen can be enjoyed even on the tail end of a day's scenic train ride from Oslo before returning on the overnight train. But that teasing taste will make you wish you had more time. On a three-week tour of Scandinavia, Bergen is worth a whole day.

While Bergen's sights are visually underwhelming and pricey, nearly all come with thoughtful tours in English. If you dedicate

Greater Bergen

the time to take advantage of these tours, otherwise barren attractions (such as Håkon's Hall and Rosenkrantz Tower, the Bryggen quarter, the Leprosy Museum, and Gamle Bergen) become surprisingly interesting. For a busy day, you could do this (enjoying tours at all but the last): 9:00—Stroll through the Fish Market; 10:00—Visit Håkon's Hall and Rosenkrantz Tower; 12:00—Take the Bryggen Walking Tour; 14:00—Take a harbor cruise or check out the Leprosy Museum; 16:00—Enjoy some free time in town (consider returning to the Bryggens Museum using your tour ticket), or catch the bus out to Gamle Bergen; 18:00—Ride up the Fløibanen funicular.

Although Bergen has plenty of attractions and charms of its own, it's most famous as the "Gateway to the Fjords." If you plan to use Bergen as a springboard for fjord country, you have three options: Pick up a rental car here (fjord wonder is a three-hour drive away); take the express boat down the Sognefjord (about four hours to Balestrand and Flåm/Aurland); or do the "Norway in a Nutshell" as a scenic loop from Bergen. The "Nutshell" option also works well as a detour midway between Bergen and Oslo (hop the train from either city to Voss or Myrdal, then take a bus or spur train into the best of the Sognefjord; scenic ferry rides depart from there). While there are a million ways to enjoy the fjords, first-timers should start with this region.

Also note that Bergen, a geographic dead-end, is actually an efficient place to begin or end your Scandinavian tour. Consider flying into Bergen and out of another city, such as Helsinki (or vice versa).

Orientation to Bergen

Bergen clusters around its harbor—nearly everything listed in this chapter is within a few minutes' walk. The busy Torget (the square with the Fish Market) is at the head of the harbor. As you face

the sea from here, Bergen's TI is to the left of the Fish Market. The town's historic Hanseatic Quarter, Bryggen (BREW-gun), lines the harbor on the right. Express boats to the Sognefjord (Balestrand and Flåm) and Stavanger dock at the harbor on the left.

Protected from the open sea by a lone sheltering island, Bergen is a place of refuge from heavy winds for the giant working boats that serve the North Sea oil rigs. (Much of Norway's current affluence is funded by the oil it drills just offshore.) Bergen is also one of the most popular cruise-ship ports in northern Europe, hosting hundreds of ships a year and up to seven ships a day in peak season. Each morning is rush hour, as cruisers hike past the fortress and into town.

Charming cobbled streets surround the harbor and climb the encircling hills. Bergen's popular Fløibanen funicular climbs high above the city to the top of Mount Fløyen for the best view of the town. Surveying the surrounding islands and inlets, it's clear why this city is known as the "Gateway to the Fjords."

Tourist Information

The centrally located TI is in a new building next to the Fish Market (June-Aug daily 8:30-22:00; May and Sept daily 9:00-20:00; Oct-April Mon-Sat 9:00-16:00, closed Sun; at the corner of Strandkaien and Torget, tel. 55 55 20 00, www.visitbergen.com). The TI covers Bergen and western Norway, provides information and tickets for tours, has a fjord information desk, books rooms, and maintains a very handy events board listing today's and tomorrow's slate of tours, concerts, and other events. Pick up this year's edition of the free *Bergen Guide* (also likely at your hotel), which has a fine map and lists all sights, hours, and special events. This booklet can answer most of your questions. If you need assistance and there's a line, take a number.

Bergen Card: You have to work hard to make this greedy little card pay off. It gives you free use of the city buses, half off the Mount Fløyen funicular, free admission to most museums (but not the Hanseatic Museum), and discounts on some tours, events, and sights—such as a measly 10 percent discount on the Bryggen Walking Tour and a 50 percent discount on Edvard Grieg's Home. It also covers the aquarium—if you're here in the winter (220 kr/24 hours, 260 kr/48 hours, sold at TI, train station, and most hotels).

Arrival in Bergen

By Train or Bus: Bergen's train and bus stations are on Strømgaten, facing a park-rimmed lake. The small, manageable train station has an office open long hours for booking all your travel in Norway—get your Nutshell reservations here if you haven't already (Mon-Fri 6:45-19:30, Sat 7:30-16:10, Sun 7:30-19:30). There are luggage lockers (30 kr/day, daily 6:30-23:30), pay toilets, a newsstand, sandwich shop, and coffee shop. (To get to the bus station, follow the covered walkway behind the Narvesen newsstand via the Storcenter shopping mall.) Taxis wait to the right (with the tracks at your back). From the train station, it's a 10-minute walk to the TI: Cross the street (Strømgaten) in front of the station and take Marken, a cobbled street that eventually turns into a modern retail street. Continue walking in the same direction until you reach the water.

By Plane: Bergen's cute little Flesland Airport is 12 miles south of the city center. The airport bus runs between the airport and downtown Bergen, stopping at the Radisson Blu Royal Hotel in Bryggen, the harborfront area near the TI (if you ask), the SAS Hotel Norge (in the modern part of town at Ole Bulls Plass), and the bus station (95 kr, pay driver, 4/hour at peak times, less in slow times, 30-minute ride). Taxis take up to four people and cost about 400 kr for the 20-minute ride (depending on the time of day). Airport info: tel. 67 03 15 55; SAS info: tel. 81 52 04 00.

By Car: Driving is a headache in Bergen—avoid it if you can. Approaching town on E16 (from Voss and the Sognefjord area), follow signs for *Sentrum*, which spits you out near the big, modern bus station and parking garage. Parking is difficult and costly—ask at your hotel for tips. Note that all drivers entering Bergen must pay a 15-kr toll, but there are no toll-collection gates (since the system is automated). Assuming they bill you, it'll just show up on your credit card (which they access through your rental car company). For details, ask your rental company or see www.autopass.no.

By Cruise Ship: Ships dock at the Skolten cruise terminal, a 10-minute walk from the fortress and the historic Bryggen district. You can also take the City Sightseeing hop-on, hop-off bus from here (described later, under "Tours in Bergen"). Taxis between the terminal and central Bergen cost about 65 kr. If you're connecting to Bergen's Flesland Airport, note the airport bus stops at the Radisson Blu Royal Hotel in Bryggen.

Helpful Hints

Museum Tours: Many of Bergen's sights are hard to appreciate without a guide. Fortunately, many include a wonderful and intimate guided tour with admission. Make the most of the following sights by taking advantage of their included tours: Håkon's Hall and Rosenkrantz Tower, Bryggens Museum, Hanseatic Museum, Leprosy Museum, Gamle Bergen, and Edvard Grieg's Home.

Crowd Control: In high season, cruise-ship passengers mob the waterfront between 10:00 and 15:00; to avoid the crush, consider visiting an outlying sight during this time, such as Gamle Bergen or Edvard Grieg's Home.

Internet Access: Kanel in the Galleriet Shopping Mall is a convenient Internet café (2 kr/minute, 20-kr minimum, Mon-Fri 7:30-21:00, Sat 9:00-18:00, closed Sun, located on ground floor next to Body Shop, tel. 40 62 22 27). The **Bergen Public Library,** next door to the train station, offers free access in their downstairs café (30-minute limit, Mon-Thu 8:30-20:00, Fri 8:30-16:30, Sat 10:00-16:00, closed Sun, Strømgaten 6, tel. 55 56 85 60).

Laundry: Jarlens Vaskoteque is at Lille Øvregate 17, one block uphill from the church called Korskirken (2-hour drop-off service for 110 kr, self-service for 80 kr, Mon-Fri 10:00-18:00, Wed-Thu until 20:00, Sat 10:00-15:00, closed Sun, tel. 55 32 55 04).

Getting Around Bergen

Most in-town sights can easily be reached by foot; only the aquarium and Gamle Bergen (and farther-flung sights such as the

BERGEN

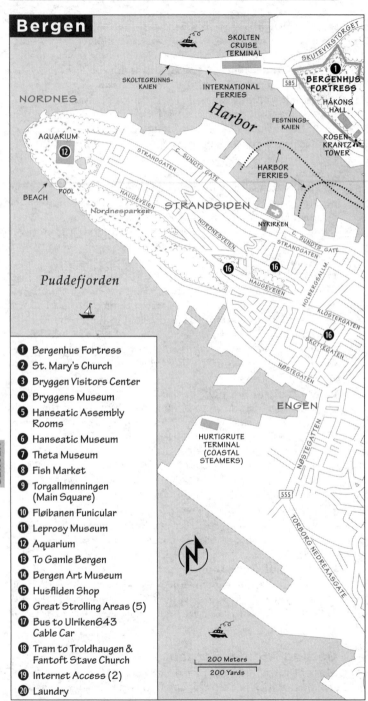

Bergen

NORDNES

AQUARIUM
12

BEACH

POOL

Nordnesparken

Puddefjorden

STRANDGATEN

C. SUNDTS GATE

HAUGEVEIEN

STRANDSIDEN

NORDNESVEIEN

16

16

HAUGEVEIEN

SKOLTEGRUNNS-
KAIEN

SKOLTEN
CRUISE
TERMINAL

INTERNATIONAL
FERRIES

Harbor

FESTNINGS-
KAIEN

HARBOR
FERRIES

NYKIRKEN

C. SUNDTS GATE

STRANDGATEN

HOLBERGSALLM.

KLOSTERGATEN

16

SKOTTEGATEN

NØSTEGATEN

ENGEN

HURTIGRUTE
TERMINAL
(COASTAL
STEAMERS)

NØSTEGATEN

555

TORBORG NEDREAASGATE

SKUTEVIKSTORGET

585

1 BERGENHUS
FORTRESS

HÅKONS
HALL

ROSEN-
KRANTZ
TOWER

N

200 Meters
200 Yards

1 Bergenhus Fortress

2 St. Mary's Church

3 Bryggen Visitors Center

4 Bryggens Museum

5 Hanseatic Assembly
Rooms

6 Hanseatic Museum

7 Theta Museum

8 Fish Market

9 Torgallmenningen
(Main Square)

10 Fløibanen Funicular

11 Leprosy Museum

12 Aquarium

13 To Gamle Bergen

14 Bergen Art Museum

15 Husfliden Shop

16 Great Strolling Areas (5)

17 Bus to Ulriken643
Cable Car

18 Tram to Troldhaugen &
Fantoft Stave Church

19 Internet Access (2)

20 Laundry

BERGEN

Fantoft Stave Church, Edvard Grieg's Home at Troldhaugen, and the Ulriken643 cable car) are more than a 10-minute walk from the TI.

By Bus: City buses cost 25 kr per ride (pay driver). The best buses for a Bergen joyride are #20 (north along the coast) and #11 (into the hills).

By Tram: Bergen's recently built light-rail line is a convenient way to visit Edvard Grieg's Home or the Fantoft Stave Church. Buy your 25-kr ticket from the machine prior to boarding (to use a US credit card, you'll need to know your PIN code). You'll get both a paper ticket and a gray *minikort* pass. Validate the pass when you board by holding it next to the card reader (watch how other passengers do it).

By Ferry: The *Beffen,* a little orange ferry, chugs across the harbor every half-hour, from the dock a block south of the Bryggens Museum to the dock—directly opposite the fortress—a block from the Nykirken church (20 kr, Mon-Fri 7:30-16:00, plus Sat only in July 11:00-16:00, never on Sun, 3-minute ride). The *Vågen* ferry runs from the Fish Market every half-hour to a dock near the aquarium (45 kr, June-Aug 10:00-18:00, 10 minutes). These short "poor man's cruises" have good harbor views.

By Taxi: For a taxi, call 07000 or 08000 (not as expensive as you might expect).

Tours in Bergen

▲▲▲**Bryggen Walking Tour**—This tour of the historic Hanseatic district is one of Bergen's best activities. Local guides take visitors on an excellent 1.5-hour walk through 900 years of Bergen history via the old Hanseatic town (20 minutes in Bryggens Museum, 20-minute visit to the medieval Hanseatic Assembly Rooms, 20-minute walk through Bryggen, and 20 minutes in Hanseatic Museum). Tours leave from the Bryggens Museum (next to the Radisson Blu Royal Hotel). When you consider that the price includes entry tickets to all three sights, the tour more than pays for itself (100 kr, June-Aug daily at 11:00 and 12:00, none Sept-May, tel. 55 58 80 10). While the museum visits are a bit rushed, your tour ticket allows you to re-enter the museums for the rest of the day.

City Walking Tours—**Bergen Guide Service** offers 1.5-hour bilingual walking tours of the city center daily in peak season (in Norwegian and English, 95 kr, mid-June-mid-Aug daily at 15:00, departs from TI, tel. 55 30 10 60, www.bergenguideservice.com).

Local Guides—**Sue Lindelid** and **Jim Paton** are British expats who have spent more than 25 years showing visitors around Bergen (600 kr for 1.5-hour group tour, less for individuals, mobile 90 78 59 52, suelin@hotmail.no). You can also contact Bergen Guide Service (see above) to hire a local guide.

▲**Bus Tours**—The TI sells tickets for various bus tours, including a three-hour tour that goes to Edvard Grieg's Home at Troldhaugen—a handy way to reach that distant sight (300 kr, May-Sept daily at 11:00, departs from curb across from Fish Market). Buses are comfy, with big views and a fine recorded commentary. There are also several full-day tour options from Bergen, including bus/boat tours to nearby Hardanger and Sogne fjords. The TI is packed with brochures describing all the excursions.

Hop-On, Hop-Off Bus—City Sightseeing's hop-on, hop-off bus links most of Bergen's major sights and also stops at the Skolten cruise terminal. Buy tickets on board or at the TI (150 kr/24 hours, late May-Aug 9:00-16:30, 2/hour, convenient stop right in front of Fish Market, tel. 97 78 18 88, www.citysightseeing-bergen.net).

▲**Harbor Tours**—The *White Lady* leaves from the Fish Market daily in summer at 14:30 for a 50-minute cruise. The ride is both scenic and informative, with a relaxing sun deck and good—if scant—recorded narration (130 kr, June-Aug). A four-hour fjord trip is also available (480 kr, May-mid-Sept daily at 10:00, July-late Aug also daily at 15:30, tel. 55 25 90 00, www.whitelady.no).

Tourist Train—The tacky little "Bergen Express" train departs from in front of the Hanseatic Museum for a 55-minute loop around town (150 kr, 2/hour in peak season, otherwise hourly; runs daily May 10:00-16:00, June-Aug 10:00-19:00, Sept 10:00-15:00; headphone English commentary).

Sights in Bergen

▲▲**Bergen Town Walk**—For a quick and historic orientation walk through Bergen, start at the fortress and tower, head up to St. Mary's Church, peruse the old wooden Hanseatic Quarter, and loiter through the Fish Market. Then head into the modern center of town, the Torgallmenningen square, and finish with a stroll around the little lake. (These sights are all described below, in the order of this walk.) Ideally, you'll get side-tracked in the museums and will take advantage of their excellent tours (included with admission). As you explore, remember two points that shape the city you'll see:

While the city dates from 1070, little survives from before the last big fire in 1702. In its earlier heyday, Bergen was one of the largest wooden cities in Europe. Congested wooden buildings, combined with lots of small fires (to provide heat and light in this cold and dark corner of Europe), spelled disaster for Bergen. Over the centuries, the city suffered countless fires, including 10 devastating blazes. Each time the city burned, the destroyed material was tossed into the harbor, creating a haphazard landfill upon which much of the old town you see today was eventually built. After 1702, the city rebuilt using more stone and brick, and suffered fewer fires.

One of the biggest explosions of World War II, which occurred in the harbor on April 20, 1944, also shaped the city. An ammunition ship loaded with 120 tons of dynamite blew up just in front of the fortress. The blast leveled entire neighborhoods on either side of the harbor (notice the ugly 1950s construction opposite the fortress) and did serious damage to Håkon's Hall and Rosenkrantz Tower. How big was the blast? There's a hut called "the anchor cabin" a couple of miles away in the mountains. That's where the ship's anchor landed. The blast is considered to be accidental, despite the fact that April 20 happened to be Hitler's birthday and the ship blew up about 100 yards away from the Nazi commander's headquarters (in the fortress).

▲Bergenhus Fortress: Håkon's Hall and Rosenkrantz Tower—Back in the 13th century, Bergen was the Kingdom of Norway's first capital. (Prior to the 13th century, kings would circulate, staying on royal farms.) This fortress was a garrison, with a tower for the king's residence and a large hall for his banquets. Today the fortress grounds are used for big events (Bruce Springsteen filled it in 2009).

The tower and hall, sitting boldly out of place on the harbor just beyond Bryggen, are reminders of Bergen's medieval importance. Both sights feel vacant and don't really speak for themselves; the included guided tours, which provide a serious introduction to Bergen's history, are essential for grasping their significance. While each sight is covered by a separate ticket and tour, it's best to consider them as one and start at Håkon's Hall (tours leave at the top of the hour). Stick with your guide, as the Rosenkrantz Tower is part two of the tour.

Håkon's Hall, dating from the 13th century, is the largest secular medieval building in Norway. It's essentially a giant, grand reception hall (used today for banquets) under a ceiling that feels like an upturned Viking boat. While recently rebuilt, the ceiling's design is modeled after grand wooden roofs of that era. Beneath the hall is a whitewashed cellar. Banquets were a men-only affair. The raised seats gave royal, church, and military dignitaries the appropriate elevation.

Rosenkrantz Tower, the keep of a 13th-century castle, has a jumbled design, thanks to a Renaissance addition. The tour brings it to life. There's a good history exhibit on the top floors and a fine view from the rooftop.

Cost and Hours: Tower and hall—50 kr each, includes guided tour; mid-May-Aug—both open daily 10:00-16:00; Sept-mid-May—hall open daily 12:00-15:00, tower open Sun only 12:00-15:00; tel. 55 31 60 67.

St. Mary's Church (Mariakirken)—Dating from the 12th century, this is Bergen's oldest building, though it's closed through

2015 while a 100-million-kroner renovation is underway. This stately church of the Hanseatic merchants has a dour stone interior, enlivened by a colorful, highly decorated pulpit. Behind the church is the back wall of the Hanseatic Quarter and the entrance to the communal Hanseatic Assembly Rooms (Schøtstuene).

Bergen's Hanseatic Quarter (Bryggen)—A horrific plague decimated the population and economy of Norway in 1350, killing

about half of its people. A decade later, German merchants arrived and established a Hanseatic trading post, bringing order to that rustic society. For the next four centuries, the port of Bergen was German territory.

Bergen's old German trading center was called "the German wharf" until World War II, and is now just called "the wharf," or "Bryggen." From 1370 to 1754, German merchants controlled Bergen's trade. In 1550, it was a Germanic city of 1,000 workaholic merchants—surrounded and supported by some 5,000 Norwegians.

The German merchants were very strict and lived in a harsh, all-male world (except for Norwegian prostitutes). This wasn't a

The Hanseatic League, Blessed by Cod

Middlemen in trade, the clever German merchants of the Hanseatic League ruled the waves of northern Europe for 500 years (c. 1250-1750). These sea-traders first banded together in a *Hanse*, or merchant guild, to defend themselves against pirates. As they spread out from Germany, they established trading posts in foreign lands, cut deals with local leaders for trading rights, built boats and wharves, and organized armies to protect ships and ports.

By the 15th century, these merchants had organized more than a hundred cities into the Hanseatic League, a free-trade zone that stretched from London to Russia. The League ran a profitable triangle of trade: Fish from Scandinavia was exchanged for grain from the eastern Baltic and luxury goods from England and Flanders. Everyone benefited, and the German merchants—the middlemen—reaped the profits.

At its peak in the 15th century, the Hanseatic League was the dominant force—economic, military, and political—in northern Europe. This was an age when much of Europe was fragmented into petty kingdoms and dukedoms. Revenue-hungry kings and robber-baron lords levied chaotic and extortionist tolls and duties. Pirates plagued shipments. It was the Hanseatic League, rather than national governments, that brought the stability that allowed trade to flourish.

Bergen's place in this Baltic economy was all about cod—a form of protein that could be dried, preserved, and shipped anywhere. Though cursed by a lack of natural resources, the city

military occupation, but a mutually beneficial economic partnership. The Norwegian cod fishermen of the far north shipped their dried cod to Bergen, where the Hanseatic merchants marketed it to Europe. Norwegian cod provided much of Europe with food (a source of easy-to-preserve protein) and cod oil (which lit the lamps until about 1850).

The wharf area is mostly reclaimed from the sea. Each time the warehouses burned, the merchants would toss the refuse into the bay and rebuild. Gradually, the land crept out, and so did the buildings. (Looking at the Hanseatic Quarter from the harborfront, you can see how the buildings have settled. The foundations, composed of debris from the many fires, settle as they rot.) The long "tenements" (rows of warehouses) we see today date from the early 1700s—built after that last great fire in 1702. To prevent future blazes, the Germans forbade all fires and candles for light or warmth except in isolated and carefully guarded communal houses behind each tenement. It was in these communal houses that apprentices studied, people dried out their soggy clothes, hot food was cooked, and the men drank and partied. One of these was blessed with a good harbor conveniently located between the rich fishing spots of northern Norway and the markets of Europe. Bergen's port shipped dried cod and fish oil southward and imported grain, cloth, beer, wine, and ceramics.

Bryggen was one of four principal Hanseatic trading posts *(Kontors)*, along with London, Bruges, and Novgorod. It was the last *Kontor* opened (c. 1360), the least profitable, and the final one to close. Bryggen had warehouses, offices, and living quarters. Ships docked here were unloaded by counterpoise cranes. At its peak, as many as a thousand merchants, journeymen, and apprentices lived and worked here.

Bryggen was a self-contained German enclave within the city. The merchants came from Germany, worked a few years here, and retired back in the home country. They spoke German, wore German clothes, and attended their own churches. By law, they were forbidden to intermarry or fraternize with the Bergeners, except on business.

The Hanseatic League peaked around 1500, then slowly declined. Rising nation-states were jealous of the Germans' power and wealth. The Reformation tore apart old alliances. Dutch and English traders broke the Hanseatic monopoly. Cities withdrew from the League and *Kontors* closed. In 1754, Bergen's *Kontor* was taken over by the Norwegians. When it closed its doors on December 31, 1899, a sea-trading era was over, but the city of Bergen had become rich...by the grace of cod.

medieval Hanseatic Assembly Rooms is preserved and open to the public (the Schøtstuene—separate entrance behind St. Mary's Church, included in Bryggen Walking Tour, difficult to appreciate without a guide).

Half of Bryggen (the stretch between the old wooden facades and the Hanseatic Museum—standing apart from the others at the head of the bay) was torn down around 1900. The man who owned the wooden building that now houses the Hanseatic Museum recognized the value of the city's heritage and kept his building as it was. Considered a nutcase back then, today he's celebrated as a visionary, as his decision has left visitors with a fine example of an old merchant house that they can tour.

After World War II, Bryggen was again slated for destruction. Most of the locals wanted it gone—it reminded them of the Germans who had occupied Norway for several miserable years. Then excavators discovered rune stones indicating that the area predated the Germans. This boosted Bryggen's approval rating, and the quarter was saved.

From the front of Bryggen, look down at the Rosenkrantz

Tower. The little red holes at its top mark where cannons were once pointed at the German quarter by Norwegian royalty. The threat was never taken seriously, however, because everyone knew that without German grain, the Norwegians would starve.

Bryggen is now touristy and boutiquey, but still lots of fun. Strolling through it, you feel swallowed up by history. Explore its wooden core, with medieval-style double tenements—long rows of planky buildings leaning haphazardly across narrow alleys. Wander. You'll find plenty of art and artisan shops, sweater shops, atmospheric restaurants, and two worthwhile museums within a five-minute walk of each other (the Bryggens and Hanseatic museums, described later). The little **visitors center** plans to add exhibits about maintenance and restoration of the tenement houses (good 80-kr Bryggen guidebook, daily May-Aug 9:00-17:00, Sept 10:00-17:00, closed off-season, at the back end of the narrow wooden lane called Bellgården).

The **Bryggen Walking Tour**, which leaves from Bryggens Museum, is your best bet for seeing this area and its museums (see "Tours in Bergen," earlier.)

▲▲**Bryggens Museum**—This modern museum explains the 1950s archaeological dig to uncover the earliest bits of Bergen (1050-1500). Brief English explanations are posted. From September through May, when there is no tour, ask to borrow the good museum guidebook (or buy it for 25 kr). The manageable, well-presented permanent exhibit occupies the ground floor. First up are the foundations from original wooden tenements dating back to the 12th century (displayed right where they were excavated) and a giant chunk of the hull of a 100-foot-long, 13th-century ship that was found here. Next, an exhibit (roughly shaped like the long, wooden double-tenements outside) shows off artifacts and explains lifestyles from medieval Bryggen. Behind that is a display of items you might have bought at the medieval market. You'll finish with exhibits about the church in Bergen, the town's role as a royal capital, and its status as a cultural capital. Upstairs are two floors of temporary exhibits.

Cost and Hours: 60 kr; in summer, entry included with Bryggen Walking Tour described earlier; mid-May-Aug daily 10:00-16:00; Sept-mid-May Mon-Fri 11:00-15:00, Sat 12:00-15:00, Sun 12:00-16:00; inexpensive cafeteria with soup-and-bread specials; in big, modern building just beyond the end of Bryggen and the Radisson Blu Royal Hotel, tel. 55 58 80 10, www.bymuseet.no.

▲▲**Hanseatic Museum (Hanseatiske Museum)**—This little museum was founded in the late 1900s to preserve a tenement interior. Its creaky old rooms—with hundred-year-old cod hanging from the ceiling—offer a time-tunnel experience back to Bryggen's glory days. It's located in an atmospheric old merchant house furnished with dried fish, antique ropes, an old oxtail (used for wringing spilled cod-liver oil back into the bucket), sagging steps, and cupboard beds from the early 1700s—one with a medieval pinup girl. Admission includes a good 45-minute guided **tour** (3/day in English, May-mid-Sept only). Even if you tour the museum with the Bryggen Walking Tour, you're welcome to revisit (using the same ticket) and take this longer tour.

Cost and Hours: 60 kr; in summer, entry included with Bryggen Walking Tour; daily May-mid-Sept 9:00-17:00; mid-Sept-April Tue-Sat 11:00-14:00, Sun 11:00-16:00, closed Mon; tel. 55 54 46 96, www.museumvest.no.

Theta Museum—This small museum highlights Norway's resistance movement (specifically, a 10-person local group called Theta) during the Nazi occupation in World War II. It's housed in Theta's former headquarters—a small room in a wooden Bryggen building.

Cost and Hours: 30 kr, June-Aug Tue and Sat-Sun 14:00-16:00, closed Mon, Wed-Fri, and off-season, Enhjørningsgården, tel. 55 31 53 93.

▲▲Fish Market (Fisketorget)—A fish market has thrived here since the 1500s, when fishermen rowed in with their catch and

haggled with hungry residents. While it's now become a food circus of eateries selling fishy treats to tourists—no local would come here to actually buy fish—this famous market still offers lots of smelly photo fun and free morsels to taste. Many stands sell pre-made smoked-salmon *(laks)* sandwiches, fish soup, and other

snacks ideal for a light lunch (confirm prices before ordering). To try Norwegian jerky, pick up a bag of dried cod snacks *(torsk)*. The red meat is minke whale, caught off the coast of northern Norway. You'll also find local fruit in season and hand-knit sweaters (June-Aug daily 7:00-19:00, less lively on Sun; Sept-May Mon-Sat 7:00-16:00, closed Sun). Watch your wallet: If you're going to get pickpocketed in Bergen, it'll likely be here.

Bergen's Main Square, Torgallmenningen—*Allmenningen* means "for all the people." *Torg* means "square." And, while this is the city's main gathering place, it was actually created as a fire break. The residents of this fire-plagued city—once one of the biggest wooden cities in Europe—knew fires were inevitable. The street plan was designed with breaks, or open spaces like this square, to help contain the destruction. In 1916, it stopped a fire, which is why it has a more modern feel today.

The **Seafarers' Monument** (which locals have nicknamed "the cube of goat cheese" for its shape) dates from about 1950. It celebrates Bergen's contact with the sea and remembers those who worked on it and died in it. Study the faces: All classes are represented. The statues relate to the scenes depicted in the reliefs above. Each side represents a century: 10th century—Vikings with a totem pole recalling the pre-Columbian Norwegian discovery of America; 18th century—equipping Europe's ships; 19th century—whaling; 20th century—shipping and war. For the 21st century, see the real people—a cross-section of today's Norway—sitting at the statue's base. Major department stores (Galleriet, Xhibition, and Telegrafen) are all nearby.

The "blue stone," a popular meeting point at the far end of the square, marks the center of a park-like swath known as **Ole Bulls Plass,** leading from the National Theater (above on right) to a little lake (below on left). The theater, built in Art Nouveau style in 1909, was founded by violinist Ole Bull in 1850 and was the first to host plays in the Norwegian language. After 450 years of Danish and Swedish rule, 19th-century Norway enjoyed a cultural awakening, and Bergen became an artistic power. Ole Bull (a pop idol and heartthrob in his day—women fainted when they heard him play his violin) collaborated with the playwright Henrik Ibsen. Ibsen commissioned Edvard Grieg to write the music for his *Peer Gynt.* These three lions of Norwegian culture all lived and worked together right here in Bergen. The park that spills downhill from the theater has a pleasantly bustling urban ambience. It leads past a popular fountain of Ole Bull (under the trees) to a cast-iron pavilion given to the city by Germans in 1889, and on to the little man-made lake (Lille Lungegårdsvann), which is circled by an enjoyable path. This green zone is considered a park and is cared for by the local parks department.

▲▲**Fløibanen Funicular**—Bergen's popular funicular climbs 1,000 feet in seven minutes to the top of Mount Fløyen for the best view of the town, surrounding islands, and fjords all the way to the west coast. The top is a popular picnic or pizza-to-go dinner spot (a Peppe's Pizza is tucked behind the Hanseatic Museum, a block away from the base of the lift). The recommended

Fløien Folkerestaurant, at the top of the funicular, offers afford-able self-service food all day and fancier dinners in the evenings (both restaurant and cafeteria open daily in summer; off-season only the cafeteria is open and only on weekends). Sunsets are great here. The top is also the starting point for many peaceful hikes (ask for the *Fløyen Hiking Map* at the Fløibanen ticket window at the base). It's a pleasant but steep walk back down into Bergen. To save your knees, get off at the Promsgate stop halfway down and then wander through the delightful cobbled and shiplap lanes (note that only the :00 and :30 departures stop at Promsgate). This funicular is regularly used by locals commuting into and out of downtown.

Cost and Hours: 80 kr round-trip, May-Aug Mon-Sat 8:00-24:00, Sun 9:00-24:00, off-season until 23:00, departures generally 4/hour—on the quarter-hour most of the day, runs continuously if busy, tel. 55 33 68 00, www.floibanen.no.

Leprosy Museum (Lepramuseet)—Leprosy is also known as "Hansen's Disease" because in the 1870s a Bergen man named

Armauer Hansen did ground-breaking work in understanding the ailment. This unique museum is in St. Jørgens Hospital, a lep-rosarium that dates back to about 1700. Up until the 19th century, as much as 3 percent of Norway's population had leprosy. This hos-pital—once called "a graveyard for the living" (its last patient died in 1946)—has a meager exhibit in a thought-provoking shell attached to a 300-year-old church. It's really only worth your time and money if you stick around for one of the free tours, which generally leave at the top of the hour or by request.

Cost and Hours: 50 kr, mid-May-Aug daily 11:00-15:00, closed Sept-mid-May, between train station and Bryggen at Kong Oscars Gate 59, tel. 55 96 11 55, www.bymuseet.no.

▲Aquarium (Akvariet)—Small but fun, this aquarium claims to be the second-most-visited sight in Bergen. It's wonderfully laid out and explained in English. Check out the informative exhibit downstairs on Norway's fish-farming industry.

Cost and Hours: 200 kr, kids-150 kr, cheaper off-season, daily May-Aug 9:00-19:00, Sept-April 10:00-18:00, feeding times at the top of most hours in summer, cheery cafeteria with light sandwiches, Nordnesbakken 4, tel. 55 55 71 71, www.akvariet.no.

Getting There: It's at the tip of the peninsula on the south end of the harbor—about a 20-minute walk or short ride on bus #11 from the city center. Or hop on the handy little Vågen "Akvariet" ferry that sails from the Fish Market to near the aquarium (40 kr one-way, 60 kr round-trip, 2/hour, daily May-Aug 10:00-18:00).

Nearby: The lovely park behind the aquarium has views of the sea and a popular swimming beach (described later, under "Activities in Bergen"). The totem pole erected here was a gift from Bergen's sister city in the US—Seattle.

▲**Gamle Bergen (Old Bergen)**—This Disney-cute gathering of 50-some 18th- and 19th-century shops was founded in 1934 to save old buildings from destruction as Bergen modernized. Each of the houses was moved from elsewhere in Bergen and reconstructed here. Together, they create a virtual town that offers a cobbled look at the old life. It's free to wander through the town and park to enjoy the facades of the historic buildings, but to get into the 20 or so museum buildings, you'll have to join a tour (departing on the hour 10:00-16:00).

Cost and Hours: Free entry, 50-kr tour (in English) required for access to buildings; mid-May-early Sept daily 9:00-17:00, closed off-season, tel. 55 39 43 04, www.gamlebergen.museum.no.

Getting There: Take any bus heading west from Bryggen (such as #20, direction: Lonborg) to Gamle Bergen (first stop after the tunnel). You'll get off at a freeway pullout and walk 200 yards, following signs to the museum. Any bus heading back into town takes you to the center (buses come by every few minutes). With the easy bus connection, there's no reason to taxi.

▲**Bergen Art Museum (Bergen Kunstmuseum)**—If you need to get out of the rain (and you enjoyed the National Gallery in Oslo), check out this collection of collections in several neighboring buildings. You'll see works by leading Norwegian painters such as Harriet Backer, J. C. Dahl, Christian Krohg, and Edvard Munch, plus an interesting modern art section. Small description sheets in English are in each room.

Cost and Hours: 80 kr, daily 11:00-17:00, closed Mon mid-Sept-mid-May, Rasmus Meyers Allé 3, tel. 55 56 80 00, www.kunstmuseene.no.

Activities in Bergen

▲**Strolling**—Bergen is a great town for wandering. The harborfront is a fine place to kick back and watch the pigeons mate. Other good areas to explore are over the hill past Klostergaten, Knosesmauet, and Ytre Markevei; near Marken; and the area behind Bryggen.

Swimming—Bergen has two seaside public swimming areas: one at the aquarium and the other in Gamle Bergen. Each is a great local scene on a hot sunny day. **Nordnes Sjøbad,** near the aquarium, offers swimmers an outdoor heated pool and a protected area of the sea (40 kr, kids-20 kr, mid-May-Aug Mon-Fri 7:00-19:00, Sat 7:00-14:00, Sun 10:00-14:00, Sat-Sun until 19:00

in good weather, closed off-season, Nordnesparken 30, tel. 55 90 21 70). **Sandviken Sjobad,** at Gamle Bergen, is free. It comes with changing rooms, a roped-off bit of the bay (no pool), a high dive, and lots of sunbathing space.

▲▲The Bergen Folklore Show— Enjoy an intimate and charming hour-long program of traditional music and dance in the historic Schøtstuene (Hanseatic Assembly Rooms). Dancers are accompanied by musicians playing the mouth organ and Hardanger fiddle (120-kr tickets sold by TI and at door, mid-June-late Aug, Tue at 21:00, a few steps below St. Mary's Church, tel. 55 55 20 06, mobile 97 52 86 30).

Sights near Bergen

▲Ulriken643 Cable Car—It's amazingly quick and easy to zip to the 643-meter-high (that's 2,110 feet) summit of Ulriken, the

tallest mountain near Bergen. Stepping out of the cable car, you enter a different world, with views stretching to the ocean. A chart clearly shows the many well-marked and easy hikes that fan out over the vast rocky and grassy plateau above the tree line (circular walks of various lengths, a 40-minute hike down, and a 4-hour hike to the top of the **Fløibanen funicular**). For less exercise, you can simply sunbathe, crack open a picnic, or enjoy the Ulriken restaurant.

Getting There: To get from downtown Bergen to the cable car, you can take a blue Bergen Sightseeing hop-on, hop-off bus (245 kr includes cable-car ride, ticket valid 24 hours, May-Sept daily 10:00-17:30, 2/hour, departs Fish Market and Bryggen, also stops at aquarium, buy ticket on board or at TI). The cable-car ride takes five minutes (prices without bus ride: 145 kr round-trip, 80 kr one-way, 8/hour, daily 9:00-21:00, off-season until 17:00, tel. 53 64 36 43, www.ulriken643.no).

▲▲Edvard Grieg's Home, Troldhaugen—Norway's greatest composer spent his last 22 summers here (1885-1907), soaking up inspirational fjord beauty and composing many of his greatest works. Grieg fused simple Norwegian folk tunes with the bombast of Europe's Romantic style. In a dreamy Victorian setting, Grieg's "Hill of the Trolls" is pleasant for anyone and essential for Grieg fans. You can visit his house on your own, but it's more enjoyable if you take the included 20-minute tour. The house and adjacent museum are full of memories and artifacts, including the composer's Steinway. The walls are festooned with photos of the musical and literary superstars of his generation. When the hugely popular Grieg died in 1907, 40,000 mourners attended his funeral. His little studio hut near the water makes you want to sit down and modulate.

Cost and Hours: 80 kr, includes guided tour in English, daily May-Sept 9:00-18:00, Oct-April 10:00-16:00, tel. 55 92 29 92, www.troldhaugen.com.

Concerts: Ask at the TI about piano performances in the concert hall at Grieg's home—a gorgeous venue with the fjord stretching out behind the big black grand piano (220 kr, concerts roughly mid-June-late Aug Sun and Wed at 18:00, free shuttle bus from TI if you show concert ticket). Delightful 30-minute lunch piano concerts are offered daily at 13:00 in peak season (20 kr plus entry ticket, daily June-Aug, Mon-Sat in Sept).

Getting to Troldhaugen: Bergen's slick **tram** drops you a long 20-minute walk from Troldhaugen. Catch the tram in the city center at its terminus on Kaigaten and get off at the stop called Hop. Walk in the direction of Bergen (about 25 yards), cross at the crosswalk, and follow signs to Troldhaugen. Part of the way is on a pedestrian/bike path; you're halfway there when the path crosses over a busy highway. If you want to make the 13:00 lunchtime concert, leave Bergen at 12:00.

To avoid the long walk from the tram stop, consider the three-hour city bus tour promoted by the TI, which comes with informative recorded narration, gets you to within a five-minute walk of Troldhaugen, and includes a brief tour of the house (300 kr, May-Sept daily at 11:00). If you're driving into Bergen from the east (such as from the Sognefjord), you'll drive right by Troldhaugen on your way into town.

Fantoft Stave Church—This huge, preserved-in-tar stave church burned down in 1992. It was rebuilt and reopened in 1997, but it will never be the same. Situated in a quiet forest next to a mysterious stone cross, this replica of a 12th-century wooden church is bigger, though no better, than others covered in this book. But it's worth a look if you're in the neighborhood, even after-hours, for its atmospheric setting.

Cost and Hours: 42 kr, mid-May-mid-Sept daily 10:30-18:00, interior closed off-season, no English information, tel. 55 28 07 10.

Getting There: The church is located three miles south of Bergen on E39 in Paradis. Take the tram to the Paradis stop, walk uphill to the parking lot on the left, and find the steep footpath to the church.

Shopping in Bergen

Most shops, including Husfliden (described below), are open Mon-Fri 9:00-17:00, Thu until 19:00, Sat 9:00-15:00, and closed Sunday. Many of the tourist shops at the harborfront strip along Bryggen are open daily—even during holidays—until 20:00 or 21:00.

Bryggen is bursting with sweaters, pewter, and trolls. The **Husfliden** shop is popular for its handmade Norwegian sweaters and goodies (fine variety and quality but expensive, just off Torget, the market square, at Vågsallmenninge 3, tel. 55 54 47 40).

The **Galleriet** shopping center on Torgalmenningen has six floors of shops, cafés, and restaurants. You'll find a pharmacy, photo shops, clothing, sporting goods, bookstores, mobile-phone shops, an Internet café, and a basement grocery store (Mon-Fri 9:00-20:00, Sat 9:00-18:00, closed Sun).

Sleeping in Bergen

Busy with business travelers and increasingly popular with tourists, Bergen can be jammed any time of year. But with economic problems plaguing Norway, once proud and pricey hotels may be willing to make deals. You might save a bundle by emailing the bigger hotels and asking for their best price. Otherwise, Bergen has some fine budget alternatives to normal hotels that can save you a bundle.

Hotels

$$$ Hotel Havnekontoret, with the best location in town, fills a grand old shipping headquarters dating from the 1920s. It's an especially fine value on weekends and in the summer, for those who eat the included dinner. While part of a chain, it has a friendly

---

Sleep Code

(5 kr = about $1, country code: 47)

S = Single, **D** = Double/Twin, **T** = Triple, **Q** = Quad, **b** = bathroom, **s** = shower. You can assume that staff speak English, breakfast is included, and credit cards are accepted unless otherwise noted.

   To help you sort easily through these listings, I've divided the accommodations into three categories, based on the price for a standard double room with bath during high season:

$$$ Higher Priced—Most rooms 1,400 kr or more.

  $$ Moderately Priced—Most rooms between 900-1,400 kr.

   $ Lower Priced—Most rooms 900 kr or less.

   Prices can change without notice; verify the hotel's current rates online or by email. For other updates, see www.ricksteves.com/update.

---

spirit. Guests are welcome to climb its historic tower (with a magnificent view) or enjoy its free sauna and exercise room downstairs. The hotel's 116 rooms are expensive during the week, and half-price on weekends and through most of the summer. If you aren't interested in fancy dining, the room price includes virtually all your food—a fine breakfast, self-service waffles in the afternoon, fruit and coffee all day, and a light dinner buffet each evening. If you take advantage of them, these edible extras are easily worth 600 kr per day per couple, making the cost of this fancy hotel little more than a hostel (Db during business peak-2,300 kr, Db Fri-Sun and most of summer-1,500-1,700 kr, extra bed-300 kr, book online to save, free Wi-Fi, facing the harbor across the street from the Radisson Blu Royal Hotel at Slottsgaten 1, tel. 55 60 11 00, www.choicehotels.no, cc.havnekontoret@choice.no).

$$$ Hotel Park Pension is classy, comfortable, and in a fine residential neighborhood a 15-minute uphill walk from the town center (10 minutes from the train station). It's tinseled in Old World, lived-in charm, yet comes with all of today's amenities. The 35 rooms are split between two buildings, with 22 in the classy old-fashioned hotel and 13 in the modern annex across the street (Sb-1,150 kr, Db-1,550 kr, extra bed-350 kr, winter weekend discounts, free Wi-Fi, Harald Hårfagres Gate 35, tel. 55 54 44 00, fax 55 54 44 44, www.parkhotel.no, booking@parkhotel.no).

$$$ Thon Hotel Rosenkrantz, with 129 rooms, is one block behind Bryggen, between the Bryggens Museum and the Fløibanen funicular station—right in the heart of Bergen's appealing old quarter. However, the next-door nightclub is noisy on

Friday and Saturday nights—be sure to request a quiet room (average rates: Sb-1,295 kr, Db-1,695 kr, elevator, free Internet access and Wi-Fi, Rosenkrantzgate 7, tel. 55 30 14 00, www.thonhotels .no/rosenkrantz, rosenkrantz@thonhotels.no).

$$ P-Hotel has 43 basic rooms just up from Ole Bulls Plass. While it's not particularly charming and some rooms come with street noise, it's got a prime location. Ask for a room facing the courtyard in the renovated wing (Sb-950 kr, Db-1,250 kr, credit card only—no cash, box breakfast in your room, elevator, free Wi-Fi, Vestre Torggate 9, tel. 80 04 68 35, www.p-hotels.no, bergen@p-hotels.no).

$$ Thon Hotel Bergen Brygge, beyond Bryggen near Håkon's Hall, is part of Thon's cheaper "Budget" chain. However, the 229 spartan rooms can be just about as nice as those in its sister hotels. Because of its relatively good prices and great location, it fills up quickly—book ahead. Light sleepers, beware: Many rooms face the fortress grounds, which sometimes host summer evening concerts. Ask for a room on the quiet side, bring earplugs, or go elsewhere (Db-1,100-1,400 kr, discounts unlikely but you save if you book online, elevator, free Internet access and Wi-Fi, Bradbenken 3, tel. 55 30 87 00, fax 55 32 94 14, www.thonhotels .com/bergenbrygge, bergenbrygge@thonhotels.no).

$ Hotel Victoria is an old hotel turned into a college dorm that becomes a utilitarian, minimalist budget hotel each summer. There are no public spaces, the tiny reception is open only 9:00-23:00, and you won't get your towels changed. But its 40 modern, bright, simple rooms are plenty comfortable for the price (open June-Aug only, Sb-795 kr, Db-895 kr, Tb-1,295 kr, free Wi-Fi, Kong Oscarsgate 29, tel. 55 31 44 04, www.basichotels.no, victoria @basichotels.no).

$ Citybox is a unique, no-nonsense hotel concept: plain, white, clean, and practical. It rents 55 rooms online and provides you with a confirmation number. Check-in is automated—just punch in your number and get your ticket. The reception is staffed daily 9:00-16:00 (S-500 kr, Sb-600 kr, D-700 kr, Db-900 kr, extra bed-150 kr, family room for up to four-1,200 kr, 50-kr service fee if booking by phone, no breakfast, elevator, just away from the bustle in a mostly residential part of town at Nygårdsgaten 31, tel. 55 31 25 00, www.citybox.no, post@citybox.no).

Private Homes and Pensions

If you're looking for local character and don't mind sharing a shower, these accommodations—far more quiet, homey, and convenient than hostel beds—might just be the best values in town. Both require guests to climb outdoor stairways, which may be tough for those not packing light.

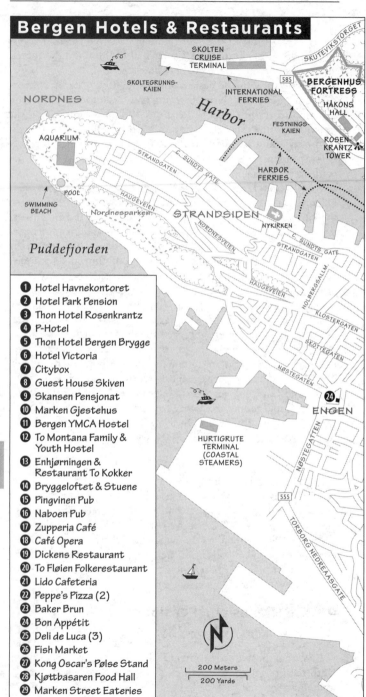

Bergen Hotels & Restaurants

SKUTEVIKSTORGET

SKOLTEN CRUISE TERMINAL

585

BERGENHUS FORTRESS

SKOLTEGRUNNS-KAIEN

INTERNATIONAL FERRIES

HÅKONS HALL

NORDNES

Harbor

FESTNINGS-KAIEN

ROSEN-KRANTZ TOWER

AQUARIUM

STRANDGATEN

C. SUNDTS GATE

HARBOR FERRIES

HAUGEVEIEN

POOL

SWIMMING BEACH

Nordnesparken

STRANDSIDEN

NORDNESVEIEN

NYKIRKEN

C. SUNDTS GATE

Puddefjorden

STRANDGATEN

HOLBERGSALM.

HAUGEVEIEN

KLOSTERGATEN

SKOTTEGATEN

NØSTEGATEN

24

ENGEN

HURTIGRUTE TERMINAL (COASTAL STEAMERS)

NØSTEGATTEN

555

TORBORG NEDREAASGATE

N

200 Meters

200 Yards

1. Hotel Havnekontoret
2. Hotel Park Pension
3. Thon Hotel Rosenkrantz
4. P-Hotel
5. Thon Hotel Bergen Brygge
6. Hotel Victoria
7. Citybox
8. Guest House Skiven
9. Skansen Pensjonat
10. Marken Gjestehus
11. Bergen YMCA Hostel
12. To Montana Family & Youth Hostel
13. Enhjørningen & Restaurant To Kokker
14. Bryggeloftet & Stuene
15. Pingvinen Pub
16. Naboen Pub
17. Zupperia Café
18. Café Opera
19. Dickens Restaurant
20. To Fløien Folkerestaurant
21. Lido Cafeteria
22. Peppe's Pizza (2)
23. Baker Brun
24. Bon Appétit
25. Deli de Luca (3)
26. Fish Market
27. Kong Oscar's Pølse Stand
28. Kjøttbasaren Food Hall
29. Marken Street Eateries

BERGEN

BERGEN

$ Guest House Skiven is a humble little place beautifully situated on a steep, traffic-free cobbled lane called "the most painted street in Bergen." Alf and Elizabeth Heskja (who live upstairs) rent four non-smoking doubles that share a shower, two WCs, and a kitchen (D-550 kr for Rick Steves readers, no breakfast, free Wi-Fi, 4 blocks from station at Skivebakken 17, tel. 55 31 30 30, mobile 90 05 30 30, www.skiven.no, rs@skiven.no). From the train station, go down Kong Oscars Gate, uphill on D. Krohns Gate, and up the stairs at the end of the block on the left.

$ Skansen Pensjonat (not to be confused with the nearby Skansen Guest House) is situated 100 yards directly behind the entrance to the Fløibanen funicular. Jannicke Alvær rents seven tastefully decorated rooms with views over town (small non-view S-450 kr, larger S-500 kr, D-700 kr, fancy D on corner with view and balcony-800 kr, apartment-850 kr, includes breakfast, 2 showers on ground floor, 2 WCs, sinks in rooms, family room with TV; all non-smoking, free Wi-Fi, Vetrlidsalmenning 29, tel. 55 31 90 80, www.skansen-pensjonat.no, mail@skansen-pensjonat.no). Follow the switchback road behind the Fløibanen funicular station to the paved plateau with benches, and look for the sign.

Dorms and Hostels

$ Marken Gjestehus is a quiet, tidy, and conveniently positioned 100-bed place between the station and the harborfront. Its rooms, while spartan, are modern and cheery (dorm bed in 8-bed room-195 kr, in 4-bed room-225 kr, S-495 kr, D-570 kr, Db-895 kr, extra bed-135 kr, sheets-65-kr one-time fee, towels-15 kr, breakfast-115 kr at nearby hotel, free Wi-Fi, elevator, kitchen, laundry, open all year but with limited reception hours, fourth floor at Kong Oscars Gate 45, tel. 55 31 44 04, fax 55 31 60 22, www.marken-gjestehus.com, post@marken-gjestehus.com).

$ Bergen YMCA Hostel, located a block in front of the TI and two blocks from the Fish Market, is the best location for the price, and its rooms are nicely maintained (bunk in 12- to 32-bed dorm with shared shower and kitchen-180 kr, bunk in 4-6-bed family room with private bathroom and kitchen-280-320 kr, Db with kitchen-900 kr, includes sheets, breakfast-65 kr, pay Internet access, free Wi-Fi, roof terrace, fully open June-Aug, no dorm beds off-season, Nedre Korskirkeallmenningen 4, tel. 55 60 60 55, www.bergenhostel.com, ymca@online.no).

Away from the Center: **$ Montana Family & Youth Hostel (IYHF),** while one of Europe's best, is high-priced for a hostel and way out of town. Still, the bus connections (#31, 20 minutes from the center) and the facilities—modern rooms, classy living room, no curfew, huge free parking lot, and members' kitchen—are excellent (dorm bed in 20-bed room-215 kr—cheaper off-season, bed in Q-280 kr, Sb-660 kr, Db-830 kr, 10 percent cheaper for members, sheets-70 kr, includes breakfast, 30 Johan Blytts Vei, tel. 55 20 80 70, www.montana.no, booking@montana.no).

Eating in Bergen

Bergen has numerous choices: restaurants with rustic, woody atmosphere, candlelight, and steep prices (main dishes around 300 kr); trendy pubs and cafés that offer good-value meals (100-190 kr); cafeterias, chain restaurants, and ethnic eateries with less ambience where you can get quality food at lower prices (100-150 kr); and take-away sandwich shops, bakeries, and cafés for a light bite (50-100 kr).

You can always get a glass or pitcher of water at no charge, and fancy places give you free seconds on potatoes—just ask. Remember, if you get your food to go, it's taxed at a lower rate and you'll save 12 percent.

Splurges in Bryggen

You'll pay a premium to eat at these three restaurants, but you'll have a memorable meal in a pleasant setting. If it's beyond your budget, remember that you can fill up on potatoes and drink tap water to dine for exactly the price of the dinner plate.

Enhjørningen Restaurant ("The Unicorn") is *the* place in Bergen for fish. With thickly painted walls and no right angles, this dressy-yet-old-time wooden interior wins my "Bryggen Atmosphere" award. The dishes, while not hearty, are close to gourmet and beautifully presented (300-330-kr main dishes, 530-600-kr multi-course meals, nightly 16:00-22:30, #29 on Bryggen harborfront—look for anatomically correct unicorn on the old wharf facade and dip into the alley and up the stairs, tel. 55 30 69 50).

Restaurant To Kokker, down the alley from Enhjørningen (and with the same owners), serves more meat and game. The prices and quality are equivalent, but even though it's also in an elegant old wooden building, I like the Unicorn's atmosphere much better (most main dishes around 350 kr, 600-685-kr multicourse meals, Mon-Sat 17:00-23:00, closed Sun, tel. 55 30 69 55).

Bryggeloftet & Stuene Restaurant, in a brick building just before the wooden stretch of Bryggen, is a vast eatery serving seafood, vegetarian, and traditional meals. To dine memorably yet affordably, this is your best Bryggen bet. Upstairs feels more elegant and less touristy than the main floor—if there's a line downstairs, just head on up (145-165-kr lunches, 200-350-kr dinners, Mon-Sat 11:00-23:30, Sun 13:00-23:30, #11 on Bryggen harborfront, try reserving a view window upstairs, tel. 55 30 20 70).

Deals near Ole Bulls Plass

Bergen's "in" cafés are stylish, cozy, small, and open very late—a great opportunity to experience its yuppie scene. Around the cinema on Neumannsgate, there are numerous ethnic restaurants, including Italian, Middle Eastern, and Chinese.

Pingvinen Pub ("The Penguin") is a homey place in a charming neighborhood, serving traditional Norwegian home cooking to an enthusiastic local clientele. The pub has only indoor seating, with a long row of stools at the bar and five charming, living-room-cozy tables—a great setup for solo diners. After the kitchen closes, the place stays open very late as a pub. For unpretentious Norwegian cooking in a completely untouristy atmosphere, this is one of your best budget choices (140-190-kr main dishes, Sun-Thu 14:00-12:45, Fri-Sat 12:00-20:45, Vaskerelven 14 near the National Theater, tel. 55 60 46 46).

Naboen (which means "neighbor") is another good deal, but only if you skip the tableclothed main-floor dining room and go straight downstairs to the popular pub. The bar menu features Swedish specialties for 100-160 kr—the plank steak with potatoes and veggies is a bargain. The draft beers (*Fatøl*) are also relatively inexpensive—for Norway (daily 16:00-23:00 except Sun until 22:00, bar open much later, Sigurdsgate 4, tel. 55 90 02 90).

Zupperia, a café in the basement of the Bergen Art Gallery's Stenersen wing, has cool ambience and even cooler prices. The cuisine has a slight Asian twist (the Thai soup is a local favorite), but you can also find burgers, salads, and Norwegian standards (75-150 kr). The 109-kr lasagna special (includes bread and salad) is a steal in this high-price city. If you're not very hungry, you can order off the lunch menu any time of day (Sun-Thu 12:00-22:00, Fri-Sat until 22:30; facing the museum, go to the entrance on the ground level at the right, Nordahl Bruns Gate 9, tel. 55 55 81 14).

Café Opera, with a playful-slacker vibe, is the hip budget choice for its loyal, youthful following. With two floors of seating and tables out front across from the theater, it's a winner (light 30-40-kr sandwiches until 16:00, 100-150-kr dinners, daily 10:00-24:00, occasional live music, live locals nightly, English newspapers in summer, chess, around the left side of the theater at Engen 18, tel. 55 23 03 15).

Dickens is a lively, checkerboard, turn-of-the-century-feeling place serving fish, chicken, and steak. The window tables in the atrium are great for people-watching, as is the fine outdoor terrace, but you'll pay higher prices for the view. To save money, go for lunch and skip the view (150-kr lunches, 250-300-kr dinners, Mon-Sat 11:00-23:00, later on Fri and Sat, Sun 13:00-23:00, reservations smart, Kong Olav V's Plass 4, tel. 55 36 31 30).

Atop Mount Fløyen, at the Top of the Funicular

Fløien Folkerestaurant offers meals with a panoramic view. The cheaper cafeteria section has a light menu, with coffee, cake, and sandwiches for around 60 kr and a 139-kr soup buffet (May-Aug daily 10:00-22:00, Sept-April Sat-Sun only 12:00-17:00). The restaurant section has decent, expensive dinners with an emphasis on locally caught fish for about 300-350 kr (150-200-kr lighter dishes, May-Aug daily 17:00-23:00, restaurant closed Sept-April, tel. 55 33 69 99).

Cafeteria Overlooking the Fish Market

Lido offers basic, affordable food with great harbor and market views, better ambience than most self-serve places, and a museum's worth of old town photos on the walls. For cold items (such as open-face sandwiches and desserts, 50-80 kr), grab what you want, pay the cashier, and find a table. For hot dishes (120-170-kr Norwegian standards, including one daily special discounted to 109 kr), grab a table, order and pay at the cashier, and they'll bring your food to you (June-Aug Mon-Fri 10:00-22:00, Sat-Sun 13:00-22:00; Sept-May Mon-Sat 10:00-19:00, Sun 13:00-19:00; second floor at Torgalmenningen 1a, tel. 55 32 59 12).

Good Chain Restaurants

You'll find these tasty chain restaurants in Bergen and throughout Norway. All of these are open long hours daily (shorter off-season). In good weather, enjoy a take-out meal with sun-worshipping locals in Bergen's parks.

Peppe's Pizza has cold beer and good pizzas (medium size for 1-2 people-175-200 kr, large for 2-3 people-200-250 kr, take-out possible; consider the Moby Dick, with curried shrimp, leeks, and bell peppers). There are six Peppe's in Bergen, including one behind the Hanseatic Museum near the Fløibanen funicular station and another inside the Zachariasbryggen harborfront complex, next to the Fish Market (with views over the harbor).

Baker Brun makes 50-70-kr sandwiches, including wonderful shrimp baguettes and pastries such as *skillingsbolle*—cinnamon rolls—warm out of the oven (open from 9:00, seating inside or take-away; several locations including Bryggen and the Storsenter shopping mall next to the bus station).

Bon Appétit sells 60-kr baguette sandwiches and wraps, plus ice cream (locations include Baneveien 15 and Bryggen). Restaurant desserts run 100 kr; strolling with an ice-cream cone can save plenty.

Deli de Luca is a cut above other take-away joints, adding sushi and calzones to the normal lineup of sandwiches. While a bit more expensive than the others, the variety and quality are appealing (open 24/7; other branches in train station and near Ole Bulls Plass at Torggaten 5—with indoor seating, on corner of Engen and Vaskerelven, tel. 55 23 11 47).

Budget Bets

The **Fish Market** has lots of stalls bursting with salmon sandwiches, fresh shrimp, fish-and-chips, and fish cakes. For a tasty, memorable, and inexpensive Bergen meal, assemble a seafood picnic here (ask for prices first; June-Aug daily 7:00-19:00, less lively on Sun; Sept-May Mon-Sat 7:00-16:00, closed Sun).

Kong Oscar's Pølse Stand, your classic hot-dog stand, sells a wide variety of sausages (various sizes and flavors—including reindeer). The well-described English menu makes it easy to order your choice of artery-clogging guilty pleasures (20-kr tiny weenie, 50-kr medium-size weenie, 75-kr jumbo, open daily 11:00-5:00 in the morning, you'll see the little hot-dog shack a block up Kong Oscar Gate from the harbor, Kenneht is the boss).

Kjøttbasaren, the restored meat market of 1887, is a genteel-feeling food hall with stalls selling groceries such as meat, cheese, bread, and olives—a great opportunity to assemble a bang-up picnic (Mon-Fri 10:00-17:00, Thu until 18:00, Sat 9:00-16:00, closed Sun).

Marken Pedestrian Street Eateries

This cobbled lane, leading from the train station to the harbor, is lined with creative little restaurants and trendy cafés. Strolling along here, you can choose among cheap chicken and burgers, the elegant **Bambus 33** for Vietnamese (daily 14:00-23:00, seating indoors and out, Marken 33, tel. 55 56 00 60), the **Taste of Indian** (69-kr daily special, daily 13:00-24:00, Marken 12, tel. 55 31 11 55), and the **Aura Café** for classy sandwiches and salads (Mon-Sat until 22:00, Sun until 19:00, indoors and out, Marken 9).

Bergen Connections

Bergen is conveniently connected to **Oslo** by plane and train (trains depart Bergen daily at 7:58, 10:28, 15:58, and 22:58—but no night train on Sat, arrive at Oslo seven scenic hours later, additional departures in summer and fall, confirm times at station, 50-kr seat reservation required—but free with first-class railpass, book well in advance if traveling mid-July-Aug). From Bergen, you can take the Norway in a Nutshell train/bus/ferry route; for information, see the Norway in a Nutshell chapter. Train info: tel. 81 50 08 88, www.nsb.no.

To get to **Stockholm** or **Copenhagen,** you'll go via Oslo. Before buying a ticket for a long train trip from Bergen, look into cheap flights.

By Express Boat to Balestrand and Flåm (on Sognefjord): A handy express boat links Bergen with Balestrand (4 hours) and Flåm (5.5 hours).

By Bus to Kristiansand: If you're heading to Denmark on the ferry from Kristiansand, catch the Haukeli express bus (departing Bergen daily at 7:30). After a nearly two-hour layover in Haukeli, take the bus at 14:40, arriving at 18:55 in Kristiansand in time for the evening ferry to Denmark.

By Boat to Stavanger: Flaggruten catamarans sail to Stavanger (1-2/day, 4.5 hours, 770 kr one-way, 990 kr round-trip; nearly half-price for students and railpass-holders; tel. 55 23 87 00 or 05505, www.tide.no). From Stavanger, trains run to Kristiansand and Oslo, and ships sail to Denmark.

By Boat to Denmark: Fjordline runs a boat from Bergen to Hirtshals, Denmark (17 hours; departs Mon and Wed at 13:00, Fri generally at 11:00; boat from Hirtshals runs Sun, Tue, and Thu; seat in reclining chair-around 1,500 kr, tel. 81 53 35 00, www .fjordline.com).

By Boat to the Arctic: Hurtigruten coastal steamers depart

nearly daily (mid-April-mid-Sept at 20:00, mid-Sept-mid-April at 22:30) for the seven-day trip north up the scenic west coast to Kirkenes on the Russian border.

This route was started in 1893 as a postal and cargo delivery service along the west coast of Norway. Although no longer delivering mail, their ships still fly the Norwegian postal flag by special permission and deliver people, cars, and cargo from Bergen to Kirkenes. A lifeline for remote areas, the ships call at 34 fishing villages and cities.

For the seven-day trip to Kirkenes, allow from $1,599 and up per person based on double occupancy (includes three meals per day, taxes, and port charges). Prices vary greatly depending on the season (highest June-July), cabin, and type of ship. Their fleet includes those with a bit of brass built in the 1960s, but the majority of the ships were built in the mid-1990s and later. Shorter voyages are possible (including even just a day trip to one of the villages along the route). Cabins should be booked well in advance. Ship services include a 24-hour cafeteria, a launderette on newer ships, and optional port excursions. Check online for senior and off-season (Oct-March) specials at www.hurtigruten.com.

Call Hurtigruten in New York (US tel. 866-552-0371) or in Norway (tel. 81 00 30 30). For most travelers, the ride makes a great one-way trip, but a flight back south is a logical last leg (rather than returning to Bergen by boat—a 12-day round-trip).

BERGEN

SOUTH NORWAY

Stavanger • Setesdal Valley • Kristiansand

South Norway is not about must-see sights or jaw-dropping scenery—it's simply pleasant and pretty. Spend a day in the harborside town of Stavanger. Delve into your Scandinavian roots at the Norwegian Emigration Center or into the oil industry at the surprisingly interesting Petroleum Museum. Window-shop in the old town, cruise the harbor, or hoof it up Pulpit Rock for a fine view.

A series of time-forgotten towns stretch across the Setesdal Valley, with sod-roofed cottages and locals who practice fiddles and harmonicas, rose painting, whittling, and gold- and silverwork. The famous Setesdal filigree echoes the rhythmical designs of the Viking era and Middle Ages. Each town has a weekly rotating series of hikes and activities for the regular, stay-put-for-a-week visitor. The upper valley is dead in the summer but enjoys a bustling winter.

In Kristiansand, Norway's answer to a seaside resort, promenade along the strand, sample a Scandinavian zoo, or set sail to Denmark.

Planning Your Time

Even on a busy itinerary, Stavanger warrants a day. If you are an avid genealogist, consider two. The port town is connected by boat to Bergen (and Hirtshals, Denmark) and by train to Kristiansand.

Frankly, without a car, the Setesdal Valley is not worth the trouble. There are no trains in the valley, bus schedules are as sparse as the population, and the sights are best for joyriding. If you're in Bergen with a car, and want to get to Denmark, this route is more interesting than repeating Oslo. On a three-week Scandinavian trip, I'd do it in one long day, as follows: 7:00—Leave Bergen;

9:00—Catch Kvanndal ferry to Utne; 10:00—Say good-bye to the last fjord at Odda; 13:00—Lunch in Hovden at the top of Setesdal Valley; 14:00—Frolic south with a few short stops in the valley; 16:30—Arrive in Kristiansand for dinner. Spend the night and catch the 9:00 boat to Denmark the next morning.

Kristiansand is not a destination town, but rather a place to pass through, conveniently connecting Norway to Denmark by ferry.

Stavanger

This burg of about 117,000 feels more cosmopolitan than most Norwegian cities. This is thanks in part to the oil industry, with its multinational workers and the money they bring into the city. Known as Norway's festival city, Stavanger hosts several lively events, including jazz in May (www.maijazz.no), chamber music in August (www.icmf.no), and a wooden boats festival in early September. With all of this culture, it's no surprise that Stavanger was named a European Capital of Culture for 2008.

Orientation to Stavanger

The most scenic and interesting parts of Stavanger surround its harbor. Here you'll find the Norwegian Emigration Center, lots of shops and restaurants, the indoor fish market, and a produce market (Mon-Fri 9:00-16:00, Sat 9:00-15:00, closed Sun). The artificial Lake Breiavatnet—bordered by Kongsgaten on the east and Olav V's Gate on the west—separates the train and bus stations from the harbor.

Tourist Information

The helpful staff at the TI can help you plan your time in Stavanger, and can also give you hiking tips and day-trip information. Pick up a free city guide and map (June-Aug daily 9:00-20:00; Sept-May Mon-Fri 9:00-16:00, Sat 9:00-14:00, closed Sun; Domkirkeplassen 3, tel. 51 85 92 00, www.regionstavanger.com).

Arrival in Stavanger

By Boat: Express boats from Bergen dock at Fiskepiren. From here, it's a five-minute walk to the center of town or to the train station. A taxi to a downtown hotel costs about 100 kr (tel. 51 90 90 90 or 51 90 90 50).

By Train and Bus: Stavanger's train and bus stations are a five-minute walk around Lake Breiavatnet to the harbor (train

Stavanger

1. Thon Hotel Maritim
2. Skansen Hotell & Gjestehus
3. Stavanger B&B
4. Nye La Piazza Restaurant
5. Vertshuset Mat & Vin Restaurant
6. Meny Supermarket
7. N. B. Sorensen's Dampskibsexpedition Pub & Restaurant
8. Sjøhuset Skagen Restaurant
9. Bølgen og Moi Restaurant
10. Fish Market
11. Boats to Lysefjord
12. Boats to Pulpit Rock & Bergen
13. Flybussen Stops (Airport Bus)
14. Bus to Fjordline Terminal (Ferries to Hirtshals, Denmark)

ticket and reservation office Mon-Fri 7:00-17:30, Sat 9:00-16:30, Sun 10:00-16:15). Luggage lockers and Norway-wide train time-tables are available at the train station.

By Plane: Stavanger's Sola Airport, about nine miles outside the city, is connected to downtown by the Flybussen (95 kr, buy ticket on bus, Mon-Fri 7:45-24:15, 3-4/hour, less Sat-Sun, 30 minutes, tel. 51 59 90 60, www.flybussen.no). This airport bus shuttles travelers to the bus station (Byterminalen) and train station (next to each other), the city center, and the boat terminal (Fiskepiren). To get to the airport from the city center, catch the shuttle at any of these stops.

Sights in Stavanger

▲▲Norwegian Petroleum Museum (Norskolje Museum)— This entertaining, informative museum—dedicated to the discovery of oil in Norway's North Sea in 1969 and the industry built up around it—offers something for everyone. With half of Western Europe's oil reserves, Norway is the Arabia of the North. Since the discovery of oil here in 1969, the formerly poor agricultural nation has been transformed into a world-class player. It's ranked

third among the world's top oil exporters, producing 3.2 billion barrels a day.

This museum describes how oil was formed, how it's found and produced, and what it's used for. There are interactive exhibits covering everything from the "History of the Earth" (4.5 billion years displayed on a large overhead globe, showing how our planet has changed—stay for the blast that killed the dinosaurs), to day-to-day life on an offshore platform, to petroleum products in our lives. Kids love the model drilling platform that they can climb on. The museum's architecture was designed to echo the foundations of the oil industry—bedrock (the stone building), slate and chalk deposits in the sea (slate floor of the main hall), and the rigs (cylindrical platforms). While the museum has its fair share of propaganda, it also has several good exhibits on the environmental toll of drilling and consuming oil.

Cost and Hours: 100 kr; June-Aug daily 10:00-19:00; Sept-May Mon-Sat 10:00-16:00, Sun 10:00-18:00; tel. 51 93 93 00, www.norskolje.museum.no. The small museum shop sells various petroleum-based products. The museum's Bølgen og Moi restaurant, which has an inviting terrace over the water, serves lunch and dinner (see listing under "Eating in Stavanger," later).

▲**Norwegian Emigration Center (Det Norske Utvandrer-senteret Ble)**—This fine museum, in an old warehouse near the wharf where the first boats sailed with emigrants to "Amerika" in 1825, is worth ▲▲▲ for anyone seeking his or her Norwegian roots. On the second floor you'll find a study center and library. It's free to use the computers and microfilm viewers to look up your relatives. The library is lined with shelves of *bygdebøker*—books from farm districts all over Norway, documenting the history of landowners and local families. For 300 kr per hour, the staff will give you a step-by-step consultation. Otherwise, they'll help answer questions and steer you in the right direction at no charge. If you want to look up relatives, do some homework ahead of time and bring at least two or three of the following: family surname, farm name, birth year, and emigration year. The third floor has a small exhibit everyone will enjoy. It tells the story of the first emigrants who left for America—why they left, the journey, and what life was like in the New World.

Cost and Hours: Library—free, museum—20 kr, Mon-Fri 9:00-15:00, closed Sat-Sun, Standkaien 31, tel. 51 53 88 60, www.emigrationcenter.com.

Stavanger Museum—This "museum" is actually nine different buildings/museums covered by one 100-kr ticket: highlights include the **Stavanger Museum,** featuring the history of the city and a zoological exhibit (Muségate 16); Stavanger **Sjøfartsmuseum,** the maritime museum (Nedre Strandgate 17-19); **Norsk Hermetikkmuseum,** the Norwegian canning museum (*brisling*—herring—is smoked mid-June-mid-Aug Tue and Thu, Øvre Strandgate 88A); **Ledaal,** a royal residence and manor house (Eiganesveien 45); and **Breidablikk,** a wooden villa from the late 1800s (Eiganesveien 40A). Pick up the handy brochure and buy your ticket from the TI.

Cost and Hours: Museums open mid-June-mid-Aug daily 11:00-16:00; off-season Tue-Sun 11:00-16:00, closed Mon, except Ledaal and Breidablikk—open Sun only; www.stavanger.museum.no.

Gamle Stavanger—Stavanger's "old town" centers on Øvre Strandgate, on the west side of the harbor. Wander the narrow, winding back lanes and peek into a workshop or gallery to find ceramics, glass, jewelry, and more.

Cost and Hours: Free, shops and galleries open roughly daily 10:00-17:00, coinciding with the arrival of cruise ships.

Stavanger Cathedral (Domkirke)—The cathedral was originally built in 1125 in a Norman style, with basket-handle Romanesque arches. After a fire badly damaged the church in the 13th century, a new chancel was added in the pointy-arched Gothic style. Have a look inside and see where the architecture changes about three-quarters of the way up the aisle.

Cost and Hours: Free; June-Aug daily 11:00-19:00; Sept-May Tue-Thu and Sat-Sun 11:00-16:00, closed Mon and Fri; tel. 51 84 04 00.

Day Trips to Lysefjord and Pulpit Rock

The nearby Lysefjord is an easy day trip. Those with more time (and strong legs) can hike to the top of the 1,800-foot-high Pulpit Rock (Preikestolen). The dramatic 270-square-foot plateau atop the rock gives you a fantastic view of the fjord and surrounding mountains. The TI has brochures for several boat tour companies and sells tickets.

Boat Tour of Lysefjord—Rodne Clipper Fjord Sightseeing offers 3.5-hour round-trip excursions from Stavanger to Lysefjord (including a view of Pulpit Rock). Boats depart from the east side of the harbor, in front of Skansegaten, along Skagenkaien. Buy your ticket on board or at the TI (390 kr; July-Aug daily at 10:30 and 14:30, Sat also at 12:00; May-June and Sept daily at 12:00; Oct-April Wed-Sun only at 12:00; tel. 51 89 52 70, www.rodne .no).

Ferry and Bus to Pulpit Rock—The Pulpit Rock trail's starting point, about an hour from Stavanger by a ferry-and-bus combination, is easily reached in summer by public transit. Then comes the hard part: the two-hour hike to the top. The total distance is 4.5 miles and the elevation gain is roughly 1,000 feet. It takes about two hours to get back down. Pack a lunch and plenty of water and wear good shoes.

There used to be ferry-and-bus packages to the trailhead from Stavanger, and the TI hopes to bring them back eventually. But for now you have to buy separate tickets for the ferry and the public bus. The following are approximate departure times—reconfirm all times at the TI before you go: Ferries leave from the Fiskepiren boat terminal to Tau (about 200-kr; mid-May-mid-Sept daily 2/ hour, best times are 8:00, 8:30, 9:00, and 9:30; mid-April-mid-May and late Sept daily at 9:45 only; no buses Oct-mid-April, ferry tel. 55 23 87 00, www.tidereiser.com). After you cross the fjord to Tau, buses meet the incoming ferries and head to Pulpit Rock cabin or to Preikestolen Fjellstue, the local youth hostel. Be sure to time your hike so that you can catch the last bus leaving Pulpit Rock cabin for the ferry (mid-April-Sept last bus leaves daily at 19:55). Pick up the helpful leaflet and confirm details at the TI. They can also give you details about more strenuous hikes.

Sleeping in Stavanger

$$$ Thon Hotel Maritim, about two blocks from the train station, near the artificial Lake Breiavatnet, can be a good deal for a big-business class hotel (Sb-1,225 kr, Db-1,525 kr; weekends Sb-795 kr, Db-1,195 kr; includes breakfast, elevator, free Wi-Fi, Kongsgaten 32, tel. 51 85 05 00, fax 51 85 05 01, www.thonhotels .no/maritim, maritim@thonhotels.no).

$$ Skansen Hotell & Gjestehus splits 28 rooms between its hotel (newer, more expensive rooms) and guesthouse (less expensive for essentially the same quality). Most of the rooms are on the street and can be noisy, but you're just off the harbor in a great location (Sb or Db-995 kr; about 200 kr cheaper on Fri-Sun nights, includes breakfast, non-smoking floors, elevator to most floors, Skansengate 7, tel. 51 93 85 00, fax 51 93 85 01, www.skansenhotel .no, post@skansenhotel.no).

$$ Stavanger B&B is your best home-away-from-home in Stavanger. This large red house among a sea of white houses has 14 tidy (and tiny) rooms, each with its own shower (but the toilet's down the hall). Waffles, coffee, and friendly chatter are served up every evening at 21:00 (Ss-790 kr, Ds-890 kr, Ts-990 kr, extra bed-150 kr, includes breakfast, 10-minute uphill walk behind train station in residential neighborhood, Vikedalsgate 1A, tel. 51 56 25 00, fax 51 56 25 01, www.stavangerbedandbreakfast.no, peck@online .no). If you let them know in advance, they may be able to pick you up or drop you off at the boat dock or train station.

Sleep Code

(5 kr = about $1, country code: 47)
S = Single, **D** = Double/Twin, **T** = Triple, **Q** = Quad, **b** = bathroom, **s** = shower. All of these places accept credit cards.

To help you sort easily through these listings, I've divided the accommodations into three categories, based on the price for a standard double room with bath during high season:

$$$ Higher Priced—Most rooms 1,000 kr or more.
$$ Moderately Priced—Most rooms between 600-1,000 kr.
$ Lower Priced—Most rooms 600 kr or less.

Prices can change without notice; verify the hotel's current rates online or by email. For other updates, see www .ricksteves.com/update.

Eating in Stavanger

Casual Dining

Nye La Piazza, just off the harbor, has an assortment of pasta and other Italian dishes, including pizza, for 145-200 kr (Mon 13:00-24:00, Tue-Sat 12:00-24:00, Sun 12:00-22:00, Rosenkildettorget 1, tel. 51 52 02 52).

Vertshuset Mat & Vin, in an elegant setting, serves up big portions of traditional Norwegian food and pricier contemporary fare (230-250 kr, light meals-100-150 kr, open daily 11:00-22:30, a block behind main drag along harbor at Skagen 10 ved Prostbakken, tel. 51 89 51 12).

Meny is a large supermarket with a good selection and a fine deli for super-picnic shopping (Mon-Fri 9:00-20:00, Sat until 18:00, closed Sun, in Straen Senteret shopping mall, Lars Hertervigs Gate 6, tel. 51 50 50 10).

Dining Along the Harbor with a View

The harborside street of Skansegata is lined with lively restaurants and pubs, and most serve food. Here are a couple options:

N. B. Sorensen's Dampskibsexpedition consists of a lively pub on the first floor (200-300 kr for pasta, fish, meat, and vegetarian dishes; Mon-Sat 11:00-24:00, Sun 13:00-23:00) and a fine-dining restaurant on the second floor, with tablecloths, view tables overlooking the harbor, and entrées from 300 kr (Mon-Sat 18:00-23:00, closed Sun, Skagenkaien 26, tel. 51 84 38 20). The restaurant is named after an 1800s company that shipped from this building, among other things, Norwegians heading to the US. Passengers and cargo waited on the first floor, and the manager's office was upstairs. The place is filled with emigrant-era memorabilia.

Sjøhuset Skagen, with a woodsy interior, invites diners to its historic building for lunch or dinner. The building, from the late 1700s, housed a trading company. Today, you can choose from local seafood specialties with an ethnic flair, as well as plenty of meat options (150-190-kr lunches, 230-345-kr dinners, Mon-Sat 11:30-24:00, Sun 13:00-22:00, Skagenkaien 16, tel. 51 89 51 80).

Bølgen og Moi, the restaurant at the Norwegian Petroleum Museum, has fantastic views over the harbor (150-kr lunches served daily 11:00-17:00, 200-300-kr dinners served Tue-Sat 18:00-24:00—reservations recommended, Kjeringholmen 748, tel. 51 93 93 53).

Stavanger Connections

From Stavanger by Train to: Kristiansand (4-7/day, 3.5 hours), **Oslo** (4/day, 8-8.5 hours, overnight possible).

By Boat to Bergen: Flaggruten catamarans sail between Bergen and Stavanger (1-2/day, 4.5 hours, 770 kr one-way, 990 kr round-trip; nearly half-price for students and railpass-holders; tel. 55 23 87 00, www.tide.no).

By Boat to Hirtshals, Denmark: For details on this boat, see the "Sailing Between Norway and Denmark" sidebar.

The Setesdal Valley

Welcome to the remote, and therefore very traditional, Setesdal Valley. Probably Norway's most authentic cranny, the valley is a

mellow montage of sod-roofed water mills, ancient churches, derelict farmhouses, yellowed recipes, and gentle scenery.

The Setesdal Valley joined the modern age with the construction of the valley highway in the 1950s. All along the valley you'll see the unique two-story storage sheds called *stabburs* (the top floor was used for storing clothes; the bottom, food) and many sod roofs. Even the bus stops have rooftops the local goats love to munch.

In the high country, just over the Sessvatn summit (3,000 feet), you'll see herds of goats and summer farms. If you see an *ekte geitost* sign, that means genuine, homemade goat cheese is for sale. (It's sold cheaper and in more manageable sizes in grocery stores.) To some, it looks like a decade's accumulation of earwax. I think it's delicious. Remember, *ekte* means all-goat—really strong. The more popular and easier-to-eat regular goat cheese is mixed with cow's-milk cheese.

For more information on the Setesdal Valley, see www.setesdal.com.

From Odda to Hovden

Attractions from here to Kristiansand are listed roughly from north to south.

Odda—At the end of the Hardanger Fjord, just past the huge zinc and copper industrial plant, you'll hit the industrial town of Odda (well-stocked **TI** for whole region and beyond; in summer Mon-Fri 9:00-19:00, Sat-Sun 11:00-17:00; off-season Mon-Fri 9:00-15:00, closed Sat-Sun; on market square at Torget 2-4, tel. 53 65 40 05, www.visitodda.com). Odda brags that Kaiser Wilhelm came here a lot, but he's dead and I'd drive right through. If you want to visit the tongue of a glacier, drive to Buar and hike an hour to Buarbreen. From Odda, drive into the land of boulders. The many mighty waterfalls that line the road seem to have hurled huge rocks (with rooted trees) into the rivers and fields. Stop at the giant double waterfall (on the left, pullout on the right, drive slowly through it if you need a car wash).

Røldal—Continue over Røldalsfjellet and into the valley below, where the old town of Røldal is trying to develop some tourism. Drive on by. Its old church isn't worth the time or money. Lakes are like frosted mirrors, making desolate huts come in pairs. Haukeliseter, a group of sod-roofed buildings filled with cultural clichés and tour groups, offers pastries, sandwiches, and reasonable hot meals (from 100 kr) in a lakeside setting. Try the traditional *rømmegrøt* porridge.

Haukeligrend—Haukeligrend is a bus/traffic junction, with daily bus service to/from Bergen and to/from Kristiansand (TI inside the café, open daily all year 10:00-19:00, brochures available all the time, TI staff available periodically, Internet access, tel. 35 07 03 67).

Hovden

A ski resort at the top of the Setesdal Valley (2,500 feet), Hovden is barren in the summer and painfully in need of charm. Still, it makes a good home base if you want to explore the area for a couple of days. Locals come here to walk and relax for a week.

Tourist Information: The TI is open all year (Mon-Fri 9:00-16:00, summer Sat 10:00-15:00, July also Sun 10:00-15:00, otherwise closed Sat-Sun, tel. 37 93 93 70, www.hovden.com, post @hovden.com).

Sights and Activities in Hovden

Canoe Rental—Hegni Center, on the lake at the south edge of town, rents canoes (230 kr/day, 120 kr/half-day, hourly rentals also possible, cash only, mid-June-mid-Aug daily 10:00-20:00, mid-Aug-mid-Sept daily 11:00-18:00, mid-Sept-mid-Oct Sat-Sun only 11:00-16:00, closed mid-Oct-mid-June, tel. 91 32 25 81).

Hikes near Hovden—Good walks offer you a chance to see reindeer, moose, arctic fox, and wabbits—so they say. The TI and most hotels stock brochures, maps, and other information about moderate to strenuous hikes in the area. Berry picking is popular in late August, when small, sweet blueberries are in season. A chairlift sometimes takes sightseers to the top of a nearby peak, with great views in clear weather (90 kr, July daily 11:00-14:00, Aug-mid-Oct Wed and Sat-Sun only). Hunting season starts in late August for reindeer (only in higher elevations) and later in the fall for grouse and moose.

Moose Safari—Per Johanson offers a 2.5-hour *Elg Safari* (that's Norwegian for "moose"). Learn more about this "king of the forest" during a late-night drive through Setesdal's back roads with a stop for moose-meat soup (340 kr, June-mid-Sept only; generally Tue, Fri, and Sun at 22:00—more often based upon demand; 50 percent money-back guarantee if you don't see a moose, tel. 37 93 93 70).

Museum of Iron Production (Jernvinnemuseum)—Learn about iron production from the late Iron Age (about 1,000 years ago) with the aid of drawings, exhibits, and recorded narration from a "Viking" (available in English). The museum is about 100 yards behind the Hegni Center (look for the sign from the road to *Jernvinnemuseum*).

Cost and Hours: Free, mid-June-mid-Aug daily 11:00-17:00, otherwise ask for the key at the TI or Hegni Center.

Swimming Pool—A super indoor spa/pool complex, the Hovden Badeland, provides a much-needed way to spend an otherwise dreary and drizzly early evening here.

SOUTH NORWAY

Cost and Hours: 125-145 kr for 3 hours or more, cheaper for shorter visits, daily 10:00-19:00 in summer, shorter hours off-season, tel. 37 93 93 93.

Sleeping and Eating in Hovden

$$ Hovden Fjellstoge is a big, old ski chalet renting Hovden's only cheap beds. Even if you're just passing through, their café is a good choice for lunch or an early dinner. Check out the mural in the balcony overlooking the lobby—an artistic rendition of this area's history. Behind the mural is a frightening taxidermy collection (hotel: Sb-750 kr, bunk-bed Db-990 kr, includes breakfast; cabins: from 650 kr for 2-4 people with bathroom and kitchen; dorms: dorm bed-200 kr, D-500 kr, 25 kr extra if you're not a hostel member, breakfast-70 kr, sheets-100 kr, towel-20 kr; tel. 37 93 95 43, www.hovdenfjellstoge.no, post@hovdenfjellstoge.no).

From Hovden to Kristiansand

▲**Dammar Vatnedalsvatn**—Nine miles south of Hovden is a two-mile side-trip to a 400-foot-high rock-pile dam (look for the *Dammar* signs). Enjoy the great view and impressive rockery. This is one of the highest dams in northern Europe. Read the chart. Sit out of the wind a few rows down the rock pile and ponder the vastness of Norwegian wood.

▲**Bykle**—The most interesting folk museum and church in Setesdal are in the teeny town of Bykle. The 17th-century church has two balconies—one for men and one for women (free, late June-mid-Aug daily 11:00-17:00, closed off-season; tel. 37 93 85 00, www.setesdalsmuseet.no). Drivers should note that the Bykle tollbooth accepts only exact change.

Grasbrokke—On the east side of the main road (at the *Grasbrokke* sign) is an old water mill (1630). A few minutes farther south, at the sign for *Sanden Såre Camping*, exit onto a little road to stretch your legs at another old water mill with a fragile, rotten-log sluice.

Flateland—The **Setesdal Museum** (Rygnestadtunet) offers more of what you saw at Bykle (30 kr, two buildings; late June-Aug daily 11:00-17:00; closed off-season; 1 mile east of the road, tel. 37 93 63 03, www.setesdalsmuseet.no). Unless you're a glutton for culture, I wouldn't do both.

Honneevje—Past Flateland is a nice picnic and WC stop, with a dock along the water for swimming...for hot-weather days or polar bears.

▲**Valle**—This is Setesdal's prettiest village (but don't tell Bykle). In the center, you'll find fine silver- and gold-work, homemade crafts next to the TI, and old-fashioned *lefse* cooking demonstrations (in the small log house by the Valle Motell). The fine suspension bridge attracts kids of any age (b-b-b-b-bounce) and anyone interested in a great view over the river to strange mountains that look like polished, petrified mudslides. European rock climbers, tired of the over-climbed Alps, often entertain spectators with their sport. Is anyone climbing? (TI tel. 37 93 75 27.)

Sleeping in Valle: **$$ Valle Motell** rents basic rooms (Sb-625 kr, Db-790 kr, includes breakfast, cabins with kitchen and bath but no breakfast-725-875 kr, tel. 37 93 77 00, www.valle-motell.no, post@valle-motell.no).

Nomeland—The Sylvartun silversmith shop sells Setesdal silver in a 17th-century log cabin (May-Sept daily 10:00-17:00, closed Oct-April, tel. 37 93 63 06).

Grendi—The Ardal Church (1827) has a rune stone in its yard. Three hundred yards south of the church is a 900-year-old oak tree.

Evje—A huge town by Setesdal standards (3,500 people), Evje is famous for its gems and mines. Fancy stones fill the shops here. Rock hounds find the nearby mines fun; for a small fee, you can hunt for gems. The TI is by Route 9 in the center of Evje (daily 10:00-15:00; tel. 37 93 14 00). The **Setesdal Mineral Park** is on the main road, two miles south of town (110 kr; July-mid-Aug daily 10:00-18:00, mid-Aug-mid-Oct Mon-Sat 10:00-16:00, Sun 10:00-17:00; May-June Mon-Sat 10:00-16:00, Sun 10:00-17:00, closed mid-Oct-April; tel. 38 00 30 70, www.mineralparken.no).

Kristiansand

This "capital of the south" has 80,000 inhabitants, a pleasant Renaissance grid-plan layout (Posebyen), a famous zoo with Norway's biggest amusement park (6 miles toward Oslo on the main road), a daily bus to Bergen, and lots of big boats going to Denmark. It's the closest thing to a beach resort in Norway. Markensgate is the bustling pedestrian market street—a pleasant place for good browsing, shopping, eating, and people-watching. Stroll along the Strand Promenaden (marina) to Christiansholm Fortress.

Orientation to Kristiansand

The TI is at Rådhusgata 6, a few blocks south of the boat, bus, and train station (mid-June-mid-Aug Mon-Fri 9:00-18:00, Sat 10:00-18:00, Sun 12:00-16:00; mid-Aug-mid-June Mon-Fri 9:00-15:30, closed Sat-Sun; tel. 38 12 13 14, www.visitkrs.no). The bank at the

Sailing Between Norway and Denmark

Two companies sail between the tips of Norway and Denmark. **Color Line** and **Fjordline** sail fast boats between Kristiansand, Norway, and Hirtshals, Denmark (2.25-3.25 hours). In addition, Fjordline boats connect Stavanger, Norway, and Hirtshals (11.5 hours, covered below). They also link Bergen with Hirtshals, though at 19.5 hours, it's a long haul.

Both Color Line and Fjordline offer car packages (covering up to 5 people and the car) and have various on-board amenities such as restaurants, coffee bars, duty-free shops, and several classes of travel. I've listed prices in euros, as they appear on the companies' websites.

Sailing Between Kristiansand and Hirtshals, Denmark: Color Line ships generally sail twice daily, all year, with a few more sailings added during summer, but mysteriously they sail only once a day in mid-April. Sailing from Norway to Denmark, Color Line boats usually leave Kristiansand at 8:00 and 16:30, arriving in Hirtshals at 11:15 and 19:45. Going from Denmark to Norway, the boats leave Hirtshals at 12:15 and 20:45, arriving in Kristiansand at 15:30 and midnight. Fares vary with day of week and season (cheaper weekdays and off-season). During the summer, one-way passenger fares start at €23/person mid-week, €33/person on weekends; car packages start at €77 mid-week and €102 on weekends.

Fjordline's seasonal ferry makes the crossing three times a day from late June to mid-August in a speedy 2.25 hours. The schedule is cut back to twice a day in late spring and early fall, with no ferries from October to April. In high season, sailing from Norway to Denmark, Fjordline boats leave Kristiansand at 7:00, 13:30, and 20:00, arriving in Hirtshals at 9:15, 15:45, and 22:15. Going from Denmark to Norway, the boats leave Hirtshals at 10:15, 16:45, and 23:15, arriving in Kristiansand at

Color Line terminal opens for each arrival and departure (even the midnight ones). The Fønix Kino cinema complex is within two blocks of the ferry and TI (70-100 kr, seven screens, movies shown in English, schedules at the entrance, tel. 38 10 42 00).

Sleeping in Kristiansand

(5 kr = about $1, country code: 47)
Kristiansand hotels are expensive and nondescript.

12:30, 19:00, and 1:30 in the morning. One-way passenger fares start at €25/person mid-week; car packages start at €60 mid-week.

Sailing Between Stavanger and Hirtshals, Denmark: Fjordline ships sailing from Norway to Denmark travel overnight, which can save you the cost of a hotel. Enjoy an evening in Stavanger, then sleep (or vomit) as you sail to Denmark. The boat generally sails four times a week (usually Mon, Wed, Fri, and Sat; departing Stavanger at either 19:00 or 21:00; arriving in Hirtshals at either 7:00 or 9:00 the next day). Ships sailing from Denmark to Norway leave Hirtshals in the morning or afternoon, arriving in Stavanger at night, not as desirable an option. These boats also sail four days a week (typically Tue, Thu, Sat, and Sun; departing Hirtshals at either 8:30, 12:30, 13:00 or 15:00; arriving in Stavanger at either 20:00, 00:15, 00:45, or 02:30 in the morning).

Fares vary, depending on how far in advance you book, the time of year, the day of the week, and the type of accommodation you want. Basic one-way fares range from €13 to €102, plus the cost of meals (€14 breakfast, €38 dinner) and accommodations (an airline-type seat or cabin). A seat, referred to as a "sleeperette," starts at €8.50. But if you're efficient enough to spend a night traveling, you owe yourself the comfort of a private room. Cabins start at €71 for a basic, two-berth, inside cabin, and go up to €420 for a "Fjord Class" cabin with a double bed and ocean view. Car packages range from €52 to €438.

Reservations: To get the best fare, book online and early—as soon as you can commit to a firm date (http://fjordline.no and www.colorline.com). This is especially true for Fjordline. Many cheaper fares are non-refundable and non-changeable, so be sure to check the details carefully when you book. Days of the week and departure/arrival times can vary—confirm specific schedules when you make your reservations.

Discounts: Color Line gives a discount off its regular fares to Eurailpass-holders, but you must call Color Line directly to book (Norway tel. 81 50 08 11 or 22 94 42 00; Denmark tel. 99 56 19 77). Fjordline doesn't offer discounts to Eurailers.

SOUTH NORWAY

$$$ Rica Hotel Norge is a modern option (Sb-1,395 kr, Db-1,595 kr, prices are averaged—rates vary with demand, Dronningensgate 5, tel. 38 17 40 00, fax 38 17 40 01, www.hotel-norge .no, firmapost@hotel-norge.no).

$$$ Thon Hotel Wergeland is inviting for a large chain hotel. It's within earshot of the church bells and busy Kirkegate—ask for a quieter room away from the street (Sb-1,395 kr, Db-1,695 kr, prices are averaged—rates vary with demand, includes breakfast, non-smoking rooms, no elevator, Internet access and Wi-Fi,

Kirkegate 15, tel. 38 17 20 40, fax 38 02 73 21, www.thonhotels.no
/wergeland, wergeland@thonhotels.no).

$$ At **Frobusdalen Rom,** Arild and Inger Nilssen rent seven
clean, bright rooms and two apartments in a beautiful guesthouse.
You'll have access to the garden, a full kitchen, and a large sit-
ting room filled with lovely antiques and wooden wainscot-
ing (Sb-400-500 kr, Db-600-800 kr, Db with balcony-1,200 kr,
apartment for 4-6 people-1,200-2,400 kr, higher prices are for
slightly larger room, no breakfast, laundry service available, free
parking; 5-minute walk from the boat, bus, and train terminals at
Frobusdalen 2; tel. 91 12 99 06, www.gjestehus.no, imsan@start
.no).

Eating in Kristiansand

The otherwise uninteresting harbor area has a cluster of wooden
buildings called **Fiskebasaren** ("Fish Bazaar"). The indoor fish
market is only open during the day, but numerous restaurants (serv-
ing fish, among other dishes) provide a nice atmosphere for dinner.
Follow Vester Strandgate past the Fønix movie theater to Østre
Strandgate, take a right, and follow the signs to Fiskebrygga.

Kristiansand Connections

From Kristiansand by Train to: Stavanger (4-7/day, 3.5 hours),
Oslo (4/day, 4.5 hours).

By Boat to Hirtshals, Denmark: For details on this boat, see
the "Sailing Between Norway and Denmark" sidebar.

Route Tips for Drivers
Bergen to Kristiansand via the Setesdal Valley (10 hours): Your
first key connection is the Kvanndal-Utne ferry (departures hourly
6:00-23:00, less on weekends, reservations not possible or even
necessary if you get there 20 minutes early, breakfast in cafeteria,
www.tide.no). If you make the 9:00, your day will be more relaxed.
Driving comfortably, with no mistakes or traffic, it's two hours
from your Bergen hotel to the ferry dock. Leaving Bergen is a bit
confusing. Pretend you're going to Oslo on the road to Voss (Route
E16, signs for *Nestune, Landås, Nattland*). About a half-hour out
of town, after a long tunnel, leave the Voss road and take Route 7
heading for Norheimsund, and then Kvanndal. This road, treach-
erous for the famed beauty of the Hardanger Fjord it hugs as well
as for its skinniness, is faster and safer if you beat the traffic (which
you will with this plan).

The ferry drops you in Utne, where a lovely road takes you to
Odda and up into the mountains. From Haukeligrend, turn south

and wind up to Sessvatn at 3,000 feet. Enter the Setesdal Valley. Follow the Otra River downhill for 140 miles south to the major port town of Kristiansand. Skip the secondary routes. South of Valle, you'll have to pass a 30-kr tollbooth. The most scenic stretch is between Hovden and Valle. South of Valle, there is a lot more logging (and therefore less scenic). As you enter Kristiansand, pay a 21-kr toll and follow signs for Denmark.

PRACTICALITIES

This section covers just the basics on traveling in this region (for much more information, see *Rick Steves' Scandinavia*). You'll find free advice on specific topics at www.ricksteves.com/tips.

Money

Norway uses the Norwegian kroner: 1 krone equals about $0.20. To roughly convert prices in kroner to dollars, divide prices by 5 (100 kr = about $20). Check www.oanda.com for the latest exchange rates.

The standard way for travelers to get kroner is to withdraw money from a cash machine (ATM) using a debit or credit card, ideally with a Visa or MasterCard logo. Before departing, call your bank or credit-card company: Confirm that your card will work overseas, ask about international transaction fees, and alert them that you'll be making withdrawals in Europe.

Dealing with "Chip and PIN": Much of Northern Europe (including Norway) is adopting a "chip-and-PIN" system for credit cards. These "smartcards" come with an embedded microchip, and cardholders enter a PIN code instead of signing a receipt. If your US card is rejected at a store, a cashier will probably be able to process your card the old-fashioned way. A few merchants might insist on the PIN code—making it helpful for you to know the code for your credit card (ask your credit-card company before you go). The easiest solution is to pay for your purchases with cash you've withdrawn from an ATM. Your US credit card may not be accepted at automated pay points, such as ticket machines at train and subway stations, parking garages, luggage lockers, and self-serve pumps at gas stations. But in Norway, I've found that my US credit card will usually work in these machines, as long as I enter the PIN when the machine asks for the "kode."

To keep your valuables safe, wear a money belt. But if you do lose your credit or debit card, report the loss immediately to the respective global customer-assistance centers. Use this toll-free number in Norway—800-190-11—to place a collect call to these 24-hour US numbers: Visa (410/581-9994), MasterCard (636/722-7111), and American Express (623/492-8427).

Phoning

Smart travelers use the telephone to reserve or reconfirm rooms, reserve restaurants, get directions, research transportation connections, confirm tour times, phone home, and lots more.

To call Norway from the US or Canada: Dial 011-47 and then the local number. (The 011 is our international access code, and 47 is Norway's country code.)

To call Norway from a European country: Dial 00-47 followed by the local number. (The 00 is Europe's international access code.)

To call within Norway: Dial the local number.

Tips on Phoning: To make calls in Norway, you can buy two different types of phone cards—international or insertable—sold locally at newsstands. Cheap international phone cards, which work with a scratch-to-reveal PIN code, allow you to call home to the US for pennies a minute, and also work for domestic calls. You can use these cards from any phone, including the one in your hotel room, but some hotels charge for calls to the "toll-free" access line (ask before you dial). Insertable phone cards, which must be inserted into public pay phones, are reasonable for calls within Norway (and work for international calls as well, though not as cheaply as the international phone cards). Note that insertable phone cards—and most international phone cards—work only in the country where you buy them. Calling from your hotel-room phone *without* using an international phone card is usually expensive.

A mobile phone—whether an American one that works in Europe, or a European one you buy when you arrive—is handy, but can be pricey. For more on phoning, see www.ricksteves.com/phoning.

Making Hotel Reservations

To ensure the best value, I recommend reserving rooms in advance, particularly during peak season. Email the hotelier with the following key pieces of information: number and type of rooms; number of nights; date of arrival; date of departure; and any special requests. (For a sample form, see www.ricksteves.com/reservation.) Use the European style for writing dates: day/month/year. For example, for a two-night stay in July, you could request:

"1 double room for 2 nights, arrive 16/07/12, depart 18/07/12." Hoteliers typically ask for your credit-card number as a deposit.

In these times of economic uncertainty, some hotels are willing to deal to attract guests—try emailing several to ask their best price. Most Scandinavian business hotels use "dynamic pricing," which means they change the room rate depending on demand—just like the airlines change their fares. This makes it extremely difficult to predict what you will pay. For many hotels, I list a range of prices. If the rate you're offered is at or near the bottom of my printed range, it's likely a good deal. In general, hotel prices can soften if you do any of the following: offer to pay cash, stay at least three nights, or travel off-season. You can also try asking for a cheaper room (for example, with a bathroom down the hall), or offer to skip breakfast. In Oslo, business-class hotels drop prices to attract tourists with summer rates (from July through mid-August) and weekend rates (Friday and Saturday, but not Sunday). You need to ask about these discounts. Any time of year, the TI's Oslo Package is a good deal for couples and great for families with young children; see www.visitoslo.com.

Eating

Restaurants are often expensive. Alternate between picnics (outside or in your hotel or hostel); cheap, forgettable, but filling cafeteria or fast-food fare ($20 per person); and atmospheric, carefully chosen restaurants popular with locals ($35 per person and up). Ethnic eateries—Indian, Turkish, Greek, Italian, and Asian—offer a good value and a break from Norwegian fare.

The *smörgåsbord* (known in Norway as the *store koldt bord*) is a revered Scandinavian culinary tradition. Seek it out at least once during your visit. Begin with the fish dishes, along with boiled potatoes and *knekkebrød* (crisp bread). Then move on to salads, egg dishes, and various cold cuts. Next it's meatball time! Pour on some gravy as well as a spoonful of lingonberry sauce. Still hungry? Make a point to sample the Nordic cheeses and the racks of traditional desserts, cakes, and custards.

Hotel breakfasts are a huge and filling buffet, generally included but occasionally a $10-or-so option. It usually features fruit, cereal, various milks, breads and crackers, cold cuts, pickled herring, caviar paste, and boiled eggs. The brown cheese with the texture of earwax and a slightly sweet taste is *geitost* ("goat cheese").

In Norway, alcohol is sold only at state-run liquor stores called Vinmonopolet (though weak beer is also sold at supermarkets). To avoid extremely high restaurant prices for alcohol, many Norwegians—and tourists—buy their wine, beer, or spirits at a store and then drink at a public square; this is legal and openly practiced. One local specialty is *akvavit*, a strong, vodka-like spirit distilled from potatoes and flavored with anise, caraway, or other herbs and spices—then drunk ice-cold.

Service: Good service is relaxed (slow to an American). When you want the bill, say, *"Regningen, takk."* Throughout Norway, a service charge is included in your bill, so there's no need to leave an additional tip. In fancier restaurants or for great service, round up the bill (about 5 percent of the total check).

Transportation

By Train and Bus: Trains cover many of my recommended Norwegian destinations. To see if a railpass could save you money, check www.ricksteves.com/rail. If you're buying tickets as you go, note that prices can fluctuate. To research train schedules and fares, visit the Norwegian train website: www.nsb.no. Nearly any long-distance train ride requires you to make a reservation before boarding (the day before is usually fine). If you're taking the Norway in a Nutshell route in mid-July or August, it's smart to make reservations at least a week in advance for the Oslo–Bergen train and the Flåm-Gudvangen fjord cruise.

Don't overlook long-distance buses, which are usually slower than trains but have considerably cheaper and more predictable fares. On certain routes (e.g., Oslo-Stockholm), the bus is less expensive but slower than the train. Norway's biggest bus carrier is Nor-Way Bussekspress (www.nor-way.no).

By Car: It's cheaper to arrange most car rentals from the US. For tips on your insurance options, see www.ricksteves.com/cdw, and for route planning, consult www.viamichelin.com. Bring your driver's license. Local road etiquette is similar to that in the US. Use your headlights day and night; it's required in most of Scandinavia. A car is a worthless headache in any big city—park it safely (get tips from your hotelier).

By Boat: Boats are both a necessary and spectacular way to travel through Norway's fjords or along its coast (for various routes, see www.fjordtours.no, www.fjord1.no, and www.tide.no). Reserve ahead if you're planning on taking overnight boats in summer or on weekends to link Oslo and Copenhagen (www.dfdsseaways.com). Other worthwhile ferry routes connect Norway and northern Denmark; see www.fjordline.com and www.colorline.com.

Helpful Hints

Emergency Help: To summon the **police** or an **ambulance,** call 112. For passport problems, call the **US Embassy** (in Oslo: tel. 21 30 85 40; passport services available Mon–Fri 8:30–12:00, www.norway.usembassy.gov). For information on what to do in case of theft or loss, see www.ricksteves.com/help. For other concerns, get advice from your hotelier.

PRACTICALITIES

Time: Europe uses the 24-hour clock. It's the same through 12:00 noon, then keep going: 13:00, 14:00, and so on. Norway is six/nine hours ahead of the East/West Coasts of the US.

Holidays and Festivals: Europe celebrates many holidays, which can close sights and attract crowds (book hotel rooms ahead). For information on holidays and festivals in Norway, check the Scandinavia Tourist Board website: www.goscandinavia.com. For a simple list showing major—though not all—events, see www.ricksteves.com/festivals.

Numbers and Stumblers: What Americans call the second floor of a building is the first floor in Europe. Europeans write dates as day/month/year, so Christmas is 25/12/12. Commas are decimal points and vice versa—a dollar and a half is 1,50, and there are 5.280 feet in a mile. Europe uses the metric system: A kilogram is 2.2 pounds; a liter is about a quart; and a kilometer is six-tenths of a mile.

Resources from Rick Steves

This Snapshot guide is excerpted from the latest edition of *Rick Steves' Scandinavia,* which is one of more than 30 titles in my series of guidebooks on European travel. I also produce a public television series, *Rick Steves' Europe,* and a public radio show, *Travel with Rick Steves.* My website, www.ricksteves.com, offers free travel information, a Graffiti Wall for travelers' comments, guidebook updates, my travel blog, an online travel store, and information on European railpasses and our tours of Europe. If you're bringing a mobile device on your trip, you can download free information from Rick Steves Audio Europe, featuring podcasts of my radio shows, free audio tours of major sights in Europe, and travel interviews about Norway (downloadable via www.ricksteves.com/audioeurope, iTunes, or the Rick Steves Audio Europe free smartphone app).

Additional Resources

Tourist Information: www.goscandinavia.com
Passports and Red Tape: www.travel.state.gov
Packing List: www.ricksteves.com/packlist
Travel Insurance: www.ricksteves.com/insurance
Cheap Flights: www.skyscanner.net
Airplane Carry-on Restrictions: www.tsa.gov/travelers
Updates for This Book: www.ricksteves.com/update

How Was Your Trip?

If you'd like to share your tips, concerns, and discoveries after using this book, please fill out the survey at www.ricksteves.com/feedback. Thanks in advance—it helps a lot.

Norwegian Survival Phrases

Norwegian can be pronounced quite differently from region to region. These phrases and phonetics match the mainstream Oslo dialect, but you'll notice variations. Vowels can be tricky: *å* sounds like "oh," *æ* sounds like a bright "ah" (as in "apple"), and *u* sounds like the German *ü* (purse your lips and say u). Certain vowels at the ends of words (such as *d* and *t*) are sometimes barely pronounced (or not at all). In some dialects, the letters *sk* are pronounced "sh." In the phonetics, Ī / ī sounds like the long i in "light."

Hello. (*formal*)	**God dag.**	goo dahg
Hi. / Bye. (*informal*)	**Hei. / Ha det.**	hī / hah deh
Do you speak English?	**Snakker du engelsk?**	SNAHK-kehr dew ENG-ehlsk
Yes. / No.	**Ja. / Nei.**	yah / nī
Please.	**Vær så snill.**	vayr soh sneel
Thank you (very much).	**(Tusen) takk.**	(TEW-sehn) tahk
You're welcome.	**Vær så god.**	vayr soh goo
Can I help you?	**Kan jeg hjelpe deg?**	kahn yī YEHL-peh dī
Excuse me.	**Unnskyld.**	EWN-shuld
(Very) good.	**(Veldig) fint.**	(VEHL-dee) feent
Goodbye.	**Farvel.**	fahr-VEHL
one / two	**en / to**	ayn / toh
three / four	**tre / fire**	treh / FEE-reh
five / six	**fem / seks**	fehm / sehks
seven / eight	**syv / åtte**	seev / OH-teh
nine / ten	**ni / ti**	nee / tee
hundred	**hundre**	HEWN-dreh
thousand	**tusen**	TEW-sehn
How much?	**Hvor mye?**	voor MEE-yeh
local currency: (Norwegian) crown	**(Norske) kroner**	(NORSH-keh) KROH-nehr
Where is...?	**Hvor er...?**	voor ehr
..the toilet	**...toalettet**	toh-ah-LEH-teh
men	**menn** *Or:* **herrer**	mehn / HEHR-rehr
women	**damer**	DAH-mehr
water / coffee	**vann / kaffe**	vahn / KAH-feh
beer / wine	**øl / vin**	uhl / veen
Cheers!	**Skål!**	skohl
The bill, please.	**Regningen, takk.**	RĪ-ning-ehn tahk

INDEX

A

Accommodations: *See* Sleeping; *and specific destinations*
Aegir Bryggeri (Flåm): 85
Airports: Bergen, 140; Copenhagen, 14–15; Stavanger, 172
Air travel resources: 190
Aker Brygge: 18; eating, 67–68
Akersgata: 53
Akershus Castle: 31
Akershus Fortress Complex: 27, 30–32
Akers River: 50, 51, 53, 54–55
Akvavit: 189–190
Almanac: 4–5
Åmotbrua: 55
Amundsen, Roald: 47–48, 49
Amusement park: 50–51
Aquariums: Balestrand, 100, 102; Bergen, 153–154
Arctic: boat travel, 167–168
Ardal Church: 181
Armed Forces Museum: 32
Art museums: Bergen Art Museum, 154; Edvard Munch Museum, 27, 49–50; National Gallery, 26, 32–39; Stavanger Museum, 173; Vigeland Museum, 42–43
ATMs: 15, 186–187
Aurland: 82, 90–92, 120–121
Aurlandsfjord: 82, 90
Aurlandsvegen "Snow Road": 87–88, 120–121

B

Backer, Harriet: 154
Balestrand: 95–110; eating, 107–108; map, 99; planning tips, 98; sleeping, 105–107; tourist information, 98–99; transportation, 108–110

Balestrand Harborfront: 100–101, 102
Båtservice: 17
Beaches: Bergen, 154–155; Oslo, 50
Beer: 65, 69–70, 85, 164, 188
Bergen: 137–168; eating, 163–166; helpful hints, 141; maps, 138, 142–143, 160–161; orientation, 139; planning tips, 137–139; shopping, 157; sights/activities, 145–157; sleeping, 157–163; tourist information, 140; tours, 144–145; transportation, 77, 78–79, 81, 84, 140–141, 144, 166–168
Bergen Art Museum: 154
Bergen Card: 140
Bergen Fish Market: 139, 151, 166
Bergen Folklore Show: 155
Bergen Guide: 140
Bergenhus Fortress (Bergen): 146–147
Bergen Public Library: 141
Bernadotte, Jean-Baptiste: 20
Besseggen: 134
Biking (bike rentals): Balestrand, 102–103; Flåm Valley, 86; Oslo, 16, 50; Urnes, 116–117
Bjørnson, Bjørnstjerne: 24, 54
Boat travel and cruises: 190; Balestrand, 108; Bergen, 109, 141, 144, 145, 167–168; Copenhagen, 71, 190; Denmark, 167, 177, 182–183; Fjærlandsfjord, 104–105; Gudvangen, 81–82; Lustrafjord, 119–120; Lysefjord, 174; Nærøyfjord, 82, 85–86;

INDEX

Oslo, 15, 71; Sogndal, 119–120; Sognefjord, 75, 109; Stavanger, 170, 177
Bogstadveien: 18, 25, 57
Borgund: 87
Borgund Stave Church: 88
Breheimsenteret Glacier Information Center: 113
Breidablikk (Stavanger): 173
Breivik, Anders Behring: 54–55
Bryggen (Bergen): 139, 147–152; eating, 163–164
Bryggens Museum (Bergen): 150
Buses: 190; Bergen, 144, 145, 167; Gudvangen, 82–83; Oslo, 14, 16, 17, 71; Solvorn, 114, 119; Stavanger, 170, 172
Bygdøy: 43–49; eating, 45; map, 44; transportation, 44–45
Bykle: 180
Byporten: 13, 19, 57

C

Cabs: *See* Taxis
Café Bacchus: 22
Campgrounds: 90, 102, 107, 117, 128
Canning museum, in Stavanger: 173
Canoeing: 179
Car travel (driving): 190; Balestrand, 108; Bergen, 141; Gudbrandsdal Valley, 127, 136; Jotunheimen Mountains, 134–135, 136; Kristiansand, 184–185; Lustrafjord, 110–111; Sognefjord, 120–122
Changing of the Guard: 31
Cheese: 6, 86, 93, 108, 177, 188
Churches and cathedrals: Dale Church (Luster), 111–112; Gamle Aker Church, 54;

Oslo Cathedral, 20–22; St. Mary's Church (Bergen), 147; Stavanger Cathedral, 173–174; Undredal church, 93. *See also* Stave churches
City Hall, Oslo: 24, 26, 28–29
Copenhagen: boat travel, 71, 190
Credit cards: 187–188
Cruises: *See* Boat travel and cruises
Currency and exchange: 5, 186–187; Oslo, 15

D

Dahl, Johan Christian: 34–35, 154
Dale Church (Luster): 111–112
Dammar Vatnedalsvatn: 180
Dance of Life (Munch): 39
Denmark, boat travel: 167, 177, 182–183
Department stores: 57
"Desolation Row": 20
Det Gylne Hus (Balestrand): 101–102
Det Norske Utvandrersenteret Ble (Stavanger): 173
Dining: *See* Eating; *and specific destinations*
Discounts: *See* Money-saving tips
Dragsvik: 108
Drammen: 78
Driving: *See* Car travel
Drøbak: 56–57

E

Eating: 189–190; Aurland, 92; Balestrand, 107–108; Bergen, 163–166; Bygdøy, 45; Drøbak, 56; Flåm, 89–90; Hovden, 180; Kristiansand, 184; Oslo, 29, 64–70; Sognefjord, 75–76; Stavanger, 176

Economy: 4–5
Edvard Munch Museum: 27, 49–50
Eidsvoll Manor: 56
Elvesæter: 135
Embassies: 190
Emergencies: 190
Emigration Center (Stavanger): 173
Engangsgrill ("one-time grills"): 65
Entertainment: 13, 155
Esefjord: 102–103
Evje: 181

F
Fantoft Stave Church: 156–157
Fearnley, Thomas: 35
Ferries: *See* Boat travel and cruises
Festivals: 170, 190
Finse: 78
Fish markets: Bergen, 139, 151, 166; Kristiansand, 184; Stavanger, 170
Fiskebasaren (Kristiansand): 184
Fisketorget (Bergen): 139, 151, 166
Fjærlandsfjord: 95, 104–105
Fjordline: 167, 182–183, 190
FjordSafari: 82, 86
Fjords of Norway: 72–84, 94–122; about, 80; map, 79. *See also* Lustrafjord; Sognefjord
Fjord Tours: 16–17, 77–78
Flag, Norwegian: 5
Flåm: 84–90; boat travel, 81–82; sights/activities, 85–88; sleeping and eating, 89–90
Flåmsbana: 76, 77, 81, 84
Flåm Valley: 79, 86
Flateland: 180
Flesland Airport (Bergen): 140

Fløibanen (Bergen): 152–153, 155
Flytoget: 14
Fodnes: 119–120
Food: *See* Cheese; Eating; Markets; Pølse; *and specific destinations*
Forsvarsmuseet: 32
Fram Museum: 26, 47–48
Frilandsmuseets: *See* Open-air museums
Frognerbadet: 51
Frogner Park: 18, 26, 39–42; eating near, 68–69
Frognerseteren Hovedrestaurant: 49, 70
Funicular, in Bergen: 152–153, 155

G
Galdhøpiggen: 134–135
Galleriet Mall (Bergen): 141, 157
Gamle Aker Church (Oslo): 54
Gamle Bergen: 154
Gamle Stavanger: 173
Gaupne: 110–112
Geilo: 78
Geography: 4
Glacier Bus: 112–113, 119
Glaciers: about, 80; Jostedal, 104–105; Nigard, 105, 112–114, 119; Norwegian Glacier Museum (Fjærland), 105
GlasMagasinet: 22, 57
Gokstad (ship): 46
Golden House (Balestrand): 101–102
Gol Stave Church: 45
Government: 5, 23–24
Grand Café: 23, 66
Grand Hotel: 23
Grasbrokke: 180
Grendi: 181
Grieg (Edvard) Home: 155–156
Grønland: 19, 51, 56; eating, 69–70; map, 52

Grünerløkka: 27, 51–56; eating, 69; map, 52
Gudbrandsdal Valley: 123–129; eating, 129; map, 125; sleeping, 127–129
Gude, Hans: 35
Gudvangen: 77, 81–83, 85–86, 121
Guidebooks, Rick Steves: 190

H
Hafslo: 111
Håkon Hall (Lillehammer): 126–127
Håkon's Hall (Bergen): 146–147
Hallingdal Valley: 78
Hanseatic League: overview, 148–149
Hanseatic Museum (Bergen): 150–151
Hanseatic Quarter (Bergen): See Bryggen
Haukeligrend: 178
Hella: 108, 111
Helpful hints: 190–191; Bergen, 141; Oslo, 15–16
Henrik Ibsens Gate: 18
Herring: 173, 183
Heyerdahl, Thor: 48
Hiking: Balestrand, 100, 102; Bergen, 152–153, 154; Flåm Valley, 86; Hovden, 179; Jotunheimen Mountains, 134–135; Nigard Glacier, 113–114; Oslo, 50, 53
Hirtshals, Denmark, boat travel: 167, 177, 182–183
Historisk Museum: 18, 39
Holidays: 5, 190
Holmenkollen Ski Jump: 27, 49
Holmenkollen Ski Museum: 27, 49
Holocaust Center: 27, 47
Honneevje: 180
Honse-Lovisas Hus: 55

Hopperstad Stave Church: 103–104, 122
Hostels, in Oslo: 64
Hotels: See Sleeping; and specific destinations
House of Oslo: 18
Hovden: 179–180
Hovden Badeland: 179–180
Hurrungane: 135
Hurtigruten: 167–168
Husfliden: Bergen, 157; Oslo, 57

I
Ibsen, Henrik: 18, 23, 24, 54, 152
Internet access: Bergen, 141; Oslo, 15

J
Jostedal Glacier: 104–105. See also Nigard Glacier
Jotunheimen Mountains: 123, 130–136; map, 125
Juvasshytta: 135

K
Karl Johans Gate: 19–23, 25; eating, 66–67; map, 20–21; sleeping near, 59–62
Kaupanger: 119
King Bele's Way (Balestrand): 101, 102
Kirkeveien: 40
Kjosfossen: 81
Kon-Tiki Museum: 26, 48
Kristiansand: 181–185
Krohg, Christian: 23, 33, 36, 154
Kroner: 5, 186–187
Kvam: sleeping, 128–129
Kviknes Hotel (Balestrand): 98, 100–101, 105–106, 107

L
Lærdal Tunnel: 87, 120

Language: 6–7; survival
   phrases, 191
Laundry: Bergen, 141; Oslo, 16
Ledaal (Stavanger): 173
Leirvassbu: 135
Leprosy Museum (Bergen): 153
Lillehammer: 124–127; eating,
   129; sleeping, 127–128
"Little Pakistan": *See* Grønland
Lom: 130–132; sleeping near,
   132–133
Lom Stave Church: 131–132
Luster: 110, 111–112
Lustrafjord: 94, 110–120, 135;
   transportation, 119–120
Lysefjord: 174

M
Maihaugen Open-Air Folk
   Museum (Lillehammer):
   124–126
Mannheller: 119–120
Mariakirken (Bergen): 147
Maridalsvannet: 50
Maritime museums: *Fram*
   Museum, 26, 47–48;
   Kon-Tiki Museum, 26,
   48; Norwegian Maritime
   Museum, 27, 48; Stavanger
   Museum, 173; Viking Ship
   Museum, 26, 46–47
Markets: 57, 170. *See also* Fish
   markets
Metric system: 190
Møllergata: 53
Money: 186–187
Money-saving tips: Bergen,
   140; Oslo, 13, 58–59, 64–66
Moose Safari (Hovden): 179
Mountain Museum (Lom): 130
Mount Fløyen: 152–153; eating,
   165
Munch, Edvard: 23, 32–33,
   37–39, 53–54, 154; biographi-
   cal sketch, 38; Museum, 27,
   49–50; *The Scream*, 38

Munch Museet: 27, 49–50
Museum of Iron Production
   (Hovden): 179
Museums: *See* Art museums;
   Maritime museums; Open-
   air museums; *and specific
   museums*
Music: 155, 170
Myrdal: 77, 79, 81, 86

N
Nærøydal: 83
Nærøyfjord: 82, 85–86, 121
Nansen, Fridtjof: 29, 47–48
National Gallery: 18, 26,
   32–39; map, 34
National Historical Museum:
   18, 39
National Theater: 24
Nes: sleeping, 117
Nigard Glacier: 105, 112–114,
   119
Nobel Peace Center: 25, 27,
   29–30
Nomeland: 181
Norges Hjemmefrontmuseum:
   26, 31–32
Norsk Fjellmuseum (Lom): 130
Norsk Folkemuseum: 26, 45–46
Norsk Hermetikkmuseum
   (Stavanger): 173
Norskolje Museum (Stavanger):
   172, 176
Norsk Reiselivsmuseum: 100
Norsk Sjøfartsmuseum: 27, 48
North Sea oil: 172
Norway attacks of 2011: 54–55
Norway fjords: *See* Fjords of
   Norway
Norway in a Nutshell: 72–93,
   121; maps, 73, 79; package
   tours, 77–78; planning tips,
   73–74; self-guided tour,
   78–84; transportation, 74–77
Norwegian Emigration Center
   (Stavanger): 173

INDEX

Norwegian Folk Museum: 26, 45–46
Norwegian Glacier Museum (Fjærland): 105
Norwegian Holocaust Center: 27, 47
Norwegian language: 6–7; survival phrases, 191
Norwegian Maritime Museum: 27, 48
Norwegian Olympics Museum (Lillehammer): 126–127
Norwegian Parliament: 23–24
Norwegian Petroleum Museum (Stavanger): 172, 176
Norwegian Resistance Museum: 26, 31–32
Norwegian survival phrases: 191
Norwegian sweaters: 57–58, 157
Norwegian Travel Museum (Balestrand): 100

O
Odda: 177–178
Olaf Ryes Plass: 56
Ole Bulls Plass (Bergen): 152; eating, 164–165
Olympics Museum (Lillehammer): 126–127
Open-air museums: Maihaugen Open-Air Folk Museum (Lillehammer), 124–126; Norwegian Folk Museum, 26, 45–46
Opera House: 27, 30
Oscarsborg Fortress (Drøbak): 57
Oseberg (ship): 46
Oslo: 10–71; at a glance, 26–27; eating, 64–70; helpful hints, 15–16; orientation, 11; planning tips, 11; shopping, 57–58; sights, 28–57; sleeping, 58–64; tourist information, 12–13; tours, 16–17; tram tour, 17–18; transportation, 13–15, 16, 70–71, 77, 78–79, 81; walking tour, 19–26, 28
Oslo Airport: 14
Oslo Bymuseum: 43
Oslo Cathedral: 20–22
Oslo City Hall: 24, 26, 28–29
Oslo City Museum: 43
Oslofjord: 24–25
Oslo Fjord Tours: 16–17, 77–78
Oslo Flaggfabrikk: 58
Oslo Guide: 12
Oslo Harborfront: 24–25, 28–30; beaches, 50; eating, 67–68
Oslo Information Center: 12
Oslo National Historical Museum: 18, 39
Oslo Pass: 13, 16
Oslo Sentralstasjon: 13–14, 19; sleeping near, 59–63
Oslo Sweater Shop: 57–58
Otternes Farms: 86–87

P
Packing checklist: 190
Parliament Building: 23–24
Passports: 190
Peer Gynt Road: 127
Peterssen, Eilif: 36
Petroleum Museum (Stavanger): 172, 176
Phoning: 187
Pickpocket alert: 15
Police: 190
Pølse: 108, 166
Population: 4
Post offices: 15
Pulpit Rock: 174

R
Rådhuset: 24, 26, 28–29
Ra II: 48
Reader feedback: 190
Rockne, Knute: 83–84

Rodne Clipper Fjord
Sightseeing: 174
Roisheim: 132, 134
Røldal: 178
Rosenkrantz Tower (Bergen):
147
Rygge Airport: 15

S
St. Mary's Church (Bergen): 147
St. Olaf's Church (Balestrand):
101
St. Olav's Church (Oslo): 53
Sami (Lapp) culture: 4, 39, 45
Sandefjord Airport: 15
Scream, The (Munch): 38
Seafarers' Monument (Bergen):
152
Setesdal Mineral Park: 181
Setesdal Museum (Flateland):
180
Setesdal Valley: 177–181,
184–185; map, 178
Shopping: Bergen, 157; Oslo,
57–58
Sjøfartsmuseum (Stavanger):
173
Skjolden: 110, 111, 136
Sleeping: Aurland, 91–92;
Balestrand, 105–107;
Bergen, 157–163; Drøbak,
57; Flåm, 89–90; Hovden,
180; Kristiansand,
182–184; Kvam, 128–129;
Lillehammer, 127–128; Lom,
132–133; Oslo, 58–64; reser-
vations, 187–188; Stavanger,
175; Valle, 181
Smörgåsbord: 107, 188
"Snow Road": 87–88, 120–121
Sogndal: sleeping, 118
Sognefjell Road: 135–136
Sognefjord: 72–84, 94–110,
135–136; boat travel, 75–76,
109; maps, 73, 79, 96–97;
package deals, 77–78; plan-

ning tips, 73–74, 95; scenic
drives, 120–122; self-guided
tour, 78–84; train travel,
76–77
Sognefjorden: 82, 85
Sognsvann: 50
Sohlberg, Harald: 37
Sola Airport (Stavanger): 172
Solvorn: 114; eating, 118; sleep-
ing, 117–118; transportation,
114, 119
South Norway: 169–185
Spiterstulen: 134
Stalheim Hotel: 83, 121
Stalheimskleiva: 121
Stavanger: 170–177; eating, 176;
map, 171; sights, 172–174;
sleeping, 175; tourist infor-
mation, 170; transportation,
170, 172, 176–177
Stavanger Cathedral: 173–174
Stavanger Museum: 173
Stave churches: 7–9; Borgund,
88; Fantoft, 156–157; Gol, 45;
Hopperstad, 103–104, 122;
Lom, 131–132; Urnes, 115–117
Stegastein Viewpoint: 87–88,
121
Stortinget: 23–24
Stortorvet: 18, 22
Sundt-Hansen, Carl: 36
Sweaters: 57–58, 157
Swimming: 154–155, 179–180.
See also Beaches

T
Taxis: Bergen, 144; Oslo, 14, 16
Telephones: 187
Telthusbakken Road: 54–55
Theta Museum (Bergen): 151
Thon Hotels: 59–62
Thorvald Meyers Gate: 56
Tidemand, Adolph: 35, 36
Time zone: 190
Torgallmenningen (Bergen):
151–152

INDEX

Tour guides: Balestrand, 99;
Bergen, 145; Oslo, 17
Tourist information: 190;
Aurland, 91; Balestrand,
98–99; Bergen, 140;
Flåm, 85; Hovden, 179;
Lillehammer, 124; Lom, 130;
Oslo, 12–13; Stavanger, 170
Tours: Bergen, 144–145; Oslo,
16–17; Sognefjord, 77–78
Tøyenbadet: 51
Trafikanten Tower: 16, 19
Train travel: 190; Bergen, 77,
78–79, 81, 84, 140, 166–167;
Flåm, 84; Kristiansand,
184; Myrdal, 77, 81; Oslo,
13–14, 14, 16, 64, 70–71, 77,
78–79, 81; Sognefjord, 76–77;
Stavanger, 170, 172, 176;
Voss, 77, 84
Trams: Bergen, 144; Oslo, 16,
17–18
Transportation: 190;
Balestrand, 108–110; Bergen,
140–141, 144, 166–168;
Lustrafjord, 119–120; Oslo,
13–15, 16, 70–71; Solvorn,
114, 119; Stavanger, 170, 172,
176–177. *See also* Boat travel
and cruises; Buses; Car
travel; Train travel
Travel insurance: 190
Trefoldighets Church: 53
Tregaarden's Julehuset
(Drøbak): 56
Troldhaugen: 155–156
Tusenfryd: 50–51
Tvindefossen: 83, 121

U
Ulriken643 Cable Car: 155
Undredal: 82, 93
Urnes Stave Church: 115–117

V
Vagsnes: 122
Valle: 180–181
Vangsnes: 108
Vår Frelsers (Our Savior's)
Cemetery: 53–54
Vigeland, Gustav: biographical
sketch, 40; Frogner Park, 18,
26, 39–42; Museum, 42–43
Vik: 103–104, 122
Vikings: 2–4, 39; Ship
Museum, 26, 46–47
Viking Ship Museum: 26, 46–47
Vikingskiphuset: 26, 46–47
Vinmonopolet: 58, 188
Voss: 83–84; transportation, 77,
82–83, 84

W
Walking tours: Bergen,
145–146; guided, 144–145;
Oslo, 19–26, 28; guided, 17
Water park: 51
Wergeland, Henrik: 24
Wet Fun: 51
What's On in Oslo: 12, 13
White Lady: 145
World War II: 4–5, 29, 146;
Norwegian Holocaust
Center, 27, 47; Norwegian
Resistance Museum, 26,
31–32; Theta Museum
(Bergen), 151

Audio Europe

Rick's Free Travel App

Get your FREE **Rick Steves Audio Europe**™ app to enjoy...

- Dozens of self-guided tours of Europe's top museums, sights and historic walks
- Hundreds of tracks filled with cultural insights and sightseeing tips from Rick's radio interviews
- All organized into handy geographic playlists
- For iPhone, iPad, iPod Touch, Android

With Rick whispering in your ear, Europe gets even better.

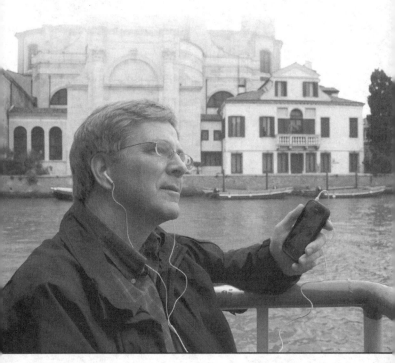

Find out more at ricksteves.com